Broken City

Broken City

Land Speculation, Inequality, and Urban Crisis

PATRICK M. CONDON

UBCPress · Vancouver

Printed in Canada on FSC-certified ancient-forest-free paper (100% post-consumer recycled) that is processed chlorine- and acid-free.

UBC Press is a Benetech Global Certified Accessible™ publisher. The epub version of this book meets stringent accessibility standards, ensuring it is available to people with diverse needs.

Library and Archives Canada Cataloguing in Publication

Title: Broken city : land speculation, inequality, and urban crisis / Patrick M. Condon.
Names: Condon, Patrick M., author.
Description: Includes bibliographical references and index.
Identifiers: Canadiana (print) 20240334973 | Canadiana (ebook) 20240335007
  | ISBN 9780774869553 (softcover) | ISBN 9780774869560 (PDF)
  | ISBN 9780774869577 (EPUB)
Subjects: LCSH: Land use, Urban. | LCSH: Housing. | LCSH: Land speculation.
  | LCSH: Equality.
Classification: LCC HD1391 .C66 2024 | DDC 333.77—dc23

Canada Council   Conseil des arts
for the Arts   du Canada

Canada

BRITISH COLUMBIA
ARTS COUNCIL

BRITISH
COLUMBIA

UBC Press gratefully acknowledges the financial support for our publishing program of the Government of Canada, the Canada Council for the Arts, and the British Columbia Arts Council.

This book has been published with the help of a grant from the Canadian Federation for the Humanities and Social Sciences, through the Scholarly Book Awards, using funds provided by the Social Sciences and Humanities Research Council of Canada.

UBC Press is situated on the traditional, ancestral, and unceded territory of the xʷməθkʷəy̓əm (Musqueam) people. This land has always been a place of learning for the xʷməθkʷəy̓əm, who have passed on their culture, history, and traditions for millennia, from one generation to the next.

UBC Press
The University of British Columbia
www.ubcpress.ca

Contents

Illustrations and Tables

TABLES

Preface

WHAT IS THIS BOOK ABOUT?

This book is about how urban land value is the largely unexamined cause of a lot of our current social justice and community health problems. It is also about practical ways of fixing them, using readily available zoning and development policy tools.

This book focuses on these problems in the English-speaking world, with occasional forays into the similar experiences of other countries. Apologies to my francophone fellow Canadians. I hope that they will forgive me for lumping them in with anglophones. Quebec continues to experience the same economic convulsions as seen in the English-speaking world, so francophones should be assured that I am speaking to their issues as well.

Such a focus is practical for two reasons. One is quite obvious: this book is written in English and unlikely to be translated in the near future (if ever), and consequently, if you are reading this, you are likely in said world. The second is that legal structures and land markets in this group of countries are similar, grounded as they are in British landowning traditions.[1] Thus the policy and financial strategies evident in one country are often reflected in the policy and financial strategies employed in the other countries of this selected group.

These countries are now confronted with a host of similarly overlapping urban crises. As I write this Preface, the global COVID-19 pandemic is finally waning and now morphing into a global-scale permanent endemic. Is there any doubt that we can expect this new danger to be a feature of future decades as well? Thus our concept of urban life has changed. It will continue to change in the future. To our more familiar urban dangers, we must now add the threat of diseases spread by human-to-human contact – on our streets, in our cafes, and while we are on our commutes to work.

Our new urban reality has added the fear of invisible killers to the other burdens of twenty-first-century city life. Among these travails, we can certainly include ever-widening income gaps (Jenkins 2021), somehow super-accelerated by the 2020 pandemic. This crisis-level inequality is most alarmingly evident in the rapidly widening threat of housing insecurity (Jowers et al. 2021).[2]

It is the hypothesis of this volume that *urban land* – its location, ownership, price, and the sacrifices that people have to make in order to access it in both its rented and mortgaged forms – is the largely unexamined link between these issues. I also argue that precedented improvements for these linked problems exist in the commonplace practices of urban land use and urban design policy.

And to avoid confusion, when I refer to "urban land" in this volume, I mean both land in traditional centre cities and land in so-called suburbs, where many – and, in some English-speaking countries, most – urban residents now reside.

THE STRUCTURE OF THIS BOOK

This book has ridiculous ambitions, particularly in a world where instantaneous information via the Internet seems to be leaving books behind.

This anxiety notwithstanding, I aim to describe how the current housing crisis is affecting a big chunk of the world and to offer practical solutions applicable beyond national boundaries.

But the main point is that the burgeoning housing crisis is not particular to one metropolitan area, one state, one province, or even one country. The problem is global. Understanding the global dimensions of the problem, and the value of similar solutions used in differing countries, avoids what I see as a frustrating myopia that gets in the way of effective solutions.

In most places, housing affordability is assumed to be a local issue, or at best a regional one. If one holds this view, housing affordability can be addressed by adjusting local variables. If housing costs too much, it must be because we are not building enough, many say. But the same problems are cropping up worldwide no matter what the local responses might be. Thus adding a burst of market-housing supply in the hope of overwhelming a global problem is a doomed exercise. That is why I have chosen such an ill-advisedly wide scope.

Nevertheless, the book as designed mitigates against this potential folly with a structure that lets you carefully read only those sections of great interest to you without losing out on the broader logics of the text. Chapters 2 and 3, which cover the underlying economics of the global housing crisis, are probably best read in their entirety, but the chapters on individual countries' variations and their individual responses to the crisis may be efficiently absorbed by selectively reading just the chapters most relevant to the reader's own concerns.

The text, too, often includes lengthy notes so that readers who are interested in a particular point can delve into the notes and associated references for deeper reading and because it is very important to be sure of the facts cited. Much of what this book has to say is not widely accepted, so fortifying evidence is called for. Speckling the text with notes can be irritating to some, and for this I apologize, but the benefit is to provide the reader with confidence in the arguments provided. For those who want the fastest way to assess this book and its content, the Introduction has been written as a summary of the whole. By reading just the Introduction, you will hopefully grasp the main thesis of the book and be able to determine if further reading is of value.

Finally, about your author. My youth was spent as a community organizer in my hometown of Brockton, Massachusetts. This mission taught me to care about how cities, particularly their housing, can influence a community's social and physical health. Concern with the role of the public realm led me to try to improve this health through neighbourhood design and the pursuit of urban design training. My formal training is in landscape architecture (University of Massachusetts), and my professional work was in city planning (Westfield, Massachusetts).

Beyond this background, I make no claims of formal training or professional experience in the methods and theories of real estate economics that are fundamental to any deep dive into why housing costs so much now, but I do claim the benefit of forty years of empirical study of cities, with an intense focus on the role of urban land. I believe that this long study has let me see the world from the ground up, literally, and I hope that this modest effort of mine will enhance the discourse.

Acknowledgments

The author would like to thank a few entities for helping this book along. I guess first would be, oddly enough, COVID-19 for collapsing my world down to my couch – and nothing beyond that – for all of 2020. 'Twas then that, absent anything else to do, and with laptop in lap, I started to write in a spirit of cold fury. I am furious about urban land prices and how land price stands in the way of equitable city design. Urban land price is, as I try to explain in this book, a hidden killer. It is the hidden killer of dreams, hidden killer of social equity, and, in the case of COVID-19, hidden killer of people.

In a more traditional vein, I want to thank Ron Kellett, the head of my school at the time of this writing, for adjusting workloads due to COVID-19 – adjustments that balanced the need to keep our academic ship afloat while not burning out students or faculty. The time allowed in seclusion made this book possible.

I would also like to thank Robert Lewis for all the help in honing this text and confirming facts contained herein, along with all of the staff at UBC Press who really contributed. Thank you all.

Finally, thanks to UBC itself. I have criticized you scores of times over my thirty years here, but I have never lost my appreciation for the opportunity you gave me to teach and write about my passions.

Broken City

Introduction

THE WORLD IS NOW URBAN

Since 2010, more of the world's people have lived in cities than in rural areas; the proportion of urban dwellers in the English-speaking world is much higher, at over 80 percent. Increasingly, wage earners are struggling to find affordable homes within cities that account for over 90 percent of their country's real estate dollar value despite covering far less than 5 percent of the land area, as seen in the United States, New Zealand, Australia, and Canada, for example.[1] This overwhelming imbalance in land value between the city and the countryside is a relatively new and accelerating trend. On average, the value of American urban land, adjusted for inflation, has increased by over 100 percent in just fifteen years.[2] In some coastal US cities, land values have increased much more dramatically – 500 percent in just seven years in most of central Los Angeles, for example (American Enterprise Institute n.d.). The situation in other developed countries is often worse. The average price of urban land in Canada, the United Kingdom, and New Zealand has doubled in less than ten years. This inflation in the cost of urban land is pricing anyone without wealth out of property markets.[3]

The problems taken up herein do not lack for attention from the media, academics, and citizens. Economic inequality, stagnant wages, unaffordable housing, and most recently, global pandemics are exhaustively covered, albeit with precious few solutions to point to, but hardly anyone mentions how these nested issues all connect to the price of urban land.

In most major cities, the price of urban land now far exceeds the value of the buildings erected on it (Christophers 2018).[4] Urban land prices have inflated so much that the cost to buy or rent homes has increasingly risen out of reach of average wage earners. Increasingly, front-line service workers cannot live close to where they work. Thus those who fought the pandemic (think orderlies and grocery clerks – now deemed essential) had to endanger themselves and others through long commutes and exposed workplaces.

What distinguishes this volume from other works on these topics is the contention that it is the price of the land under the building that is far more important than any other single factor in determining who gets sick, who struggles to keep a roof over their heads, and who lives paycheque to paycheque. Or stated another way, our most serious social and public health problems are caused by the hyper-financialization of urban land.[5]

The hyper-financialization of urban land is the result of a decades-long shift away from a housing market that once struck a rough balance between local housing costs and average wages in metropolitan areas. Real estate, throughout the English-speaking world, is now largely priced not for its value as housing but for its value as an asset in a global marketplace hungry for assets of any kind.[6] Of these assets, urban land is attracting the lion's share of global wealth (Piketty 2014). Urban land is now traded and valued just like stocks and bonds,[7] and it is similarly subject to simultaneous shifts in real estate prices on both sides of the globe. Rents are unaffordable not because building costs have risen but because the land under the apartment building has more than tripled in price in many locations. Mortgages are increasingly out of reach not because it is so much more expensive to build a home and not because planning policies are too restrictive but because the cost of a home in the hottest global markets is now governed by the price of the dirt below it. Details of how that has happened and why, and what to do about it, form the core of this book.

HOW DO WE TALK ABOUT URBAN LAND PRICE?

Urban land price is so unusual compared to other forms of wealth, and its economic significance so obscured for most of us, that we need better ways to talk about it. When economists talk about land *price*, they generally think of it as fifteen to twenty years' worth of *rent* needed to amortize the same land; or said another way, rent is how much you can afford to pay, monthly or yearly, for the land that you use. This point is crucial. In this text, I use the term "rent" as a stand-in for "land price" to align with this practice. This way of thinking about land price is exactly the same way that you think about house price. A house price is really the amount that you can pay in interest and principle every month for the fifteen to thirty years before you own it outright (or amortize the loan). That is what economists call land rent. To distinguish the commonplace meaning of "rent" (such as the monthly payment for an apartment) from the term as it is used by economists, the word "Rent" is capitalized when this second technical sense is meant. This is an important concept to grasp, and it comes up frequently in the remainder of this text.

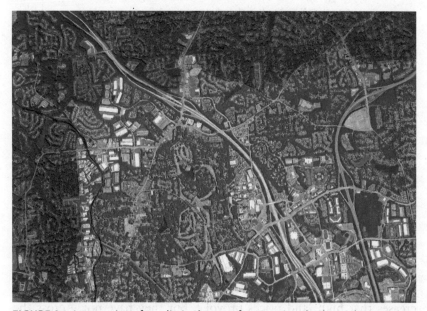

FIGURE 0.1 Intersection of two limited-access freeways in suburban Atlanta, Georgia. Land owners benefited from new infrastructure expenditures in previously rural areas. | Courtesy Google Maps.

A NEW PROBLEM: THE PANDEMIC

Recent immigrants to global cities, disadvantaged ethnic classes, and more generally, the poor were hit hardest by the 2020 pandemic. Many media voices have speculated that urban density was the cause of this disparity, or personal hygiene, or crowded buses. In contrast, in this volume, you will find evidence that inequitable exposure to disease resulted from the way that land is priced and distributed. Land cost and thus home cost are now substantially out of balance with wages in all of the English-speaking world, an imbalance that has been gradually widening since the 1970s. In the United States, for example, average home prices were only four times the average annual gross wages in the 1970s. Now, the difference is eight times the annual wages – after having completely recovered from the real estate price crash of 2008, when it fell to five times the wages. This situation is repeated in the rest of the English-speaking world but often much more dramatically. Average home prices in New Zealand, for example, are almost twelve and a half times the average wages (Longtermtrends n.d.). In Metro Vancouver, the ratio is only slightly better, at ten times the average wages (Gougeon and Moussouni 2021). Rising urban land costs don't just affect home purchase prices; they also affect the value of land under rental buildings and thus, over time, inflate rents. As a consequence, immigrant families are increasingly forced to crowd a dozen people into apartments suitable for four, creating a rich environment for the transfer of disease.

This problem might not be so hard to solve if we could just add a few more floors to a building, thus reducing the land-price component of monthly rent. But experience has shown that increasing density has the negative consequence of increasing land price, streaming most of the gains of increased density to landowners – not to renters or to first-time homebuyers. This last assertion is controversial. It's also counterintuitive. But it's true, and this book's goal is to unpack the hows, whys, and wherefores and to suggest what to do about it all.

Urban land prices would also be less of an issue if increases in service industry employees' incomes kept pace with the rent and mortgage increases that high land prices provoke, but they have not. Across the English-speaking world, as urban land prices have inexorably risen, hourly wages, after adjustment for inflation, have largely stayed flat, undercutting the long-held presumption that metropolitan-area home prices normally align with the average metropolitan-area wages (McDowell 2022) – an alignment often regarded as one of the "real estate fundamentals" ("What in the World?" 2019). Until recently, this ratio was an assumed fundamental law of real estate economics. This so-called law, as we shall see later in this volume, is currently being rewritten.

Now, throughout the English-speaking world, full-time service workers, those closest to the front line against pandemic, pay rents for housing that are higher – both in inflation-adjusted terms and in terms relative to the average median household income – than at any time in the previous seventy years.[8] Because these high rents make saving impossible, it is now extremely difficult for service workers in their key family-forming years to save enough money for the down payment on a first home as a way to access a share of the urban land necessary to build wealth (Connolly 2019)[9] – that is, real estate wealth, which has been the principal pathway to middle-class financial security in most of the English-speaking world.

DISEASE AND RACE

Racial problems manifest uniquely in the United States. Despite substantial gains in education, Black Americans have no more personal wealth now than they did in 1950 (Brooks 2020). The small gains in wealth (mostly housing wealth) made by Black Americans during the 1980s and '90s were wiped out by the Great Recession of 2008. Today, Black Americans are almost as likely to live in segregated areas as they were in the 1970s ("Segregation in America" 2018), and they are far more likely to hold front-line service jobs (such as grocery clerk, delivery driver, orderly, and bus driver) than American whites (Salsberg and Kastanis 2018). These factors combine to ensure that American Blacks are, on average, less likely to work from home and less able to stay home from work. Thus they come into far more frequent contact with other endangered and endangering people than do their white counterparts. This remains the case more than fifty years after the US Congress passed fair housing, voting rights, and anti-discrimination legislation. Much of this disparity is a unique legacy of America's original sin: slavery.

This wealth disparity between whites and Blacks is nearly the same in the United Kingdom.[10] During the pandemic, systemic factors combined to make Blacks in the United Kingdom and the United States up to four times more likely to die of COVID-19 than whites. On average, their daily routine moves them from overcrowded homes that they don't own and can hardly afford on transit systems with poor ventilation to jobs where they share air space with other similarly endangered people every day. Why is this so? The commonplace answer is that systemic racism explains these income and wealth gaps. Less acknowledged, and in many ways easier to correct, is that the invisible hand of shifts in urban land prices marginalizes groups into dangerous and unequal living circumstances, making it nearly impossible to build wealth in the form of urban land equity.

DISEASE AND INEQUALITY BROADLY

Similarly, throughout the English-speaking world, the pandemic and its aftermath have helped create a whole new underclass. College-educated millennials, barred from access to the same urban land wealth that their parents acquired, now serve in low-wage, precarious McJobs or in the gig economy, with burdensome school loans to pay off and no reasonable hope of owning a home or achieving retirement security.[11] This process has unfolded as the world's developed nations have completed shifting their economies from industry to the same service categories that are currently endangering Blacks and immigrants.[12] Members of the millennial generation are now, more than other generations in global cities, closed out of the opportunity to build the wealth enjoyed by many of their parents (again, mostly in the form of homeownership). Adjusted for inflation, wages for most classes of workers have stayed largely flat in the English-speaking world, whereas the cost of housing has more than doubled in real terms (Anderson et al. 2018). A near net-zero interest rate for much of this century[13] meant that the savings strategy of former generations, whereby saved money would compound with interest while home prices stayed more or less flat, no longer works. In some world-class cities, such as Boston, today's average wage earner would need twenty-two years to save enough money for a 20 percent down payment on a decent home. For baby boomers, it took only five years (Olick 2018).

NEOLIBERALISM: IT MATTERS

It is also crucial to acknowledge that this urban land-price inflation is occurring while the English-speaking world continues to swear fealty to its predominant economic theory. Since the 1980s, our most influential economists have coalesced around a few foundational tenets: the government that governs least governs best, the private sector can do most things more efficiently than the public sector, trade barriers between countries should be largely removed, enhanced access to home equity for the middle class would compensate for lower wages, and high taxes on wealth (including urban land wealth) will kill the goose that lays the golden egg. The technical name for this approach is "neoliberalism" (N. Smith n.d.).[14] Due to the global free flow of capital that this trend released, 400 Americans now have more combined wealth than the entire United Kingdom, with the share of national income of the bottom 50 percent of Americans having crashed from 20 percent in 1980 to 13 percent now (Piketty 2014). During those same four decades, the share of income claimed by the top 1 percent of earners in the English-speaking world doubled from approximately 10 percent of the total to around 20 percent.[15] But the even greater economic disparity is not in *income* but in *wealth*. Asset-value gains are a larger and larger share of gains in gross national product (GDP).[16] Less well known is that, by far, the largest share of this wealth is not in the form of buildings, machinery, or other physical assets but in the form of urban land (ibid.).[17]

DISEASE AND HOUSING

This shift in wealth and income might not have been so hard to accept if it hadn't been accompanied by large increases in the cost of housing – increases that were more than double the rate of inflation. As ever-increasing amounts of total wealth flowed into the pockets of those who already had wealth, both in the United States and throughout the English-speaking world, the value of all asset classes skyrocketed. This "everything bubble"[18] is nice if you own assets and the value of your investments grow and grow. It is not so great when you are living paycheque to paycheque, like almost half of Americans,[19] and when the cost of housing (really the dirt below it) gets bid up higher and higher by its capacity to store, hold, and increase value as an asset class.

In the United States, the value of urban land now exceeds the combined market capitalization of every corporation (Lloyd 2019),[20] and as this value inflates, the gap between wage-earner incomes and the cost of a home or rent continues to widen. The result is an unhealthy crowding in the homes of immigrants, people of colour, and the wage-earning class more generally – a crowding not seen since the 1930s. The data now clearly show that it is not residential density that is the vector for disease (i.e., the number of units per acre) but the number of people per square foot in the housing units themselves. Disease passes in shared kitchens and bathrooms, not in the elevators and lobbies of expensive high rises.

DISEASE AND URBAN DESIGN

The disease vector of crowded apartments is echoed in the inequitable layout of our metropolitan regions. Over the past several decades, major metropolitan areas have become ever more segregated by income. Automobility and the supporting infrastructure of limited-access highways have enabled an urban landscape where income classes are typically separated by scores of miles rather than by the mile or two more common to earlier times. In consequence, low-income and minority enclaves have become ever more confined. That is especially true in the United States. In these neighbourhoods of concentrated disadvantage, the crowding is exacerbated by the presence of similarly disadvantaged residents on the streets and in the cafes, dramatically increasing the chances that, unlike in exclusive areas, the person next to you is infected. Contemporary housing policy in many nations conspires to make this situation worse by focusing increasingly parsimonious housing-assistance funds in already poor neighbourhoods, thus missing an opportunity to dilute the disease-concentrating effects of race and class segregation (Berg 2014; Thrush 2020).

THE ISSUE OF ASSET WEALTH IN REAL ESTATE

What can be done about this? Certainly, ungluing the pieces of the urban puzzle and arranging them more equitably will take time. We might begin by simplifying the issue: a metropolitan city can be reduced to the land within its borders and to the buildings placed on that land – and to the pattern of how those buildings are distributed. I argue here that the key to understanding the problem of this moment is to under-stand the importance of urban land itself – literally the dirt under build-ings – and how much that dirt costs. What actually governs city design (as presently practised at any rate) is not primarily within the power of developers or planners but almost entirely a function of how much urban land costs in any particular location and for what purpose it is used. Globally, the most lucrative purpose for that dirt is housing.

Using this lens, we might see how increasing inequality is reflected in how average wage earners have less and less access to the land that they need yet no choice but to pay the price, as their income from their urban job depends on it. The invisible hand of land economics over-whelms any rational government response. Indeed, it reveals how the efforts of both entrepreneurs and wage earners do not primarily enrich the workers or the owners themselves but are absorbed into the price of urban land. A hundred entrepreneurs who enrich a district with an at-tractive variety of shops and services will soon be rewarded with rent increases (and associated land-value increases) that threaten their survival. Thus the benefits of their efforts accrue passively to those who own the land below their shops. As this process plays out region-wide, the pres-sure of land-value increase rises to the point where the economy strains under the weight of housing inequality for wage earners, while robbing entrepreneurs of their gains.

CAN IT BE FIXED?

To some extent, maybe even to a large extent, the problem can be fixed. Chapter 7 enumerates effective policy responses that have been put into practice worldwide, responses that are broadly applicable within legally allowable constraints on urban land use. These efforts are not, at this time, in equal measure to the problem, but they could be. It would be wise for citizens and their policy agents to insist on the continuation and expansion of these measures as the current global housing and health crises make the future ever more uncertain. To attack the systemic dys-functions in health, housing, land use, and transportation, it is necessary to point out that the cost of urban land – or its Rent – is not the conse-quence of benign forces of supply and demand but the consequence of a highly destructive form of monopoly. It is the purpose of this volume to contribute to an emerging understanding of the influence of land Rent on the critical social and epidemiological pathologies that result from the inequitable geographies of our urban landscapes, which are themselves shaped, in large part, by the continued damaging influence of land Rent.

1
Inequality, Disease, and Urban Land

WAGE-EARNER INEQUALITY AND HOUSING MILLENNIALS WORLDWIDE

Since the 1980s, in inflation-adjusted terms, the average wages in the English-speaking world have remained flat, whereas the costs of life-supporting goods such as education and housing have more than doubled (E. Martin 2017a, 2017b). Housing costs in booming global cities have become even worse, quadrupling since 1950 (Fidler and Sabir 2019). These fundamentals are increasingly out of reach at levels enjoyed by baby boomers and even Generation X. For millennials, intergenerational inequity is undermining not just health but also social stability.

The first strong evidence of broad discontent with structural inequality was seen in the Occupy Wall Street protests of 2011 (Graeber 2012) – protests that started in New York and quickly spread throughout the developed world. Before the public expression of rage subsided, protests had been held in over eighty countries (A. Taylor 2011). Here again, the protesters were largely white and young – the first time in modern history that a worldwide protest movement was sparked by purely economic issues and the first time that economic class was redefined as the 1 percent

FIGURE 1.1 Occupy Wall Street protest, September 2011. | Courtesy Paul Stein via Wikimedia Commons.

against all the rest. Their complaint was, and is, that the share of wealth going to wage earners – the lion's share of the 99 percent – represented a smaller and smaller portion of the economic pie, whereas the investor class, the 1 percent, were grabbing too much.

Their diagnosis was largely correct. For three decades after the Second World War, the share of product value (whether for a car or an insurance policy) that went to wage earners in the English-speaking world stayed steady at roughly 60 percent of the sale price (Piketty 2014; Zaveri 2020). Since 1980, despite massive gains in worker productivity, the wage-earner share has dropped to around 40 percent, with the remainder going to owners and stockholders. This change is hugely significant, as it means that additional trillions of dollars are going into the pockets of those who need it least: the small class of citizens with sufficient capital to invest and enough cash flow from these investments to leverage (or financially back up) more and more asset purchases. Enthusiasts for this system on the political right claim that it benefits the broader population since retirement plans and consumer-accessible mutual funds are also lifted up (Erturk et al. 2007). True. They also claim that the majority of people benefit due to the increased equity gains that they enjoy from their property, almost exclusively housing. Again, true.

Unfortunately, as generous corporate retirement plans become rarer and as housing and other essential costs proportionately rise, the capacity of average wage earners to acquire the benefits of surging asset value are becoming more limited. More than 50 percent of American and British (Kidd 2019) wage earners now have a negative net worth. The average member of the American middle class now has only US$4,000 saved for retirement (Horowitz 2018), enough for one month's rent for a two-bedroom apartment in San Francisco.

The COVID-19 pandemic made this discouraging diagnosis grimmer still, as the bottom 50 percent of income earners were decanted into districts where housing is offered at prices that, if not exactly affordable, are at least possible to afford. As this sorting took hold with ever greater ferocity, the same infection dangers experienced by American Blacks and Latinos spread to an ever-larger number of wage earners throughout the English-speaking world as well.

FIGURE 1.2 Diverging income equalities trajectories, United States

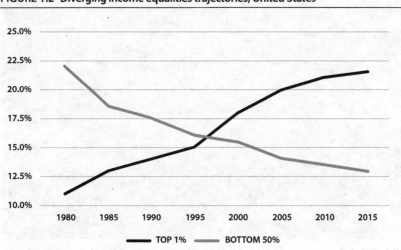

Based on data from piketty.pse.ens.fr/capital21c.

A LOOK AT JUST ONE US STATE AND THE RELATIONSHIP
BETWEEN PANDEMIC AND INCOME

Taking a look at just one US state, Massachusetts, where the data are fairly robust at the time of this writing, we can chart the incidence of infection and death against the average income levels of the state's cities and towns. Massachusetts is a geographically small state with well over 300 separate municipalities, virtually all of them small in area. These municipalities also commonly do not house residents with a wide range of incomes. Residents of rich communities are almost all rich (a result effectuated largely by restrictive zoning laws), whereas other communities (largely older former mill towns) are home to residents with primarily lower-middle or low incomes. In the ten richest towns in the Commonwealth of Massachusetts, the average COVID-19 infection rate was less than 1 percent (Data USA 2020). In the ten poorest cities, the average rate was more than four times higher, at over 4 percent. In Newton, the richest city (Sparkes 2019), the rate was 0.66 percent, whereas in the poorest, Springfield (Massachusetts Department of Public Health 2020), the rate was over six times higher, at 4.25 percent. Fitchburg, also

FIGURE 1.3 Aerial view of Fitchburg, Massachusetts, one of the state's poorest cities and with the highest infection rate in May 2020. The city is 78 percent white and 5 percent Black. | Courtesy Nick Allen via Wikimedia Commons.

on the list of the top ten poor communities, had an even higher infection rate, at 4.9 percent. Yet the population of Fitchburg is only 5 percent Black versus 78 percent white – giving it a Black population nearly 3 percent lower than the state average. This suggests that although Black Americans are uniquely exposed to the dangers of pandemic, they are not alone. Housing areas segregated by income, not race by itself, seem to be the dominant vector for COVID-19 infection (Data USA 2020).

MILLENNIAL WHITES INCREASINGLY ALSO CLOSED OUT OF LAND WEALTH

The pandemic also revealed that geographic inequality, the vector for the disease, is a problem increasingly shared by previously advantaged racial groups, particularly those under the age of forty. Younger people of all races, particularly those living in jobs-rich global cities, are experiencing daunting gaps between the cost of housing and what they can afford to pay. Throughout the English-speaking world, house prices have doubled in the past twenty years (E. Martin 2017a). In some global cities, prices have quadrupled (Fidler and Sabir 2019). But these raw price increases don't tell the whole story. Those who already own homes, older on average than those looking to purchase their first home, escape the worst.

In fact, those lucky enough to have purchased their homes twenty or more years ago are, again on average, sitting on substantial wealth gains (and are naturally loath to see them reduced). But absent very dramatic decreases in home prices, and absent a doubling of wages for those under forty (the trends there don't look promising to say the least), homeownership or even reasonable rents are increasingly out of reach for younger wage earners worldwide.

That is of course unless millennials can access the bank of Mom and Dad for the six-figure down payment required – which is, increasingly, the only way for young people to get on the first rung of the home equity ladder (E. Martin 2019).[1] Again, much of this reality is generally known, but a few facts to support such broad assertions are merited. Millennials with a college degree or a high school diploma make roughly 85 percent as much, in constant dollars, as baby boomers earned at the same age (Bialik and Fry 2019). And even though millennial college graduates make 9 percent more than baby boomer college grads did at the same age (ibid.), they carry an average of roughly US$40,000 dollars in educational debt into their first professional job (Stolba 2019) – not to mention that with housing costs now double in real terms, their standard of living is substantially lower than that of their parents.

But that's not all. On average, their baby boomer parents also carry about US$40,000 in educational debt (Stolba 2019). What gives? Are those sixty year olds going back to school in huge numbers? No, they are obligating themselves through the Parent PLUS student loan program, and others like it, to finance the huge costs of their children's education (ibid.).[2]

These unprecedented educational debts explain why the average net worth of US millennials – only US$8,000 dollars – is 36 percent lower than that of Generation X at a similar age. This figure is itself skewed by breathtaking inequality levels. For example, the estimated net worth of social media mogul Mark Zuckerberg was US$86 billion in 2020, equal to the average net worth of over 10 million of the roughly 80 million US millennials (Duffin 2020). Because of these unprecedented strains, US millennials are giving up on the idea of marriage and childbirth or putting it off by six years on average (Stahl 2020), having fewer children on average, at 1.7 per female and trending down, far below the replacement rate of 2.1 (Editorial Board 2019), living with their parents at nearly twice the rate as in 2000, a trend rapidly accelerated by the pandemic (Pinsker 2020), and giving up on or putting off purchasing a home, with the result that they are half as likely to own a home by age thirty-five as were baby boomers (D. Thompson 2014).

These financial constraints show up in indicators for pandemic risk that are not unlike those experienced by American minorities: the acceptance of more crowded living conditions due to high housing cost, with half of millennials employed in the essential workforce now spending more than 30 percent of their pre-tax income on housing (Nova 2019, citing Freddie Mac 2019);[3] the higher likelihood of employment in the high-exposure gig economy; and fewer opportunities to work from home (college-educated US millennials may do so in large numbers, to be sure, but only 39 percent of US millennials have college degrees) (Bialik and Fry 2019). Generally speaking, the massive growth in the precarious jobs that make up the gig economy is both adding to pandemic risks and limiting opportunities to acquire real estate wealth, start a family, or secure a comfortable retirement (Prudential 2019).

BUILDING TYPE, TRANSPORTATION, AND DISEASE
But what of housing type itself? What evidence links our public and private choices about housing type to communicable diseases? At the beginning of the COVID-19 pandemic in 2020, much concern was

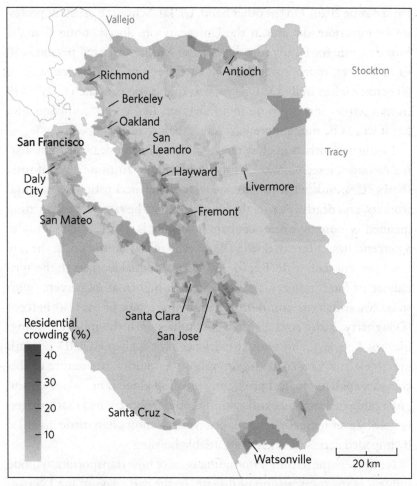

FIGURE 1.4 Residential crowding in the San Francisco Bay Area. In lower-income areas, over 50 percent of all rentals can be crowded. | Cartography by Eric Leinberger. Based on data from US Census Bureau.

expressed about high-density buildings and the possibility of shared spaces – elevators, lobbies, hallways, and common rooms – spreading the disease. At the time of this writing, the evidence strongly suggests that residential density, in multi-unit buildings, is not by itself the problem. On the one hand, models of droplet behaviour provided by Richard L. Corsi, the dean of engineering and computer science at Portland State University and a specialist in indoor air quality, suggest that given the slow rate of air exchange in elevators, droplets from an infected person can linger in elevator air long enough to infect the next rider (cited in Parker-Pope 2020). On the other hand, Dr. Ian Schwartz, assistant professor of infectious diseases at the University of Alberta, notes that the infection rate for family members living with an infected person is 10 to 20 percent, much lower than the infection rate for measles, at 70 to 90 percent (cited in ibid.).[4] One expects that if you can catch COVID-19 from a ten-second exposure in an elevator, living with someone who has it would be much more hazardous than that.

Living with others in close quarters is proving far deadlier than sharing elevators, it seems. Work by the Public Policy Institute of California shows a clear link between apartment crowding, occupations as essential workers, and deaths. Across the United States, the rate of overcrowding (defined as more than one occupant per room) is relatively low, at under 5 percent. In California, due to the severity of its housing crisis, the rate is 8.3 percent state-wide. But for low-wage essential workers in the agriculture or food industry, the rate is much higher, at 24 percent, with some lower-income communities showing a rate of over 40 percent (Dougherty 2020). And California counties with the most crowding, like Los Angeles County, also experienced the highest COVID-19 death rate (Meja and Cha 2020). Again, given the multivariate nature of this complex epidemiological problem, crowding alone is not a proven singular cause of death but exists within a multivariate context that is driven largely by ever-increasing inequality, which is most often made manifest by impeded access to suitable affordable housing.

Next, we come to the confounding issue of how transportation mode influences the transmission of disease. In the early days of the US pandemic, focused largely on New York City, many people associated New York's particularly early and severe health crisis with its subway system,

FIGURE 1.5 Typical medium-density "streetcar suburb" street in the predominantly Black East Flatbush, New York, neighbourhood where disease hit hard. This is not anyone's image of high-density life. | Courtesy Google Maps.

one that is unique in the United States. It seemed logical that crowded subways, along with high-density neighbourhoods, were vectors for the disease. This view was reinforced by early work, such as the widely disseminated study "The Subways Seeded the Massive Coronavirus Epidemic in New York City" (2020) by economist and physician Jeffrey E. Harris of the Massachusetts Institute of Technology. His title was far more inflammatory than the article, where Harris was careful not to make any claims of causation or even to narrow down correlations to one influence. Nevertheless, with the release of his paper prior to publication and peer review, his apocalyptic title caused an eruption in the media. Reaction from urbanists was swift. Salim Furth (2020), director of the Urbanity Project at George Mason University in Georgia, did an equally deep dive into the same data and came to the opposite conclusion: cars were the culprit. Furth's conclusion seems counterintuitive. How could sitting in your own car by yourself be an occasion to catch or spread disease? The answer seems to be that neither subways nor cars are the vector. Inequality is. Furth pointed out that there was a higher correlation between auto use and disease than between subway use and disease, but left largely unnoticed by him was the much stronger correlation between inequality and disease evident in the data. Indeed, over 40 percent of Manhattan residents in the top decile, or one-tenth, of income simply left town to wait out the pandemic. New Yorkers in the bottom nine-tenths of income did not have this option, nor were they rich enough to live in most parts of Manhattan (Quealy 2020). They were instead sequestered far from Manhattan in the moderate- and low-income boroughs, where disease was concentrated, where car use was more necessary, and where daily they were exposed to similarly endangered neighbours regardless of how they got to work.

FIGURE 1.6 COVID-19 deaths (per 100,000), workers in overcrowded homes (%)

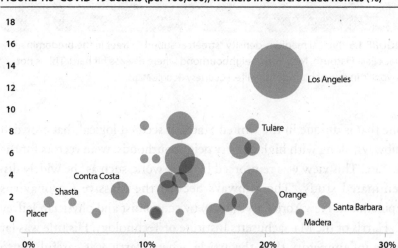

Note: Dot size relative to populations of cities surveyed, with some cities called out for reference. Based on data from Policy Institute of California.

INEQUALITY AND URBAN GEOGRAPHY

To sum up, then, inequality, more than any other factor, is the vector for pandemic. This inequality is manifest in where a home is located, how much it costs, how many people live under one roof, what job types are associated with what type of resident, and the district's concentration of families with similar characteristics. Systemic racism, both blatant and subtle, places American Black families in much higher danger than white families. However, systemic inequality is increasingly placing wage earners of all races in similar danger. The social tensions spawned by systemic inequality and racism are manifest both in recent eruptions,

FIGURE 1.7 View from 398 Westlake Ave. to the southeast up West Maryland St. This is a typical Westlake district residential street. Westlake has the most severe overcrowding in Los Angeles. | Courtesy peter boy12qq12 via Wikimedia Commons.

such as the Black Lives Matter protests and the earlier Occupy Wall Street protests, and in the populist frustrations evident in the recent growth of anti-immigrant political sentiment (see Frank 2020).

Inequality in housing is far more odious than in more benign forms. Housing is necessary for life. Citizens can't choose not to pay for a place to live. Paying the rent must come first. In this way, paying the rent is unlike paying for a flat screen television, double-shot lattes, or avocado toast. This reality makes the doubling of average home prices nationwide and the more than tripling of housing costs in jobs-rich coastal cities particularly problematic. Urban designers and those forging urban development policies now have an additional reason to address housing and urban form inequities. More than social justice, lives are at stake.

COVID-19, RACE, AND URBAN LAND IN THE UNITED STATES

The role of race as a factor in disease has assumed new importance. Data clearly indicate that Black and Brown Americans are at least three times more likely to become infected with COVID-19 than whites (State of Black America 2020).[5] It turns out that a century of systemic discrimination is a major factor, manifest both in the economic geography of

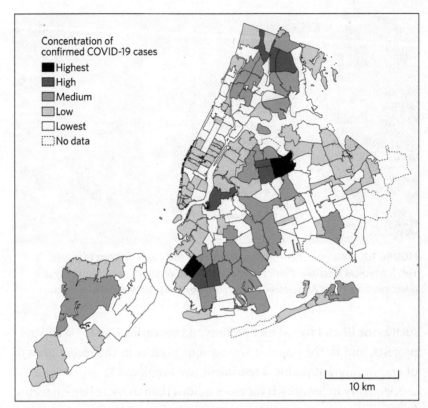

FIGURE 1.8 Concentration of COVID-19 cases in New York City in 2020 by zip code. The concentrations align with poverty, not density. | Cartography by Eric Leinberger. Based on data from US Census Bureau.

American cities and in the patterns of everyday life common to disadvantaged communities. These troubling urban economic geographies are not exclusive to American minority populations, but minority communities are clearly the hardest hit.

DENSITY AND THE "BAD HABITS" OF BLACK AMERICANS

Some have argued that residential density is the vector for disease, a premise supported by the early onset of the pandemic in the densest US city: New York. A secondary early assumption was that disease was caused by morbidity – factors such as obesity, hypertension, and other health factors that presumably affect those who don't take good care of themselves.

President Donald Trump's secretary of health and human services, Alex Azar, was not subtle in implicating what he saw as the unhealthy lifestyles of minority Americans in an on-air interview with *CNN* on May 17, 2020:

> Unfortunately, the American population is a very diverse ... population with significant unhealthy comorbidities that do make many individuals in our communities, in particular African American, [and other] minority communities particularly at risk here because of significant underlying disease health disparities and disease comorbidities. (Quoted in Holmes and Bohn 2020)

This sort of remark was confined neither to Secretary Azar nor to his time. The United States has a long history of rushing to blame the lifestyle habits of those below the poverty line or a presumably unsophisticated ethnic group for the diseases that befall them. When cholera ripped through Lower Manhattan in the mid-1800s, affecting a largely Irish American cohort, the presumably dissolute habits of the poor were also blamed (Garner 2015). It was not until 1854, when Dr. John Snow of England discovered that cholera was transmitted via contaminated food and water consumed by the poor and via the human waste of cholera victims, that New York's leaders reacted intelligently by upgrading their water and sewer systems.

LOW INCOME AS THE VECTOR FOR DISEASE

Latino and African American residents of the United States were three times more likely to become infected with COVID-19 than their white neighbours and three times as likely to die – yet urban density is not the cause (Oppel Jr. et al. 2020). In New York City, where robust data sets allow researchers to track cases down to the postal code, we learn that Manhattan, the highest-density borough of the city and one that is increasingly white and wealthy, had the lowest incidence of COVID-19 cases, whereas lower-density outer portions of the Bronx, Queens, and Brooklyn, areas with higher concentrations of Blacks and Latinos, had much higher levels of infection per capita.

What best explains this concentration of disease among minority

FIGURE 1.9 The assumed "fever nests" of New York City. Illustrations clearly depict the abodes of poor Irish immigrants of the day to make the connection between lifestyle, habits, family size, and disease. | Courtesy Healy Collection.

populations if not density, lifestyle, or special susceptibility? The driver seems to be the low income of Black Americans relative to whites – a disparity that has persisted since the 1950s despite dramatic increases in minority education.

In 1968, just 54 percent of Black adults had a high school diploma. Today, 92 percent do. That same year, just 9 percent of Blacks had a college degree. Now, 23 percent do (Brooks 2020). Yet average wages for Blacks remain stuck at just 51 percent of what whites earn nationwide (Leonhardt 2020). This shocking difference is partly caused by including in this depressing statistic the number of both whites and Blacks who are no longer in the labour force due to unemployment, who are not actively looking for work, or who are incarcerated – Blacks having a proportionately higher percentage in all three of these categories.[6]

Low pay, in and of itself, is obviously not the direct causal vector for disease. Susceptibility must somehow be tied both to the activities and life choices associated with this low pay and to the housing that you can afford given these earnings.

Black Americans, as one might expect in light of these low levels of income, are inordinately represented in low-wage jobs in retail and food services, as cab and bus drivers, in warehousing and delivery, as hospital nonprofessional staff, and so on. The proportion of these low-paying but essential jobs held by Blacks is twice that of whites (Salsberg and Kastanis 2018). Research has shown these "nonrelocatable occupations" to expose workers to higher COVID-19 risks (M.G. Baker 2020).

Conversely, the percentage of professional, managerial, and financial services jobs –relocatable jobs – held by Blacks is less than half that of whites (US Bureau of Labor Statistics 2012). During the 2020 pandemic, most nonrelocatable service workers, such as grocery clerks, were considered newly essential. Thus these low-wage workers could neither work from home nor stay home and still pay the rent.

Given that neighbourhoods in New York (where the best data come from) are highly segregated by ethnicity and income, residents with a high likelihood of becoming infected had similarly endangered persons on their streets, in their cafes, and on transit, adding to the risks of exposure that these people experienced each day.

THE COMPLEX SYSTEM OF AMERICAN INEQUALITY AND DISEASE
Proving that disease is caused by just one or even two factors is impossible, although correlations are much more than suggestive. For example, American Blacks, again because of lower income, are more likely to lack health insurance than whites. Even more odious is that the health care system has structural inequities between Black and white patients even when they have similar health care plans. A *New England Journal of Medicine* editorial puts it this way: "Slavery has produced a legacy of racism, injustice, and brutality that runs from 1619 to the present, and that legacy infects medicine as it does all social institutions" (Evans et al. 2020). In a *Washington Post* follow-up article spawned by this editorial, Tina Douroudian, an optometrist in Sterling, Virginia, discusses evidence of subtle and systemic race-based inequities affecting similarly insured patients:

> "I ask all of my diabetic patients if they have ever seen a registered dietitian," she says. "The answer is an overwhelming 'yes' from my white patients, and an overwhelming 'no' from my black patients. Is there any wonder why they struggle more with their blood sugar, or why some studies cite a fourfold greater risk of visual loss from diabetes complications in black people?" (Quoted in Russell 2020)

Thus, as we can see, the relationship of disease to income and location in the urban fabric is multifaceted. But the evidence strongly supports the conclusion that reversing this trend toward ever-greater geographic inequality for low-income American minorities would improve health outcomes.

AMERICAN INFRASTRUCTURE, RACE, POVERTY, AND DISEASE
Infrastructure decisions have also been identified as contributing to the high COVID-19 death rates among American Blacks. Urban redeveloper Robert Moses, according to journalist Robert Caro's famous biography of the man, intentionally drove disruptive limited-access highways through New York's largely minority neighbourhoods. He even insisted that the clearance heights of highway overpasses be too low for buses, presumably buses carrying minorities, to keep Long Island beaches

largely white (Caro 1974). This strategy was not unique to New York or to Moses but was typical in other cities and regions as well. Close-in streetcar neighbourhoods were plowed through by freeways in many US cities to give ready auto access to newly developing, and almost entirely white, auto-oriented suburbs. The result is that poorer, close-in neighbourhoods are typically subjected to harmful air quality, leading to a high incidence of asthma, which ultimately resulted in higher COVID-19 death rates. The effect is not insignificant. A paper from the Harvard T.H. Chan School of Public Health (n.d.) reports "an 11% increase in mortality from COVID-19 infection for every 1 microgram [per] cubic meter increase in air pollution." Many low-income neighbourhoods located next to heavily used freeways have over 8 micrograms of pollutants per cubic metre (ibid.). Robert D. Bullard – a professor of urban planning and environmental policy at Texas Southern University and the author of *The Wrong Complexion for Protection: How the Government Response to Disaster Endangers African American Communities* (1991), as well as nine other books on the relationship between race, cities, and the environment – put it this way:

> "Oftentimes, communities of color have the wrong complexion for protection," Bullard said in an interview with NPR's *Weekend Edition Sunday*. "You can't wash race out of it ... There's all kinds of studies that show that race is still the most potent variable for predicting who gets more than their fair share of the 'nasty stuff,' and who gets more than their fair share of the good stuff."
>
> Bullard argues that losing out on "the good stuff" ultimately shortens Black and brown lives. Minorities are disproportionately likely to live in areas with more pollution and in areas that are flood-prone. (Quoted in Valentine 2020)

HOUSING COST, EDUCATION, THE AMERICAN CITY, AND DISEASE
If the cost of housing is sorting residents by income and race into narrowly bracketed communities, this sorting will triple your chance of succumbing to disease. Sadly, income segregation is getting more, not less, extreme as the decades pass. Research by the Sage Foundation shows that although US schools are not more segregated by race than

FIGURE 1.10 Low-clearance overpass on the Belt Parkway in Brooklyn. According to biographer Robert Caro, Robert Moses built parkways for cars only to limit access to low-income riders presumably in buses. | Courtesy Google Maps.

they were fifty years ago, they are dramatically more segregated by income – caused by families moving to communities with better schools and amenities if they can afford to do so, leaving behind people of all races who can't. Such dramatic increases in the degree to which urban regions are segregated by income are shown to impede academic achievement for all races in disadvantaged school districts (Duncan and Murnane 2011). The aforementioned educational challenges can thus be added to the health challenges of residing in lower-income districts. A nationwide sorting of Americans by race, income, and occupation, against the background of what is commonly referred to as a housing crisis, can now be seen as especially damaging to the security, health, and educational well-being of the nation, and not only is this threat clinical in its cause and cure, but it should also, if we are reasonable, be addressed by reconsideration of the increasing inequalities of our economic geographies – inequalities that are most importantly driven by the cost of urban land.

AMERICAN RACIAL PROTEST, THE CITY, AND DISEASE

The increasing segregation of American urban areas by income and class can be measured by other evidence of political stress. During the spring of 2020, in the midst of some of the darkest days of the pandemic, Derek Chauvin, a white Minneapolis police officer, kneeled on the neck of George Floyd, a forty-six-year-old Black man, until Floyd was dead. Caught on camera (as all things are these days), the incident sparked riots and then nationwide protests involving both whites and Blacks (and every skin shade in between). In some ways, the middle of a pandemic seemed an unlikely time for throngs of protesters to hit the streets. In another way, it made perfect sense. As Frederick J. Riley (2020) wrote in a *USA Today* op-ed on July 8:

> Communities of color are disproportionately ravaged by COVID-19. Communities of color are also bending and breaking under the weight of decades of structural racism – our country's "unfinished business" – which impacts not only how policing and criminal justice are meted out but also how our educational, economic and health systems function by design.
>
> At the same time, we know that the health and economic toll of this period will cut a wide path across America, leaving vulnerable communities of all colors and stripes in its wake. At times like this, facing multiple perceived threats, our local communities and our country as a whole may struggle mightily to secure and strengthen our "bonds of affection." It's natural, it's human, to let fear divide us. It takes heart and courage to tap the deep waters that connect us.

Racial inequality can thus be seen as the most odious manifestation – and a structural one – of inequality more generally. However, the combination of the pandemic and the Black Lives Matter protests in 2020 indicates that, this time, the outrage against systemic inequality extended beyond the Black community (Washington 2020). Unlike in previous American race protests, where participants were virtually all Black, people of all colours participated this time, and in some cities, such as Seattle (Gutman 2020), white faces predominated. This fact is less surprising than one might initially think when one realizes that the pressures on white wage earners, if not equal to the pressures on American Blacks, are now beginning to resemble them, especially for Americans under the age of forty – the millennials and Generation Z.

FIGURE 1.11 A Black Lives Matter "die-in" over tram tracks on September 20, 2020, protesting alleged police brutality in Saint Paul, Minnesota. | Courtesy Fibonacci Blue via Wikimedia Commons.

A troubling conclusion seems clear: for the average American Black family, the vector for the disease was low wages. Low wages correlate with high-contact service jobs – which cannot be conducted from home. Low wages also correlate with the concentration of low-wage earners in highly income-segregated areas, where those in your neighbourhood are similarly endangered and will endanger each other in cafes, on sidewalks, at work, and in transit.

A SHORT HISTORY OF A SPECIAL CASE: US RACIAL EXCLUSION FROM URBAN LANDOWNERSHIP

The history of racial discrimination is the United States is unique in the English-speaking world and warrants additional explication. To illustrate how access to US urban land and racial inequality are linked, I start with the most obvious historical example of how government policy can either grant or deny land to an entire race, providing a brief recap of the troubling 150-year history of withholding land wealth from African Americans.

Some of what follows is relatively well known, but it bears repeating. At the time of this writing, African Americans own, on average, only about one-tenth of the wealth claimed by the average American white: US$17,150 versus US$171,000 (McIntosh et al. 2020). Most of the capital value held by American whites is in the form of urban land – largely their fully or partially paid-off home. The current low comparative wealth of Black families in the United States is a consequence of institutionally blocked access to urban land wealth. This disparity can be shown to be a still-lingering effect of slavery.

After the American Civil War, despite the exhortations of abolitionists, no serious effort was made to redistribute land to freed slaves. The history is complex and multifaceted, with the failure of one initiative, the Freedmen's Bureau (Cox 1958), standing out as especially unjust. Set up at the end of the war with President Abraham Lincoln's support, the bureau's goal was to distribute land to former slaves. The amount specified was 40 acres each, or a "quarter-quarter section" in the parlance of the Continental Land Survey (Linklater 2002, 181).[7] Importantly, the redistributed land had been "abandoned," or it was land "to which the United States shall have acquired title by confiscation or sale, or otherwise" (US Government 1865, sec. 4).

Originally, as administered during Lincoln's life, the legislation would have allowed for the "confiscation" of the white-owned plantations of southern insurrectionists, with land being parcelled off to the freed slaves who had worked it. After Lincoln's assassination in 1865, President Andrew Johnson, a Democrat from North Carolina, quickly reversed course. Henceforth, southerners who signed a "loyalty oath" would have their confiscated lands returned to them, ensuring that white plantation owners would reclaim the South's most arable lands. Blacks also had to compete with white "refugees" for what lands remained. Then, to make it completely impossible for Blacks to claim land, white owners quickly instituted vagrancy laws (without federal objection) that made it a crime for Blacks to be idle, giving them no choice but to work for the same "masters" they had been enslaved to (Daniel 1979).

One more thing. Simultaneous with the Civil War and the later failed Freedmen's Bureau initiative in the South, the federal government was opening up western lands for settlement under the terms of the

FIGURE 1.12 Racist poster from post–US Civil War South against the Freedmen's Bureau. | Courtesy National Archives and Wikimedia Commons.

Homestead Act. This legislation was designed to give free land to Americans on the western plains (and eventually beyond).[8] In modern terms, the land was *sparsely* but not entirely unoccupied. These lands were former Spanish colonies or Native American lands (Arrington 2012). These free farmsteads were theoretically available to the newly freed Black slaves. A small number of freed slaves were able to take advantage of this initiative and thus to acquire land. Unfortunately, most southern Blacks were, after Lincoln's death and in light of the prohibitive race laws passed by southern governments, no more than indentured servants under contract to work plantation lands. Breach of contract would result in jail terms, with prison labour served on the same plantation lands – but this time for no pay at all.

Comparing the results of the Homestead Act to those of the Freedmen's Bureau makes for a disheartening assessment. Relatively few of the 4 million southern Blacks ended up with land, either in the South or on the western plain, whereas 4 million whites got free land under the Homestead Act. As historian Keri Leigh Merritt (2016) points out,

> The number of adult descendants of the original Homestead Act recipients living in the year 2000 was estimated to be around *46 million people, about a quarter of the US adult population.* If that many White Americans can trace their legacy of wealth and property ownership to a single entitlement program, then the perpetuation of black poverty must also be linked to national policy. Indeed, the Homestead Acts excluded African Americans not in letter, but in practice – a template that the government would propagate for the next century and a half. (Original emphasis; see also Merritt 2017)

RACISM, HOUSING, AND AMERICAN LAND WEALTH IN THE TWENTIETH CENTURY

To reiterate, in brief because much of this history is well known and others cover this ground more completely, institutional racism has blocked access to real estate wealth for Blacks up to this day. Just after the Civil War, three constitutional amendments were passed: the Thirteenth, abolishing slavery; the Fourteenth, affording due process protection to Americans of all races; and the Fifteenth, guaranteeing the right to vote regardless of race.

The Thirteenth Amendment is the best known, but less known is that, to this day, Section 2 of this amendment still gives Congress the right to pass laws ensuring state compliance. Congress followed up in 1875 with its Civil Rights Act barring all public or private discrimination. Sadly, in 1883, the US Supreme Court declared that in passing this law, Congress had exceeded authorities granted by the Thirteenth Amendment, arguing that it did not give Congress the right to rule over the use of private property. In 1896, the Supreme Court went even further in its landmark *Plessy v. Ferguson* decision,[9] declaring specifically that "separate but equal" facilities, this time including public schools, were constitutional. These Supreme Court precedents would not be overturned until 1968 when the case of *Jones v. Alfred H. Mayer Co.* came before the high court.[10] Joseph Jones was an African American who sued the Alfred H. Mayer Company for blocking his purchase of a new home

FIGURE 1.13 Joseph Jones sued the Alfred Meyer Company for blocking his purchase of a new home in St. Louis because he was Black. The decision effectively reversed the *Plessy v. Ferguson* interpretation of Amendment 13. | Courtesy National Archives.

in St. Louis because he was Black. The decision effectively reversed the *Plessy v. Ferguson* interpretation of the Thirteenth Amendment – almost 100 years after it was passed (Rothstein 2017).[11]

Prior to 1968, private developers such as William Levitt (builder of the famous Levittowns) were free to refuse home sales to African Americans, whereas the circumstances for city officials intent on keeping white neighbourhoods white were slightly more complicated. Cities and towns throughout the United States were free to institute explicitly discriminatory zoning codes (setting aside certain parts of town for whites only) until 1917, when the US Supreme Court outlawed this practice in its *Buchanan v. Warley* decision.[12] Undeterred, many US cities continued the practice, including Palm Beach till 1960, Kansas City till 1987, and Norfolk Virginia till 1987 (Rothstein 2017). And finally, when all else failed, cities and towns could simply use zoning rules set to ensure that the vast majority of Black families, having been successfully blocked from capital accumulation for a century, could not afford to move there. Setting high minimum lot-area requirements (5-acre minimums were common) was a common tool of de facto racial discrimination and class exclusion (Babcock and Bosselman 1973).

FIGURE 1.14 Typical discriminatory 2–5-acre minimum lot size sprawl zoning in Sudbury, Massachusetts. | Courtesy Google Maps.

This practice endures to this day, and the battle rages on. The administration of President Barack Obama sought to address this inequity in the mildest of ways, issuing an order requiring suburban communities to offer a plan to end this kind of race and class discrimination as a condition for receiving federal funds of all types. He acted as the executive administrator of the Fair Housing Act of 1968 in this instance.[13] An executive order titled "Affirmatively Furthering Fair Housing" would require suburban communities to show that their housing policies conformed to the 1968 legislation (Fuchs 2020). Failing to do so would impede access to federal funds. During the 2020 US election, President Donald Trump made this order a centrepiece of his campaign, promising to kill the rule in the hope of appealing to racist fears among white suburban residents. He claimed that candidate "[Joe] Biden will destroy your neighborhood and your American Dream. I will preserve it, and make it even better!" (quoted in Olorunnipa and Itkowitz 2020). The relatively close vote in this still-incendiary election suggests that this argument may still resonate.

But suburbs in the United States have become increasingly mixed. The white share of US suburbs fell by 8 percent between 2000 and 2018 and now stands at 68 percent, trending toward rough parity (Parker et al. 2018). This fact does not contradict the increasingly stark income and wealth segregation across metropolitan areas that census information makes clear, as it indicates only that some districts within some suburbs are trending toward housing Black and Brown residents over time.

WHAT WE KNOW ABOUT THE PANDEMIC, NATIONAL RESPONSES, AND RACIAL WEALTH TRENDS

At the time of this writing, the long-term economic effects of the 2020 pandemic are not entirely clear, but certain things are already obvious. Since job losses in the United States have hit low-wage workers hard and low-wage Black and Brown workers even harder (Luhby 2020),[14] these cohorts are experiencing ever-greater financial stress. Absent continued federal requirements to extend generous unemployment support, continue mortgage forbearance, and continue various limits on evictions from rental units, housing security for low- and moderate-income Americans is further endangered – with avenues to gain land wealth further blocked. Meanwhile, efforts to keep America's corporations from collapsing led the Federal Reserve and Congress to inject trillions of dollars into the economy in order to protect shareholders – as most shares of stock are held by the upper 10 percent of Americans (Wigglesworth 2020).[15] Money went out in the form of loans that were either low-interest

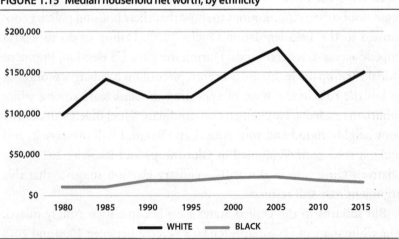

FIGURE 1.15 Median household net worth, by ethnicity

or nearly no-interest, financed using the drastically expanded balance sheet of the Federal Reserve Bank, and the recipients included everything from airlines to real estate investment trusts (REITs), protecting both rental-unit landlords and the portfolios of the investor class (Ocasio-Cortez 2020).[16]

AUSTRALIA, COVID-19, AND HOUSING STRESS

Australia's battle with COVID-19 differed from that of the United States, but certain relevant similarities prevailed. Australia took a much harder stance in trying to keep disease out of the country, with a zero-COVID strategy of barriers to immigration, contact tracing, and isolation of the afflicted. Thus its rate of COVID-19 deaths was relatively low, at 20 persons per 100,000 versus 290 per 100,000 in the United States. And although one death is too many, a performance that is well over ten times better than that of the United States is something to celebrate. However, at the time of this writing, Australia and New Zealand are infection hot spots, with infection rates far higher than in the United States (Johns Hopkins University 2023). This finding bodes ill for managing what is left of this pandemic, or the next one, or what increasingly looks like a long-term, global viral endemic.

With due appreciation for such success, it is still evident in the data that race, immigration status, and income are vectors for the disease. As of February 2022, COVID-19 death rates were three times higher for immigrant families than for nonimmigrant families (Davey and Nicholas 2022). In fact, despite making up 24 percent of the population, immigrants – many from the Middle East – accounted for almost twice as many deaths as occurred among the native born: 1,600 versus 900 respectively. The litany of causes cited by public health officials is familiar: crowded apartments, the concentration of employment in low-wage, high-contact service jobs impossible to do from home, and neighbourhood interactions on streets, in homes, and in cafes with similarly endangered families (ibid.).

AUSTRALIA AND INTERGENERATIONAL HOUSING STRESS

Homeownership rates in Australia (at 64% of all housing) are similar to those in Canada (68%), the United Kingdom (65%), New Zealand (65%), and the United States (65%). However, these rates are declining, largely due to the difficulties that millennials encounter getting their first home ("Home Ownership Rate," 2022). Since 1994, renters of both public and private housing, who constitute the remaining 36 percent of the population, have seen a substantial increase in the portion of net income flowing to rent, a change that has resulted in all of the income gains over this period among those in the bottom decile of income going to increases in rent (Karácsonyi, Dyrting, and Taylor 2021). This sad fact mirrors recent trends in wealth and income inequality. Wealth inequality concerns us most in these pages due to its direct relationship to urban landownership. Data show that between 2003 and 2018, only Australians in the top one-fifth of wealth saw any substantial increase in new worth equity (Sheil and Stilwell). And this flow of wealth was not in stocks, bonds, or bitcoins but in urban land value – not in the value of the house but in the value of the land under it (Costello 2014). This increase in land value drove the 7 percent annual increase in home prices during the past thirty years, or a doubling in dollar price every ten years (Kohler and van der Merwe 2015). It's not getting any better either, no matter how many new homes are built in Australia's capital cities. Between 2010 and 2020, the average annual increase in home prices grew by about 10 percent per year, speeding up the rate of the doubling in price to just seven years in inflation-adjusted terms (Ryan 2021). This is all great if you bought your home fifteen or twenty years ago, as did the majority of Australia's homeowners. But it's not so great if you are thirty and hoping to buy your first home. Wage-earning millennials and Generation Z Australians are, unsurprisingly, buying homes at only two-thirds the rate of their parents when they were the same age – 62% in 1980 versus 43% now – and the majority of those lucky young homeowners are lucky because they can tap into the bank of Mom and Dad to access loans drawn by their parents from their own home equity to cover their children's down payment (Wiltshire and Wood 2017). Looking into the future suggests that this lower rate of homeownership among millennials and Generation Z portends a much higher rate of renting for this cohort as they age and a concomitant reduction in family wealth during retirement (Coates and Chivers 2019). This consequence matters because housing wealth has traditionally been a cushion against disability expenses during aging in Australia. A general decrease in the percentage of citizens with such a cushion inevitably increases financial pressures on the state for their welfare and represents yet another impact of the shift in social value away from income and productive capital to the inflated price of urban land.

THE UNITED KINGDOM, COVID-19, AND HOUSING STRESS

One of the enduring features of this investigation of land wealth is the similarity of the stresses imposed on average wage earners and the young from one nation to the next. The situation in the United Kingdom conforms to this rule. The United Kingdom had the seventh highest infection rate of any country in the world, just slightly higher than the rate in the United States, which was eighth (Elflein 2022). There, as in the United States, immigrant families working in urban service industries and, more generally, those making low wages suffered COVID-19 infection and death rates that were up to four times higher than those seen among the more well-off. An exhaustive data dive examining 17 million complete but anonymous heath records of the United Kingdom's National Health Service elicited the following insight:

> Particularly compelling were the study's findings on race and ethnicity, said Sharrelle Barber, an epidemiologist at Drexel University who was not involved in the study. Roughly 11 percent of the patients tracked by the analysis identified as nonwhite. The researchers found that these individuals – particularly Black and South Asian people – were at higher risk of dying from COVID-19 than white patients.
>
> That trend persisted even after [Dr. Ben] Goldacre [of the University of Oxford] and his colleagues made statistical adjustments to account for factors like age, sex and medical conditions, suggesting that other factors are playing a major role.
>
> An increasing number of reports have pointed to the pervasive social and structural inequities that are disproportionately burdening racial and ethnic minority groups around the world with the coronavirus's worst effects. (Wu 2020)

And here again, much as in the United States, overcrowding within apartments, not the number of homes per acre in a district (also known as residential density), was the most glaring vector for disease. A diversity of health agencies concluded that districts with over 20 percent of their housing stock technically overcrowded (generally defined as more people living in an apartment than there are rooms) exhibited infection and death rates that were six times higher than in districts whose stock was only 5 percent overcrowded. No such disparity in infection rates was found between districts with high versus low numbers of dwelling units per acre (N. Barker 2020).

Of course, overcrowding is not something done for fun but out of financial necessity. Thus the singular vector for the disease is not crowded housing by itself but the high cost of adequate housing, which is at the root of the unequal danger from pandemics. It's worth considering whether there is anything new about the United Kingdom's dangerous level of housing precarity. There is. And land price, not building price, is the driver.

FIGURE 1.16 COVID-19 deaths (per 100,000) in UK residential overcrowding (%)

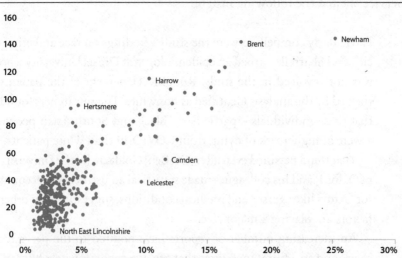

Note: Each dot represents one community plotted by residential crowding, with certain communities called out for reference. Deaths occurred during the first six weeks. Courtesy Nathaniel Barker. Based on data from British Office for National Statistics.

THE RAPIDLY INFLATING PRICE OF URBAN LAND IN THE UNITED KINGDOM

From 1990 until 2020, there was a remarkable increase in the cost of housing across the United Kingdom, with the average cost doubling in inflation-adjusted terms (UK Land Registry 2023). Further exacerbated by the pandemic, house prices climbed 8.5 percent in 2020 alone, according to figures from the Office for National Statistics (cited in ibid.). However, during these same decades, the cost of construction remained relatively stable. Thus the doubled value accruing to the asset comes not from the value of the constructed home but from the value of the land beneath it (Knoll, Schularick, and Steger 2014). In the 1930s, the value of the land under a new home was only 7 percent of the value of the home above (Christophers 2018). "In 1995, the price paid for a home was almost evenly split between the value of the land and the property [i.e., building]. In 2016, the cost of the land had risen to over 70 percent of the price paid for a home" – more than double the value of the structure itself (L. Murphy 2018, 2). This finding means that 100 percent of the increase in home price was attributable to land-price inflation alone. A publication by the British Institute for Public Policy Research has estimated that by 2036, if these trends continue (and they show only signs of accelerating), land value will constitute 83 percent of the purchase price of new homes (ibid.). Land is now the most valuable asset in the United Kingdom, growing from one-fifth of aggregate UK household net wealth in 1995 to two-fifths by 2016, with the total value increasing by 544 percent (ibid.). This figure represents an increase in the gross national asset value of urban land from £1 trillion to £5 trillion during the same period, or nearly 9 percent per year, three times faster than the annual increase in the total value of machinery, for example (ibid., 6).

INTERGENERATIONAL INEQUITY IN THE UNITED KINGDOM AS A RESULT OF URBAN LAND PRICE

This kind of growth in wealth has a distinct generational impact. Whereas one in two young people between the ages of twenty-four and thirty-five owned their own home in 1990, this number had fallen to one in four by 2017. Meanwhile, the rates of homeownership for those over sixty-five had increased from one in two in 1990 to three in four by 2017 (L. Murphy 2018, 15). For British citizens of the baby boom generation, the average ratio of income to home price hovered at around one to four for the price of the average home. From 1955 to about 1995, the ratio of wage to home price hovered at this same ratio, with the occasional boom-to-bust spikes in intervening decades (Longtermtrends n.d.). These ratios echoed those in other parts of the English-speaking world, reinforcing the belief among real estate economists that these one-to-four ratios constituted a real estate fundamental. This so-called fundamental has been far less certain in recent decades, with this ratio inflating wildly. In the past decade, the wage-to-price ratio rose to one to eight in the United Kingdom, and it has recently risen to one to nine and above. These ratios of wage to home price are considered to be dangerously unaffordable by most housing-policy professionals.

These wage-to-price ratios, as alarming as they seem, disguise the intergenerational inequity problem that exists. Housing ownership is the traditional way for middle-class Britons to gain wealth and financial

FIGURE 1.17   A street festival in the Notting Hill district of London shows the rich diversity of ethnic groups that are now a feature of London. London, the major immigration catchment metro area for many decades, is now dominated by non–Anglo Saxons. These diverse groups, due to their relatively late arrival in the UK, have missed opportunities enjoyed by other Britons to acquire housing wealth.
| Courtesy Wikimedia Commons.

security in old age. British citizens in their peak family-forming ages between twenty-five and thirty-five have seen their average wealth, in relation to the wealth held by their parents' generation at the same age, slip by a steady 10 percent per decade (Bangham and Leslie 2019).

The future looks doubly difficult for British millennials when the entry price for housing keeps rising while wages remain frustratingly stagnant. Wages for service workers in the United Kingdom, those experiencing the greatest barriers to housing affordability, have been flat, after factoring for inflation, since the 1970s (Drum 2019).

A reference to the overarching economic context seems appropriate here. This trend in intergenerational inequality, and in inequality more generally, reflects global trends in the flow of wealth away from wage earners and into the pockets of the investor class over the course of the past four decades (Piketty 2014). What the above information also makes clear is that, for the United Kingdom, much like for the rest of the English-speaking world, the contemporary flow of asset value largely shows up on the national wealth ledgers as the massively inflated price of the dirt under urban homes (Wasmer et al. 2021).

SOMETHING ESPECIALLY DEPRESSING ABOUT BRITISH LANDOWNERSHIP

One aspect of British landownership distinguishes its tradition of land regulation from that of other countries in the English-speaking world: landownership is often a closely held secret, as explained below.

The UK aristocracy (and landed gentry) of the past held the title to large estates that covered the nation. To this day, many of these families still hold their massive estates. Many of these owners, of noble and lesser noble rank, never need to apply for wage-earning employment to put food on the table but can sell parcels of their landholdings at ever-inflating prices whenever the need for cash creeps up. This situation naturally locks in place the British class structure, made all the more odious by the negative consequences of the rapidly inflating value of urban land referred to above.

The system that benefits these families was so pervasive that, according to investigative journalist Guy Shrubsole (2019), approximately half of the land in England is owned by less than 1 percent of the population.

Of this half, about 30 percent is owned by the aristocracy and landed gentry, 18 percent by corporations, and 17 percent by oligarchs and city bankers (ibid.). Despite the widely circulated rumour that vast portions of the nation are owned by the Royal Family, Shrubsole reports that these holdings represent only 1.4 percent of the nation's land (ibid.). These statistics are estimates because the National Land Registry's secretive and incomplete approach to the collection of landholding information means that residents must pay to access this information. Furthermore, the Land Registry can verify only who owns about 80 percent of the total land in the country, with ownership of the final 20 percent being a mystery even to its overseers (ibid.).

NEW ZEALAND, COVID-19, AND HOUSING STRESS

New Zealand became world-famous for its zero-COVID policy. Along with China, it was one of the very few countries to make this attempt. This undertaking involved a firm shutdown of all contacts with the outside world, including preventing New Zealanders unlucky enough to be out of their country at the time of the outbreak in spring 2020 from returning home for more than a year. This prohibition even applied to the fully vaccinated and boosted, who would have been happy to isolate if they had been allowed to do so (Power 2021). However, at the time of this writing, the damn has burst with a nearly vertical, rapid doubling and tripling of cases. There is reason to believe that COVID-19 or future pandemics will affect people of colour disproportionately in comparison to New Zealand whites. Overcrowding is increasing rapidly in New Zealand, at a rate of 10 percent every five years (Stats NZ 2018, 19). Currently, one in ten persons in New Zealand lives in crowded conditions, but for people of colour, the rate is much higher, at between two in ten for Asians and four in ten for people of Pacific ethnicity. High housing costs for large extended families are the main driver, with those same high costs (relative to income) forcing the choice of inadequate and now health-endangering housing (ibid., 29).

THE LEGACY OF COLONIAL LANDOWNERSHIP IN NEW ZEALAND

The high cost of housing and its disproportionate impact on recent immigrants and Aboriginal peoples is rooted in patterns and processes of colonial inhabitation. Descendants of settlers still maintain an advantage gained in previous centuries with regard to urban land wealth. Like in many parts of the English-speaking world, colonial practices have produced disparities in landownership patterns that remain dominant.

New Zealand was colonized somewhat later than other British dominions. First-wave British colonists were surprised to find that the Mauri had firmly established agricultural practices and the right of land use that these practices made concrete. Thus complex interactions were required by early colonizers in order to gain access to already clearly occupied and claimed land. In short, colonialists chose to establish peaceful ways of negotiating with Aboriginals in order to secure access to landholdings. Once the deal was made, colonialists would use English property laws to establish fixed and recorded metes and bounds for lands that they now claimed to own outright as individuals. In time, unsurprisingly, the system affecting most of New Zealand's land passed from one of informal ownership by Aboriginals, governed by word of mouth in their nonliterate culture, to one where landholdings were recorded in precise surveys and registered with local magistrates to ensure legally defensible ownership by white settlers (Banner 1999). This shift helps to explain why white New Zealanders have five times more wealth on average, at NZ$114,000, than do Maori, at NZ$23,000 (Stats NZ 2016). In 2017, 70 percent of this total was in the form of urban housing, a dramatic shift in the proportion of wealth types from the 1980s, when housing wealth and financial wealth were equal (M. Wong 2017). This situation was likely more extreme at the time of this writing since housing value had inflated a further 50 percent since then, whereas inflation in other asset classes has been far more moderate ("House Prices" 2021). This shift of wealth into housing value is largely a shift into land value. The ratio of an urban parcel's value to its building value has changed dramatically over the past few decades. In 1993, the parcel value was 41 percent of the total value on average. By 2018, the parcel value accounted for 67 percent of the value of the median home, with the building now worth only the remaining 33 percent. When inflation is factored in, nearly all of the dramatic increase in home prices afflicting all of New Zealand's cities was due solely to land-price inflation (C. Harris 2018).

The impeded access to urban land due to inflated price has further cemented in place the structural inequality that exists between white New Zealanders and their Aboriginal fellow citizens. One indicator of this crisis level of housing stress is that the number of Kiwis on the social-housing waiting list has exploded from 4,000 to 24,000, or 500 percent, since 2015, with 43 percent of the people on this list being Maori, even though the Maori make up just 13 percent of the population ("Govt Formally Putting" 2017; Smyth 2021).

THE EROSION OF THE FAIR GO IN NEW ZEALAND: IS SOCIAL MOBILITY STILL POSSIBLE?

In 2014, the Organisation for Economic Co-operation and Development (OECD) granted New Zealand the dubious distinction of having the OECD member states' most unaffordable housing when measured as a percentage of wages consumed by housing costs (B. Perry 2021; Rash-brooke 2014). Since then, the gap has only widened. The urban land-value shift is inordinately responsible for the gradual increase in inequality experienced by New Zealanders and undercuts a commonly understood lynchpin of Kiwi identity: the fair go.

The idea of a fair go captures the idea of New Zealand as a paradise of equal opportunity. This characterization may have been true between the Second World War and 1990, but in the successive decades, New Zealand experienced the most rapid increase in inequality, as measured by its Gini coefficient,[17] of any OECD nation. New Zealand's Gini measure rose from 0.25 to 0.35 between 1990 and today. Prior to 1990, it ranked among the most equal countries by this measure. After 2000, it shifted dramatically, such that it now ranks close to the United Kingdom by this measure and is far less equal than, for example, Germany and Norway (OECD Data n.d.). The Gini coefficient by itself should alarm New Zealanders, but it does not tell the whole story. When the cost of housing is added to the Gini computation, New Zealand's 2016 Gini coefficient is shown to have risen even further, from 0.35 to 0.40 (B. Perry 2016), which puts it close to US levels of inequality and reveals, yet again, the significant role of urban land-price inflation in accelerating economic inequality.

INTERGENERATIONAL INEQUALITY IN NEW ZEALAND:
DO THE YOUNG STILL HAVE A FAIR GO?

As in the countries discussed above, the average gauges of inequality conceal even more alarming intergenerational levels of inequality, with younger New Zealanders getting the short end of the stick. This inequality is also largely a consequence of urban land-price inflation.

The above discussion has illuminated how urban land-price inflation, not building prices and not primarily income by itself, is the underlying but often hidden pressure increasing social and systemic inequality in New Zealand, which leads the OECD pack by most measures of housing stress, or unaffordability (B. Perry 2016). It should not come as a surprise to the reader that the young – Generation Z and the millennials – are inordinately blocked from gaining the same share of land wealth as their parents. In 1998, house prices were about seven times the average gross income. For Generation Z, they are eighteen times the average. Depressed interest rates consequent to the pandemic period's quantitative easing have pushed New Zealand housing prices much higher, with the marginal benefit of reduced interest rates and thus reduced monthly payments to the bank – but not lower levels of debt.

However, historically low interest rates have not helped young buyers to secure the money needed for down payments – unless they can access the bank of Mom and Dad. Additionally, first-time homebuyers who have recently jumped the hurdle into million-dollar-plus mortgages have no equity cushion to protect them against the hikes in mortgage rates that are now occurring worldwide. New Zealand mortgages, unlike their American equivalents, are short-term, with monthly balance payments recalibrated to current rates at renewal. Current maximum-term loans with fixed rates in New Zealand are seven years, with the vast majority of home loans issued for much shorter terms. This massive debt burden is an unprecedented potential-bankruptcy time bomb that will explode as interest rates double, and it leaves this Kiwi generation far more exposed to fiscal calamity than were their parents.

A 20 percent down payment in cash is typically required of first-time buyers, and at an average home price in Auckland of NZ$1.2 million (Granwal 2022), it would take five years for typical millennials to save this amount (after taxes),[18] assuming that they did not spend a nickel on anything else. Saving a more reasonable 10 percent of income per year would push this number of years out to somewhere between fifty and infinity, depending on the direction of the housing market during that period.

CANADA, COVID-19, AND HOUSING STRESS

Canadians' response to COVID-19 closely tracked that of Americans but with less resistance to mask mandates and with higher vaccination rates than in the United States. In general, debates in Canada about public health responses did not track with political affiliations in the way that they did in the United States. People with affiliations in all parties seemed more or less equally divided in their opinions as to the efficacy of government measures, and both Conservative and Liberal governments seemed equally aggressive (or not) in applying lockdowns and other public health responses. At the time of this writing, the US COVID-19 death rate stands at 279 per 100,000, whereas in Canada the rate is much lower, at 94 per 100,000 (Debusmann Jr. 2022).

However, much as in the United States, the dangers from infections fell more heavily on people of colour and the poor than on the rest of the population. Similar to New Zealand, discussed above, apartment overcrowding (or more people sharing a dwelling than there are rooms) is a fact of life for one in ten Canadians. In major cities – notably Toronto, at 20 percent – crowding is much higher (Tencer 2019). Also, as we have come to expect, crowding is higher among immigrant families and people of colour more generally. Studies have confirmed that census areas with high levels of crowding, a concentration of recent immigrants, a high proportion of Black and Brown residents, and a high concentration of essential employees – life characteristics that tend to group together, as in the United States – recorded at least twice as many infections and deaths as districts with average rates of these demographic features (Yiqing et al. 2022). These data were generalized by census area. If these studies had focused more on just the individuals with these demographic features living within these districts, rather than on the districts that they inordinately occupied, these rates would doubtless be much higher.

LANDOWNERSHIP IN CANADA

The land of Canada is owned mostly by the Crown, which in this case means owned either by the federal or provincial governments. The occupation of this vast landscape by First Nations peoples was, for the most part, acknowledged by colonizers, and treaties were signed that shifted land rights to the Crown. These treaties are considered valid to this day, although skepticism remains about the extent to which these treaties were negotiated in good faith. The exception is British Columbia, where colonizers were injudicious about consulting with local First Nations groups for land rights. The failure of BC settlers to clarify treaty rights creates unusually galling tensions between First Nations and other citizens in British Columbia.[19] In short, the ownership of Canadian lands is an area of continuing conflict.

Colonial settlers discovered that there were at least fifty completely different First Nations civilizations across this expansive country, each with an entirely different language and its own creation myths. The small size of these nations was more extreme in British Columbia than elsewhere due to the rough typography and the natural tendency of nations in such landscapes to permanently settle close to ocean food sources rather than ranging nomadically across large open landscapes.

Throughout Canada, after securing the land base by equitable or inequitable means, federal and provincial governments set about releasing lands to white settlers at low costs to encourage immigration and colonial settlement. The most favoured locations were in agriculturally rich areas close to the rivers necessary for maintaining connections with the larger world. In time, these unique locations would grow into major cities, including Montreal, Toronto, Edmonton, and Vancouver, to name but a few.

In English-speaking areas, the land to be transferred into private hands was first surveyed using the Dominion Land Survey system (W.A. Taylor 1975), copied from the Continental Land Survey system in the United States. This system regularizes varied landscapes by imposing uniform one-mile squares whose edges align with the cardinal axes. Its legacy is an agricultural checkerboard pattern of one-mile or half-mile squares.

Cities that eventually expanded in the midst of these checkerboards conformed to the same axes when their more finely grained gridiron street patterns expanded into agricultural areas (Condon 2010).

Although this urban land was originally inexpensive, the intervening years have been kind to land speculators but unkind to those who simply need housing. Now, land used for urban housing is, at over Cdn$6 trillion in cash value, far more valuable than all other types of land combined, even though it consumes far less than 5 percent of all land in Canada. To give some sense of how out of whack this relationship is, urban housing land in Canada is now three times more valuable than Canada's annual gross domestic product (GDP), adding over Cdn$1 trillion in value just since 2017 (Punwasi 2021). To put this figure in context, the ratio of urban land value to GDP is twice the ratio seen in the United States, where urban land-price inflation has been anything but moderate.

Ethnic differences play a role in who has access to urban land in Canada, as does the number of generations that your lineage has in this country. The term "old stock Canadians" is (to some) a politically palatable way of distinguishing white families whose ancestors came to Canada more than a few generations ago from more recent Black and Brown immigrants and equally from Aboriginals ("Stephen Harper Explains" 2015). Because of the stark difference in average land wealth between these groups, this disparity also marks an important class distinction as well.

Homeownership rates for more recent African, Middle Eastern, and Latin American immigrant groups are in the range of 40 percent, similar to ownership rates among Aboriginals. Homeownership rates for Canadian whites are much higher, at just over 70 percent. This figure reflects the difference in wealth between these groups, with white Canadians having more than twice the wealth on average as racialized groups, with 58 percent of this increasing gap attributable to the rapid recent rise in home values (Billy-Ochieng 2022).

INTERGENERATIONAL INEQUALITY IN CANADA

Although the increase in land wealth is the major underlying force increasing levels of inequality in Canada, it is also important to note that this trend has not just increased the investment portfolios of the top 10 percent (or top decile) but has also increased the equity held by the over 65 percent of Canadians who own their own homes (or part of them, with the bank owning the rest). Thus the majority of Canadians are, without a doubt, hoping that urban land prices never decline, for in such a case, their situation could be dire. With Canadian mortgages seldom of longer terms than five years and with renewals contingent on paying in cash any amount outstanding below the current assessed value of one's home, a decline in assessed value of only 10 percent can lead to banks demanding a mortgage-renewal pre-payment of six figures to bridge the gap between the amount owed and the market value after the drop, which can result in default for those who are unable to come up with the difference in cash. With most first-time buyers now being millennials and members of Generation Z, this cohort is inordinately exposed to the dangers implicit in an urban land-price crash. Naturally, they are all anxiously hoping that prices will never fall.

The situation is even more dire for younger Canadians who have not been able to take the plunge into homeownership for lack of the entry fee. Younger renters have had a much harder time climbing onto this first rung of the property ladder than their parents. Canadian millennials in major cities where a high land price is common carried only half as many home mortgages per capita as their Generation X neighbours did when they were the same age (Borrowell Team 2021).

The impeded access to housing equity shows up in the difference in net worth of Canadian generations when they were of similar ages. Millennials who have been closed out of the home-purchase market (or who have chosen or been forced to rent) have a net worth of under Cdn$18,000 dollars on average, whereas millennial homeowners have a net worth ten times larger (Heisz and Richards 2019). The equity gap between owners and nonowners in the previous two decades was half the size (ibid.).

One might imagine that this gap between the haves and the have-nots has much to do with disparities in the ambitions, education, and incomes of millennials when compared to Generation X. This assertion is undercut by the fact that 70 percent of Canadian millennials have a post-secondary degree, the highest rate in history and 50 percent higher than Generation X (Heisz and Richards 2019). The educational debt still carried by these millennials partly explains their lower average net worth.

In sum, most Canadians feel enriched by dramatic spikes in urban land value. This renders policy actions that might lower land values nearly impossible to implement, as political resistance would be too high. Left out in the cold, to a large extent, are a disproportionate share of Canada's minorities – a cohort that has traditionally experienced impeded access to urban land wealth – and members of the younger generation of all ethnic groups, who now have an unprecedented financial barrier in their way as well.

And finally, as urban land values increase, so do rents. Rents in Canada's major cities have climbed, in inflation-adjusted terms, by over 30 percent since 2002, whereas hourly wages have stayed flat (O'Keefe 2018).

2

The Economics of Urban Land Value

WHY DOES LAND VALUE MATTER?

In the previous chapter, I devoted considerable attention to the issue of the rapidly inflating urban land price and its implications not only for citizen health but also as the major driver increasing inequality. I also showed how this phenomenon is not just a feature of one national economy but is, possibly, the dominant economic context influencing pandemic health and the distribution of wealth in the wider English-speaking world. Why is this happening? And what, if anything, can be done about it? As the following chapter attempts to make clear, this debate is anything but settled. In the end, it comes down to the question of whether the spike in urban land and housing price is a consequence of limits to supply (either through policy restrictions or other market friction) or whether something else is going on here. Jumping right in, I start with the core debate: is this a problem of supply and demand or not?

SUPPLY AND DEMAND FOR HOUSING: FACT OR FICTION?

Essentially, there are only two responses to the question of why housing costs too much. The most common one is that if we all just allowed for more housing construction, the laws of supply and demand would ensure that housing costs dropped. The second response is that more supply has not, and thus will not, fix the problem.

The first response conforms to all the lessons taught in most introductory economics courses. It is, in a related way, the typical response of mainstream economists.[1] Those who hold the contrary position, having no widely accepted economic canon to use as a cudgel, start off on their heels. That is because a belief in the invisible hand of the marketplace and in the laws of supply and demand has held sway in the planning discourse since at least the "Reagan-Thatcher revolution"[2] of the 1980s (Dadkhah 2009) – a shift in political economy that marked the movement of the English-speaking world toward market-based solutions to all problems, including the problem of housing affordability.

Only in the past decade or two have we seen the erosion of widespread allegiance to free-market ideals as applied to housing. The theory of supply and demand has been undercut by the observed empirical reality in many parts of the world – namely that no matter how many new housing units a metropolitan area adds, housing prices continue to rise. This outcome begs the question of what the cause of high housing prices actually *is*, if not constrained supply. The problem seems to be the way that urban land price has become an ever-larger component of the cost of housing (as discussed in Chapter 1) and that this increase in urban land price seems to be caused by factors other than the supply and demand for new homes. The increase has to do with the innate limits on the availability of urban land and with how these limits make urban land perform uniquely in the global marketplace for "real" assets.[3]

To grasp this complex subject, it is helpful to remember that there are three determinants of real estate value: location, location, and location. Tired as this aphorism may be, its ubiquity signals its veracity. When you buy or rent a home, it's not the house that you buy or rent but the location. Or in more physical terms, you buy or rent the dirt under it, so you are stuck with this cost: as American humorist Mark Twain famously said, "Buy land, they aren't making any more of it." As a result, urban land is often regarded as a natural monopoly by economists.

It follows, then, that the crucial factor is not the cost of the building – as construction costs, adjusted for inflation, have not risen much in thirty years (Zarenski 2016b)[4] – but the cost of the land on which the building sits. And over the past two decades, the proportion of the home price that is attributable to land value has exploded. To cite one example, between 2006 and 2022, the nominal dollar value of a typical building in Vancouver stayed about the same (which means that it decreased in inflation-adjusted terms), whereas the nominal value of land under a typical building increased by over 500 percent.[5] This radically different ratio between building value and land value holds true, in a way that seems to defy economic fundamentals, even for Vancouver's many large buildings on small parcels. With land prices going up so fast, you would think that bigger buildings on smaller parcels would see a more favour-able relationship between building value and parcel value, but this is not the case.

FIGURE 2.1A Land and building values in Vancouver, 2006–17

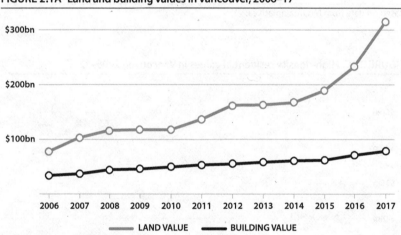

Based on data from Mountainmath.ca.

Thus a factor that, until relatively recently, was often seen as a less important influence on affordability than building cost has now emerged in many high-cost metropolitan areas as the dominant impediment standing between citizens and affordable housing. This change means that finding ways to lower building costs, although helpful, cannot fix the problem. Somehow, land prices must be brought back into control.

FIGURE 2.1B   Small detached home values in Vancouver, 2006–22

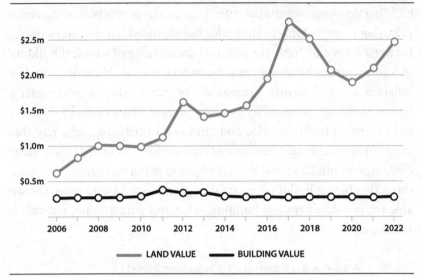

Based on data from Mountainmath.ca.

FIGURE 2.1C   High-density residential values in Vancouver, 2006–22

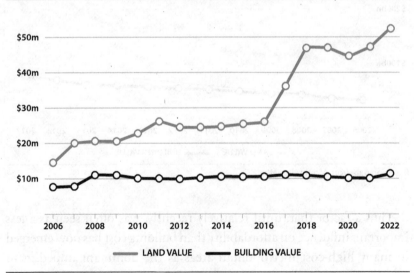

Based on data from Mountainmath.ca.

And even more alarmingly, in urban areas with high land cost (Condon 2020a), it does not seem to help to add density to a parcel in the hope of diluting the land-price component of a home. Rather, adding allowable density seems to spawn a nearly immediate increase in land price driven by the speculative value of any new density allowed.

LAND, LABOUR, CAPITAL, AND GEOGRAPHIC SHIFTING

The negative social consequences of this urban land-price explosion are both significant and accelerating. Wage earners are increasingly sifting themselves into buildings on urban lands within portions of metropolitan areas that may be far from job sites or amenities but have the advantage of being within their budget – high-priced districts with high-value land close to jobs and amenities for the wealthy, poorly served districts for the working poor, and districts somewhere between these two extremes for the middle class. Viewed in this way, metropolitan landscapes can be read as a map of inequality. Average incomes do not typically vary much inside any chosen census area. And what distinguishes rich neighbourhoods from all the others is not primarily the replacement value of buildings but the price of the land under the buildings.

Mainstream economists, classified as neoclassical within the economics discipline, claim that these land values and the map of inequality that they display are just the consequence of the invisible hand of the market and that interference will distort the land market by rendering it uneconomic, thus making housing less affordable. Free markets – understood by mainstream economists to be markets with few impediments (such as high taxes) between buyers and sellers and thus without friction – are assumed to be best. Importantly, neoclassical economists do not distinguish between above-ground capital and urban land, considering both to be forms of capital.

But in contrast to what neoclassical economists claim, many modern heterodox economists (some of whom have won the Nobel prize) argue that urban land value is not like the value of a factory building, something built with your own hands, so to speak.[6] The increased price of well-located land does not really represent a net increase in a community's wealth; rather, it is better understood as uselessly vacuuming up value created by the wage earners and entrepreneurs above it, swallowed up by the black hole of land price. It's not by the landowners' actions that urban land gains its monetary value, they say, but by the collective actions of government and private individuals such as wage earners and entrepreneurs in the area of the city around that land. In simplest terms, they argue that land has effectively no productive value until it is taken into the limits of the city and becomes "urban land." In this way, land is entirely unlike the cafe or the factory. It contributes nothing on its own to producing new wealth of the kind that is generated almost out of thin air by labour and real capital. Land is necessary for the factory or shop to exist, but the land itself does not make an economic contribution. For them, urban land is a *necessary* but *non-productive* factor of production.[7]

Given this aspect of land, the first and most famous economists in the English-speaking world – classical economists such as Adam Smith and David Ricardo[8] – argued that the production of new wealth in the emerging capitalist world would be greatly accelerated if those who collectively generated this value, namely the wage earners and the entrepreneurs, got most of the reward for their efforts, with landowners getting less – much, much less. These economists are now called classical economists throughout the English-speaking world. Classical economists argued that the taxes needed to maintain the emerging capitalist city should come largely from a tax on land, with a commensurately lower tax on wages or on the capital gains not associated with urban land-price increases.

To simplify this concept, I introduce here the concept of deadweight loss. Mainly used in economics, a deadweight loss can be applied to any deficiency caused by an inefficient allocation of resources. Inefficiently allocating resources to overpriced land is the best example of deadweight loss imaginable. Many economists agree, including the very mainstream Chicago School economist Milton Friedman ("Time May Be" 2018). Friedman admits that a tax on land is better than any other tax because land does not contribute to production and indeed can be a real drag on economic growth if its price is too high, suggesting that taxes should fall much more heavily on land than on either labour or fixed capital and capital gains.

To some extent, modern cities have followed Smith's advice by imposing property taxes that now fall largely on the deadweight value of urban land. But property taxes tend to capture only a relatively small proportion of the unearned value of urban land. This increased value is captured mostly by the lucky (or prescient) owners of that land.

An important distinction between the original classical economists and today's neoclassical economists must be noted here. Whereas classical economists included land as a separate factor of production, along with labour and capital, neoclassical economists largely lump land in with capital, blurring the distinction between the capital value of the (productive) factory and the value of the (unproductive) land on which it sits.

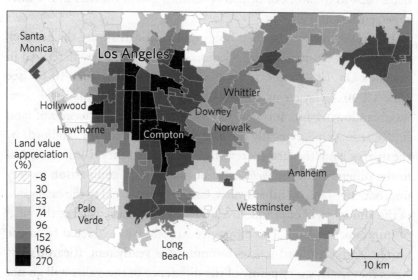

FIGURE 2.2 Seven-year increase in land value by zip code in Los Angeles. Land prices in the central Los Angeles area increased by over 300 percent in only seven years. These are the same areas where medium- and low-income residents reside. | Cartography by Eric Leinberger.

It's useful to think a bit more deeply about how urban land value may not be inherent to the land itself (as neoclassical economists would have it) but instead accrues from all the actions that occur around it (as classical economists would have it). So prepare yourself for a deep dive into the Law of Rent, an economic law not often mentioned in introductory economics classes but one that provides the alternative to the laws of supply and demand and helps to explain why housing-price increases may not be caused by constraints on supply but by the way that urban land will absorb, up to almost the last nickel, the value created by city wage earners and entrepreneurs.

THE CONCEPT OF LAND RENT

As mentioned in this book's Introduction, the word "rent" has, for centuries, been used in two ways. Its most commonplace definition is the monthly amount that you might pay for your rental home. This is similar but not identical to how economists use the term "rent," which dates back to the work of British economist David Ricardo in the early nineteenth century.

Urban landowners, be their holdings large or small, are the beneficiaries of what economists call Ricardo's law of rent, a law described in his book *On the Principles of Political Economy and Taxation* (1817) (see Hawes 2010). In lay terms, the law of rent describes the unique economics of landownership. It states that the price paid to the *owners* of land (in Ricardo's time, typically the lord of the manor, or the landlord) by the *users* of land (the farmers renting the land that they tilled) was equal to the difference in the *yield value* of rich land in comparison to very unproductive land. In other words, land rent was equal to the cash value of the annual yield of productive land minus the cash value of the yield of unproductive land. The difference in yield was extracted from the farmer by the landlord in a cash monthly or yearly rent. Ricardo's law states that nearly every penny of the difference in this value will go not to the farmers who reap that bumper crop but to the landlords who own the land in the form of the price that they demand in land rent. This view of the ability of landlords to passively acquire nearly *all* of the extra value consequent to farmers' work on their land, without the need for them to perform any labour of their own, is still the way that economists think of land Rent, or price. The landlord's gain is entirely the consequence of having somehow gained rights to a piece of land with certain innate capacities that enable the landlord to demand rent for its use – without any obligation for its maintenance.

The law of rent applies with even more ferocity in urban areas. The most productive (or valuable) land in a *city* is land at the centre of all the services and infrastructure needed to maximize its commercial value. In this volume, as explained in the Introduction, when I use the term "rent" in the Ricardian sense, I capitalize it as "Rent" to distinguish the term from its commonplace usage.

In short, Rent is paid in monthly instalments or in a one-time cash payment for the use or acquisition of land based on its productivity. The productivity of urban land is its location. What we are seeing now, in most of the world's global cities, is a new and mystifying rise in urban land Rent that is many times faster than the rise of average wages, leading to increasingly precarious housing for a larger and larger share of the population. One expects, as mainstream real estate economists have argued for many decades, that land Rent will match up with rises in local wage rates. Between 1945 and approximately 1990, they did. But not anymore. Now, land Rent is exploding while wages stay stagnant. But why? Why are real estate fundamentals no longer holding up? Again, some argue that restrictive zoning is the friction interfering with the natural fluidity of supply and demand. We shall see. But before that, we must look at the "crappy wages" side of the problem. If wages doubled, this problem would vanish. So why have wages and urban land value been separated so completely?

DOES LAND COST TOO MUCH, OR ARE WAGES TOO LOW? IT'S BOTH

It's obvious that if wages could double, the housing-affordability and urban land Rent problem would not be so severe. But a doubling of wages, given current trends, seems highly unlikely. Confoundingly, wages in most of the English-speaking world have remained frustratingly flat, whereas housing prices, in both rigidly regulated jurisdictions and much more loosely regulated jurisdictions, have risen at a pace that is wildly out of synch.[9]

Mainstream economists disagree on what to do about stagnant wages and about the four-decade decline of the middle class throughout all of the English-speaking world that is its corollary. Their approaches range from centre-right to centre-left positions. On the centre-right side of the political spectrum, they recommend pumping more and more newly created money into the pockets of investors,[10] up to and beyond the point where inflation returns, based on the principle that keeping corporations and investors healthy produces good-paying jobs and access to asset wealth for the broader public. This view held sway during the first three years of the 2020 pandemic, during which central banks reduced the interest cost of money to be used by investors as a stimulus to economic expansion. Economists on the centre-left side of the political spectrum are more inclined to suggest rebuilding the middle class by reinvigorating unions and creating new entitlements that will shore up the purchasing power of wage earners and put them in a stronger bargaining position with their bosses, thus strengthening workers in the knowledge that even if they lose a job, they will retain robust federally ensured benefits ("COVID-19 Pandemic" 2020).[11]

America's best-known Nobel Prize–winning economists, Joseph E. Stiglitz (2020; see also Hepburn et al. 2020) and Paul Krugman (2020),[12] promote the second of these two options. It follows that a more robust governmental involvement in housing would align with the centre-left economic response by shoring up the security of wage earners, thus allowing them to change jobs with a much-reduced fear of homelessness, and by clarifying that housing is critical national infrastructure (Fearn 2014).[13] Unplugging the roadblocks in the way of rising wages would surely help, but what we know for sure is that the relationship between wages and urban land price is so severely out of balance that something radical will be needed to bring them back in line with what are called, within the ranks of the real estate industry, the real estate fundamentals.

THE COLLAPSE OF THE REAL ESTATE FUNDAMENTALS

For at least five decades following the Second World War, housing economists assured us that a region's housing market was structurally linked to a region's average wages,[14] explaining that even if the market could not effectively house those in the bottom 20 percent of income, the free market was best suited to supply housing for the rest. However, in many cities – particularly those at the centre of globalized economic development like Sydney, San Francisco, Vancouver, London, and New York – the relationship between regional wages and average house prices has been completely cut. For example, what was once a dependable ratio of one to four in the United States and the United Kingdom is now over one to twelve in many major cities (Pettinger 2022). In Canada, New Zealand, and Australia, the situation is worse (Numbeo n.d.). And sadly, efforts to increase housing supply in the laudable hope that doing so will satisfy demand, and thus lower prices, do not seem to have worked. Houston, which is famous for operating without zoning controls, saw a five-year jump in average home prices of 78 percent between 2012 and 2022 (Federal Reserve Economic Data 2022b), whereas wages grew well below the rate of inflation (Douglas 2020). Vancouver, despite tripling the number of housing units within city limits since 1960, has been rewarded for its efforts with the third highest housing prices in the world.[15]

It seems that home-price increases no longer rise and fall with region-wide salary levels. But home prices in major cities *do* rise and fall in line with the rise and fall of housing prices in similar global cities. Since at least 2000, whenever the prices of homes in New York or San Francisco have gone up, so too have the prices of homes in London, Sydney, Christchurch, and Toronto (Wong 2018).

According to a study published by the Center for Economic Studies and Ifo Institute, the problem is not the cost of the house or the supply of buildings but the cost of the land on which the house sits

> This paper presents annual house price indices for 14 advanced economies since 1870. Based on extensive data collection, we show that real house prices stayed constant from the 19th to the mid-20th century, but rose strongly during the second half of the 20th century. Land prices, not replacement costs, are the key to understanding the trajectory of house prices. (Knoll, Schularick, and Steger 2014, Abstract)

After a mind-numbing presentation of formulae, global charts, and tables, this study concludes,

> After a long period of stagnation from 1870 to the mid-20th century, house prices rose strongly in real terms during the second half of the 20th century ... The decomposition of house prices into the

replacement cost of the structure and land prices reveals that rising
land prices have been the driving force for the observed trends ...
Explanations for the long-run trajectory of house prices must be
mapped onto the underlying land price dynamics and the comparatively minor role of changes in the replacement value of the structure.
(Ibid., 33–34)

But why are urban land prices no longer linked to average wages?
There seem to be two different but related ways to explain this confounding trend. The first explanation suggests that this gap between
wages and housing costs is simply one aspect of inequality more generally. The second explanation, a variant of the first, is that urban land has
a special ability to absorb value, expressed in the form of elevated land
Rent, until it becomes unaffordable by the average wage earner. The
next two sections examine these explanations in turn.

GENERAL INEQUALITY: PIKETTY ET AL. PART 1
Policy makers may disagree on the cause, but everyone – whether on
the political left or the political right – agrees that inequality is increasing dramatically in most of the world's developed economies. Whereas
wages are flat, most everything you really need to buy costs more: housing, transportation, education, health care, and so on. The most popular
explanation for this trend comes from the left-leaning French economist
Thomas Piketty. In his widely read and hugely influential book *Capital
in the Twenty-First Century* (2014),[16] he explains that given the fundamental
mechanisms of capitalism, unless interrupted, wealth will naturally
gravitate toward those who already have wealth and away from those
who must live on their wages. This tendency eventually results in an end
state that he terms "patrimonial capitalism" (ibid., 173), where a small
number of the wealthy (now often called oligarchs) and their descendants exert near monopoly control over both the economy and the politics
of a nation. Like all good economists, to explain this outcome, he provides a mathematical formula, $r > g$, where r is the 5 percent return on
capital (e.g., rents and interest) that has been generally constant throughout the centuries and where g is the rate of increase in gross national
product (ibid., 25).[17]

Piketty claims that when GNP grows faster than 5 percent, there is enough new wealth created that wage earners can increase their wealth share – relative to the investor class, that is. He takes over 600 pages to prove his point, so those interested may want to absorb his argument there. However, one key point made by Piketty should be repeated. He asks and answers the question of why, during the 1960s, '70s, and '80s, the proportionate share of total capital wealth controlled by North America's and Europe's middle class was increasing and why, in about 1980, this trend reversed. His answer is that the three great catastrophes of the early twentieth century – the Great Depression and the two world wars – played a role by bombing the factories of the rich, by raising their taxes to 90 percent of income, and by rendering their bonds worthless through wartime and postwar inflation.

Thus the postwar financial restart allowed advanced nations to rebuild rapidly (or in the case of the United States, to capitalize on its new global dominance) with very high GNP growth, which was higher than 5 percent per year for decades, with a larger than usual share of this wealth going to the growing ranks of the Western middle class.[18] Piketty (2014), following Jean Fourastié who coined the phrase, calls the years between 1950 and 1980 the "Les Trois Glorieuses" throughout his book.[19]

But these wealth gains of the middle class came to a stop in the late 1970s and early 1980s during the period of international stagflation, a time when Keynesian government approaches seem to have failed.[20] This failure set the stage for the "Reagan-Thatcher revolution" (Dadkhah 2009),[21] initiating a shift back to the unfettered free-market economic approaches of neoliberalism, which had held sway prior to the Great Depression. In Piketty's (2014, 348–50) view, this set up the machinery of the global economy to slowly produce greater and greater inequality – levels of inequality not unlike those experienced during the "Gilded Age" of the late nineteenth century.

ABSORBED VALUE: PIKETTY ET AL. PART 2

In his second book, *Capital and Ideology* (2020), Piketty takes a deeper dive (at 1,300 pages, much deeper) into political and economic history, concluding that the groundwork for three decades of progress among the middle class throughout the English-speaking world was actually laid in the late nineteenth century by the political foment of the Progressive Era in the United States (McGerr 2003)[22] and by the various socialist movements in continental Europe and Oceana. During this period, wage earners increased their power in relation to the investor class in the United States via measures such as public support for labour unions and for a steeply progressive income tax and in the United Kingdom via means that included the beginnings of a government-sponsored social safety net with retirement benefits.

Piketty (2020) illustrates that at the end of the Second World War, the ground was set for the emergence of strong social democracies in Europe and for the continuation of New Deal policies in the United States.

He observes that post-1980 globalization led to an unfortunate relaxation in financial controls around the world, setting off a competitive race to the bottom. Owners of capital were taxed less and less while austerity politics undercut the relative power of wage earners by undercutting trade unions and shrinking support for social safety nets.

FIGURE 2.3 Productivity versus average real earnings

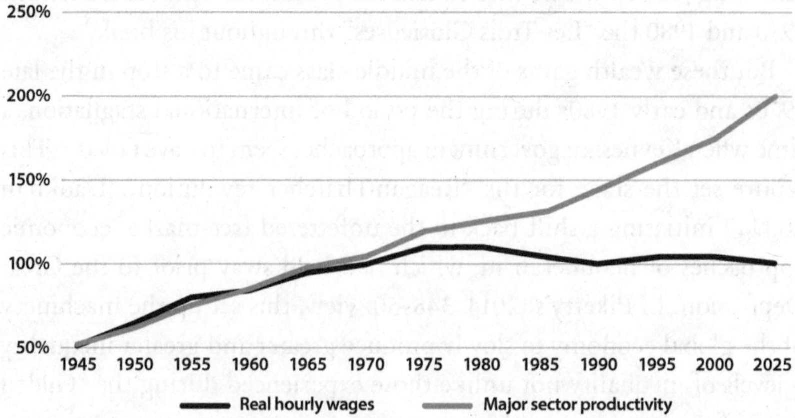

Based on data from Information Bureau of Labor Statistics.

IT'S NOT ABOUT THE 1 PERCENT REALLY BUT ABOUT THE 60 PERCENT

Piketty's work has transformed the conversation among economists, but he is not without his critics. Notable among them is Matthew Rognlie of the Massachusetts Institute of Technology. He and others argue that, yes, more money is flowing into the value of assets – a flow largely into the value of urban land – than into wages and that this development marks a shift from the golden decades between 1945 and 1980 when the middle class was king, but they assert that a closer look reveals that most of this growth has been in one asset class: housing (Rognlie 2015). For these economists, this finding suggests that increasing the production of housing will slow the rampaging engine of inequality. More production will drive down its price, they say, by increasing its supply. Although this diagnosis of the problem – the idea that increases in the asset value of housing are the major driver of our current asset-to-wages imbalance – is supported by the evidence that Rognlie supplies, his solution of adding housing supply is not.

In the face of the work of both Piketty and Rognlie, I draw a somewhat different conclusion. The evidence discounts Rognlie's contention that the constraint on housing supply is the problem, and it suggests that Rognlie and Piketty support each other. The flow of wealth into housing doesn't undercut Piketty's argument about inequality but instead hints at the emergence of an entirely new twenty-first-century class structure comprised of those who have housing assets versus those who don't.

This is probably the best point in this volume at which to introduce another uniquely modern aspect of our current global surge of inequality. Our conventionally applied categories of social class are still grounded in the way that the industrial era unfolded. Then, there were the owners (or the upper class), the middle managers (or the middle class), and those below (or the working class). The division was based on a simple taxonomy: one class of capital owners who paid salaries and two classes of wage earners who received them.

This habit of mind gets in the way of what is, today, an alternative taxonomy. In the English-speaking world, this shift in the structure of class correlates with the shift from an industrial to post-industrial society. We are witnessing a financialization of the whole of culture, with the result that what generates wealth is no longer labour and machinery but wealth itself (Adkins, Cooper, and Konings 2021). So now the classes might more rightfully be thought of in terms of only two cohorts: wage earners without wealth and those (some wage earners and some not) whose wealth generates more wealth.

FIGURE 2.4 Median home price, US versus California

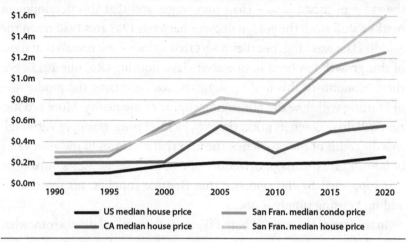

Based on data from National Association of Realtors.

FIGURE 2.5 Housing as value of France national capital (% of national income)

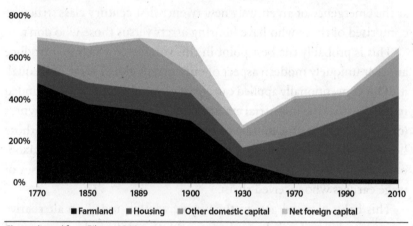

Chart adapted from Piketty 2016.

The most evident manifestation of this shift, and a clear benefit to a majority of households in the English-speaking world, can be seen in the spread of urban landownership to include over 60 percent of all households. But the obvious downside of this emerging land-asset society is that it correlates with the ever-climbing entry fee needed to get into a first home. These ever-higher entry fees require heavier and heavier debt burdens for willing home purchasers and their sponsoring banks, factors that are driving an explosion of household debt throughout the English-speaking world.[23]

But the payoff can be huge. Those who have successfully gained access to the first rung – especially those who have subsequently climbed up to the second, third, and fourth rungs – are now often "earning" much more from home-price equity gains each year than from their salary (Olick 2022). Thus the wage-earning former middle class has split in two, with the upper half now gaining equity each year from urban land-value appreciation, whereas those unable to access even a tiny share of this urban land value fall further behind. And of course, under contemporary circumstances, those folks who can't reach that first rung are either inordinately disadvantaged ethnic classes or young people without access to the bank of Mom and Dad.

THE DIFFERENCE BETWEEN LAND RENT AND ECONOMIC RENT

Readers may have encountered the term "economic rent" at some point in their education, which is a broad category that includes land Rent. Economic rent is defined as wealth that does not derive from productive capital, such as a factory, but from a locational advantage, a product monopoly, or a risk-mitigation advantage of some kind. This definition makes economic rent a difficult concept for the layperson to understand. For example, both wage increases negotiated by labour unions and the advantages of monopoly control over, well, really anything are considered economic rent. Stiglitz discusses "too big to fail" banks as an example of economic rent (Piketty and Stiglitz 2015). In his example, when the federal government agrees to bail out banks with taxpayer money, this money is a form of economic rent since it produces a reduction in risk and thus a shift in value from the public to the private sector. Owners of bank shares see the value of their holdings increase in line with their reduced risk – which is called rent seeking because you lobby for this increased wealth, ask for it, steal it, or otherwise seek to secure it without increasing productivity. Land Rent is lumped together with economic rent in this discourse.

But this definition of economic rent, for our purposes, muddies the waters (Gaffney 1994). The original eighteenth-century (and more obvious) definition of land Rent provided by David Ricardo (1817) is more useful. He focused exclusively on land Rent. Remember that Ricardo's law holds that the difference in the yield between good land and bad land is its Rent. Thus the productive value of farmers' work is distinct from the value of the land on which they grow crops – or its Rent. And Rent can be anything up to the difference in yield between productive land and barren land. In terms that include urban land, Rent is the cost paid by a land user to a landowner (or to the bank holding one's mortgage) for putting the land to some purpose.[24] Productive work (or capital formation) and land Rent are thus two different things.

Why do we care about separating land wealth (or Rent) from other kinds of wealth, including the value of the building sitting on top of the land? We care because knowing the amount of land Rent lets us separate this cost from the costs necessary for production, namely productive capital, like a factory or an apartment building, and labour (or wages). Land in this view is still a necessary factor of production, but it contributes only by virtue of its location or yield. Land, in economic terms, is worthless without labour and capital to put it to use in a fixed location. Drawing attention to land's parasitic essence might assist us in generating effective policies for mitigating the deleterious effects of land Rent.

Unfortunately, mainstream economists conflate the concept of land Rent with the broader term "economic rent." This approach obscures the distinctive quality of land Rent, reducing the commonly understood ingredients necessary for economic production to only two – capital and labour – with land and all its qualities now dumped into the definition of productive capital, along with buildings such as factories and cafes. It has also meant that we typically forget (or simply don't see) that the housing-affordability crisis is really a crisis of land Rent.

TRACING THE HISTORY OF THE LAND RENT DEBATE

The idea that land, although essential to production, is not in itself productive dates back, again, at least to the time of Adam Smith's work *The Wealth of Nations* (1776, 43), where he writes,

As soon as the land of any country has all become private property, the landlords ... love to reap where they have never sowed, and demand a rent even for its natural produce. The wood of the forest, the grass of the field, and all the natural fruits of the earth, which, when land was in common, cost the labourer only the trouble of gathering them, come ... to have an additional price fixed upon them.

Smith here sums up an issue that after 250 years is still important. Landlords, as he correctly states, monopolize the use of land (demanding Rent) without providing any capital value like a factory or any labour value in the form of actual work. In this view, land – which could under ideal circumstances be available free of charge to factory owners and their workers – absorbs most of the value of capital and labour in the form of land Rent. Most mainstream economists try to overcome this objection by merging a factory's value with the value of the land below it, assigning them both productive values (Hayek 1944).[25]

Stiglitz maintains that mainstream economists make a serious error (perhaps by design) when they conflate productive capital with unproductive land, regarding both the factory and the land on which it sits as capital and rendering land's essentially parasitic aspect invisible to economists. On the question of housing affordability, we tend to do the same, merging land value with building value in our minds, debates, and policies – never seeing urban land and the buildings on it as two very different things. Stiglitz takes a view more in line with Smith's. He complains that the growth of land Rent, if not mitigated through state controls, such as land-taxing policy, exacerbates wealth inequality by draining off the value of both productive capital and labour to create the value of the unproductive asset class of urban land. In his work, Stiglitz (2015, 430, 432–33) contrasts what he calls the "neoclassical model" (or the "standard model," which rests on a faith in the laws of supply and demand) with the "exploitation model" (which posits rent seeking as a corrupting force that disturbs the presumed equilibrium of the neoclassical model and leads to morally unsupportable and economically counterproductive growth in inequality). His discussion of Piketty's *Capital in the Twenty-First Century* (2014) gives the flavour of his thinking:

Piketty's recent book noted the enormous increases in the wealth-output ratio in most capitalist countries in the last third of a century. But these increases have been partly, and in some cases largely, related to increases in the value of (urban) land. A tax on the return to land, and even more so, on the capital gains from land, would reduce inequality and, by encouraging more investment into real capital, actually enhance growth. This is, of course, an old idea, promoted most famously by Henry George (1879). (Stiglitz 2015, 442–43; see also Piketty and Stiglitz 2015)

As this process unfolds, more and more value is absorbed in Rents for urban land, until much of the new wealth produced by capital and labour are largely absorbed in Rent. He notes that urban land is, as a largely speculative asset, "untethered" to its use function and in this way especially subject to speculative bubbles (Stiglitz 2015, 439). More odious still, because of the way that land markets work, the price of land can temporarily be pushed beyond the capacity of labour and capital to afford its price – its Rent – until the metropolitan economy teeters at the precipice of collapse. That's when we experience crashes like the one in 2008. Indeed, when looking back at economic depressions and recessions over the past 140 years, we see that they were often preceded by an urban land-price bubble.[26] Stiglitz, unsurprisingly, also maintains that land Rents are the major driver of social inequality, as the high cost of land Rent makes it increasingly hard for wage earners to afford secure housing close to workplaces (ibid.).

For Stiglitz to make this claim is not surprising. The work upon which his reputation is founded is based on land Rent. In what has come to be known as his Henry George theorem, he explains that investments in city infrastructure – in the broadest sense, inclusive of roads, parks, hospitals, schools, and so forth – are reflected in the total land value of the area served and that quite often land-value increases are larger, in the aggregate, than the level of public investment seems to warrant ("Henry George theorem" n.d.). Thus public investment is a producer of wealth; that is, taxpayer-funded civic infrastructure more than pays for itself, as reflected in increased land values. The problem is that this value gets privatized by the lucky owners of land, who likely have not contributed to this increased value.

What follows from this assessment is that public-sector investments should be financed by a heavy tax on those citizens who benefit most from this taxpayer-funded investment, and the main beneficiaries of these investments are the owners of developable urban land. Acquiring funds by taxing land to extend and enhance civic infrastructure would allow governments to reduce taxes on capital income, sales, and wages – thereby rewarding and encouraging these useful categories of economic activity. Thus a tax on land value should be the primary means of financing public infrastructure (again, broadly conceived). Stiglitz's work is called the Henry George theorem because it was Henry George, an American political economist of the Progressive Era, who first promoted this idea. I pay additional attention to the important contribution of Henry George in Chapter 3.

3

Henry George and His Relevance Today

HISTORY

Henry George was a journalist turned political economist who worked in California in the 1870s. It was while doing this work that he was struck by an insight, recounted in his seminal work, *Progress and Poverty* (1879, 274):

> For, as soon as land acquires a value, wages, as we have seen, do not depend upon the real earnings or product of labor, but upon what is left to labor after rent is taken out; and when land is all monopolized, as it is everywhere except in the newest communities, rent must drive wages down to the point at which the poorest paid class will be just able to live and reproduce, and thus wages are forced to a minimum fixed by what is called the standard of comfort – that is, the amount of necessaries and comforts which habit leads the working classes to demand as the lowest on which they will consent to maintain their numbers.

George describes a world where more and more of returns to entrepreneurs and more and more of the pay envelopes of wage earners go into land Rents, which are paid to landlords as monthly rent or to banks as mortgages, leaving workers with just enough left to "live and reproduce." The parallels with our own time are obvious, especially when considering the growing percentage of wage earners who are closed out of housing wealth throughout the English-speaking world.

HENRY GEORGE AND HIS THIRD WAY

Henry George is almost forgotten in the world of economics, overtaken by Marxism on the left and by neoliberal and neoclassical economics on the right (George Jr. 1900). But during his lifetime, he was a revolutionary figure, more famous than Mark Twain and of much greater immediate impact than Karl Marx. He deserves more attention than he gets, for unlike Marxists and socialists and unlike neoclassical conservatives, George threaded the needle between the ideological battles that in his lifetime pitted capital (or entrepreneurs) against labour (or wage earners).

To elaborate on this point, both the economics of the left (or socialism) and the economics of the right (or neoliberalism) largely describe workers and owners in a long-running competition for their fair share of newly created wealth – with wealth accumulation viewed as a zero-sum game. Those on the right feel that workers should be grateful for the wages that the job creators provide, regardless of how much their efforts enrich owners. Those on the left see owners' profits as unjust, constituting a theft of the surplus labour value, as Marx would have it, of their work. Combatants in both camps typically ignore the fact that much of their combined effort goes to filling the pockets of landowners in the form of Rents.

Marx famously minimized the power of landlords, seeing them as a historical anachronism that the newly powerful capitalist class would soon put out of business (Christophers 2021).

They didn't.

Liberal economist John Maynard Keynes also thought that land Rent would eventually be abolished and rentiers forced out of business, but his reasons differed from Marx's. Keynes argued that the golden goose of capital creation – labour and owners creating value from their collaboration – would eventually attract all of the resources of a modern economy to the productive factors of production: labour and capital.

They didn't.

Neither of these two worthies predicted that Rent, particularly urban land Rent, would assume the global dominance that it now enjoys.

But Henry George forged a different path from typical socialists or liberals. For him, the view that saw capital pitted against labour was completely wrong. He argued that by ignoring the problem of urban land, socialists and liberals were missing the real problem: Rent. George revived the classical economics idea of being three factors of production with only two of the three being productive, labour and capital, and one of the three a hugely unproductive but still necessary factor: land.

George, like Adam Smith before him, put both the owners of capital and the wage earners employed by them on the same team, happy to let both labour and capital retain all of the value that their collaboration created while taxing landlords the full value of their land Rent to pay for urban services and the social safety net.

FIGURE 3.1 Mayoral candidate Henry George strangling a large snake wrapped around New York City Hall. The snake represents "corruption," "monopoly," "rings," "deals," "spoils," "nor law," "club law," and "want." On the ground is a club emblazoned with the title of George's famous book, *Progress and Poverty*. | Courtesy Wikimedia Commons.

Or as Smith (1776, 43) so elegantly put it long before, a region's entire tax burden should be placed on "the landlords ... [who] love to reap where they have never sowed, and demand a rent even for its natural produce."

Doctrinaire socialists of George's time held a similarly dim view of landlords, but their prescription – nationalization of the land – was more extreme than his. George would simply have shifted taxes off of wages and capital, eliminating income taxes as well as business and capital-gains taxes on real capital, and he would have applied a greater tax to land, commensurate with its market price – or Rent. The money gained from this land tax would be more than enough, he argued, to pay for advanced urban infrastructure, such as schools and hospitals, and to fund a robust social safety net.

This strategy made George a unique and revolutionary figure in his day. Neither a doctrinaire socialist nor a neoclassical capitalist, he was a political economist who clearly separated out the nonproductive element of capitalist society – land Rent – and strategically targeted land Rent wealth for taxation at a rate equal to its full Rent value yearly, which would effectively drive its asset value for purchase close to zero. These taxes would henceforth provide all the funds required to maintain the common good.

Freeing the economic machinery of the "deadweight loss" associated with land Rents, George claimed, would reduce the frequency and severity of economic depressions. He explained that the recurring cycle of depressions (a relatively new feature of life in his time) was caused by land Rents. Landlords, by their nature, always push capitalism to the brink of failure by demanding maximum Rents, he argued. At these precarious levels, economic disruptions (e.g., the collapse of the real estate bubble in 2008) mean that capital owners (or entrepreneurs) can't keep up with the Rent and that low-paid workers (or labour) will end up unemployed. The knock-on effects are inevitable, he said. Recessions ensue, and overleveraged individuals and banks see their real estate equity collapse while their liabilities cannot be rolled over. The result is depression. With the global levels of land Rent and the associated household debts to banks that it demands now at historic highs (as measured in relation to GDP), we would seem to be in danger of this calamity.

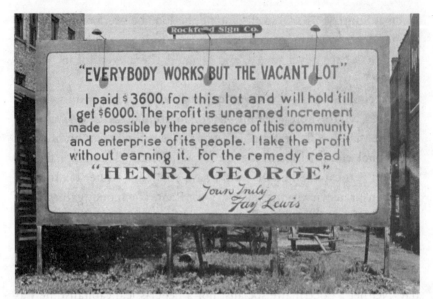

FIGURE 3.2 Sign erected on an empty urban lot in San Francisco to make Henry George's main point for him. | Courtesy Wikimedia Commons.

THE CONTEMPORARY INFLUENCE OF HENRY GEORGE

For years, George's most famous book, *Progress and Poverty* (1879), was the only book in the United States that outsold the Bible. Translated into a dozen languages, it sold millions of copies (George Jr. 1900) – unheard of for a book on political economy, at least until the publication of Thomas Piketty's *Capital in the Twenty-First Century* (2014). His insights spawned a movement in the English-speaking world, leading significantly to Progressive Era constitutional amendments in the Unted States and to land-tax policies in Australia (Pullen 2005) and the United Kingdom (P. Jones 1987).[1] His renown was such that he stood for election as mayor of New York City in 1886 and would have won if not for vote tampering by Tammany Hall. Throughout the United States and Canada, states or provinces as well as cities adopted separate property-tax valuations for land and improvements for the first time due to his work. Most US states established single-tax political groups to advance his ideas, many of which still exist. George-spawned US think tanks still thrive, propped up by the financial legacies that his followers seeded, notably the Lincoln

FIGURE 3.3 American economist Henry George, 1839–97. | Courtesy Wikimedia Commons.

Institute of Land Policy in Cambridge, Massachusetts. But his own work was halted by his untimely death due to a stroke when he was just fifty-eight years of age (George Jr. 1900).

WHY HENRY GEORGE WAS CRUSHED

Part of the reason for George's diminished standing these days is the powerful forces that were arrayed against him while he lived, powers that were invested in maintaining and extending the wealth that they had acquired from Rents. The most powerful of these interests were the fantastically wealthy railway barons of his time, who derived their wealth largely from land. This debate was lengthy, vicious, and complex, as well as profoundly political. Those wishing for the complete history should read the late Georgist scholar Mason Gaffney's essay "Neo-classical Economics as a Stratagem against Henry George" (1994). Here, I touch only on the fact that Columbia University and the Chicago School of Economics at the University of Chicago were set up, and staffed, for the specific purpose of refuting Henry George, with faculty who were unwilling to do so never lasting long.[2] As Gaffney and land-reform economist Fred Harrison point out, academic attacks on George at the behest of wealthy land barons were sustained and vicious:

> George was also in a running dispute with E.R.A. Seligman, Chairman of Columbia's Department of Economics over many, many years (circa 1880) under both Presidents Low and Butler ... Butler, in turn, was the funnel through which the wealth of Wall Street, personified by the dominating banker J.P. Morgan, patronized Columbia, making it the wealthiest American university for its times. Money poured into the Department of Economics. Under Seligman, his Department swelled from two members to "forty or fifty" ...
>
> This was a period of secularization of US colleges. Businessmen were replacing clergymen on boards. The new broom swept out some old problems, no doubt. At the same time, it posed new threats to academic freedom, threats of which Butler was the very embodiment. Clerics, after all, owe some allegiance to Moses, the Prophets and the Gospels, which are suffused with strident demands for social justice. They were displaced by others more exclusively attuned to the Gospel of Wealth. Academic tenure was a distant dream: top administrators were hired and dismissed with few checks and balances. They only needed to dismiss a radical occasionally: others got the message ...

Pressures on academics were extreme: it was placate or perish. (Gaffney and Harrison 1994, 50–51)

WHAT DID HAPPEN?

Henry George didn't precipitate a violent revolution like Marx or set the terms of the Reagan-Thatcher revolution like neoclassical economist[3] Friedrich Hayek (1944),[4] but his successes were numerous and terribly relevant to the issue of housing costs. His separately assessed and rated property tax on land has been used in fifteen Pennsylvania municipalities for over a hundred years. Maryland and twenty-eight other US states assess land and improvements separately as part of their state-wide tax policy (M.E. Bell and Bowman 2006). What is most interesting about this approach is that it provides a third way out of the seemingly intractable debate between the political left and right. George's view that land Rent is the most important cause of poverty in the midst of wealth overcame the Hobbesian view that the poor are always with us, a view long favoured by right-wing economists, thus fuelling a global progressive movement that stood for the possibility of achieving social and economic justice without resorting to the complete state ownership promoted by Marx or permitting the unfettered acquisition of wealth in the faith that it will trickle down to the masses, as promoted by neoclassicists. George and his fundamental insights are now being revived at a time when the problem of out of control land Rent is becoming increasingly dire.

THE PROBLEM WITH A TOO NARROW INTERPRETATION OF GEORGE'S THOUGHT

However, there is a danger in perceiving Henry George's insight too simplistically. George's wide-ranging proposals have been compressed into a rather unfortunate slogan, that of the single tax on land. Economist Michael Hudson (2004) criticizes many contemporary purveyors of Georgeism, suggesting that George's oeuvre has been captured by the real estate industry, on the one hand, and by ideological libertarians, on the other, because the former favours a split tax policy that shifts the burden of local taxes away from buildings and onto land and because libertarians regard the shift of taxes onto land as suggesting an overall reduction in taxes and thus a reduction in the powers of the state.[5]

That should not be the only way of applying this concept. The Henry George theorem, as interpreted by Joseph E. Stiglitz (2015), provides a way of correctly, fairly, and practically applying tax policy, such that it falls on those who benefit the most from collective public action and can be spent to benefit those who contribute most to the social and economic life of the city. This revenue can be used to build the most important infrastructure of the city: affordable housing. Coming out of the pandemic, it is clear that housing is the infrastructure that we most lack – housing to mitigate the crippling cancer of inequality, with funding derived from the landowning beneficiaries of a well-oiled and attractive city. In fact, in modest ways, as discussed in Chapters 7 and 8 with reference to the applicable precedents, this approach has already been implemented.

SUMMING UP LAND RENT

We can conclude that housing-price inflation in the past forty years may not have been driven by constraints on housing supply but by how urban land, due to its inherent monopoly – location, location, location – has a unique ability to take nearly all of the value generated by city wage earners and entrepreneurs and absorb it into the price of urban land (or its Rent) up to and over the point where the local economy is endangered and housing precarity reaches a crisis. Clearly, we are now at this point.

We might also now understand why adding allowable housing density to a city parcel will not reduce home prices but instead increase the amount of Rent demanded by the landowner up to and over the brink of affordability – unproductively emptying the pockets of wage earners and even those entrepreneurs who would like to, if land were not so expensive, provide affordable housing.

We can also conclude, along with Stiglitz, that given these dynamics, effective policies are needed to ensure that the value increases generated by the private and civic actions of citizens somehow increase the "commonwealth"[6] of these same citizens, not just the wealth of land speculators.

We obviously need policy tools if we are to pursue this outcome. Fortunately, practical and precedented planning and development tools exist to help. They just haven't been used at a scale commensurate with our current housing crisis. In following chapters, I explore some appropriate measures. But first, let's look at how land Rent is also the main driver of another critical issue very intimately related to the housing crisis: urban sprawl.

4

Land Rent, Urban Sprawl, and Transport

LAND RENT AND SPRAWL

For the past seventy years, major metropolitan areas throughout the English-speaking world have spread their populations over vast suburban landscapes. In the United States, this transformation has been the most dramatic. Now, over half of all Americans live spread out over more than five times the area of the older centre cities that spawned them. Although the United States is globally famous for first advancing the new low-density residential landscape, Australia (Coffee, Baker, and Lange 2016), New Zealand (Schrader 2014), Canada (Pope 2016), and the United Kingdom (Mathiesen 2015) have largely followed suit.

This well-known phenomenon is pejoratively known as urban sprawl, but the relationship of sprawl to land Rent is virtually unknown. Prior to the Second World War, land Rent was the largest factor holding back the growth of a global middle class. For example, in the 1920s, the cost of a home in New York City was eight times the average household income, more than twice what most housing experts consider optimal.[1] The Great Depression and the Second World War slowed and then reversed this rise, with the housing-to-income ratio falling to roughly two to one in New York City by the year 1970 (Daughherty 2022; J. Miller 2011). Sadly, after 1980, the gap between home prices and average incomes widened inexorably, with a temporary decline after the Great Recession of 2008. Now, New York City's ratio of income to home price stands at over one to ten (J. Jones 2022). New York City is not alone in this regard. This same (or worse) ratio of income to home price is echoed in Sydney, Christchurch, London, Toronto, and other major cities worldwide.

This trend raises several questions. Why did New York City home prices (relative to wages) dip during the thirty years between 1950 and 1980. Why was there an inexorable rise over the following thirty years? And why did the same trend persist globally, regardless of disparate policy regimes and economic events in distant lands? The answers, of course, must have something to do with the price of urban land, given that during these years the cost of construction stayed relatively stable, inflating in real terms only within a range of 10 to 40 percent, depending on the metro area (Zarenski 2016a).

Thus the vast majority of this global price increase must be attributable to the price of land. This finding is reinforced by the previously mentioned research of the Center for Economic Studies and Ifo Institute (Knoll, Schularick, and Steger 2014), which shows that the cause of the global run-up in housing prices that afflicted all of the world's advanced economies was the unprecedented run-up in the price of urban land.[2]

But why the run-up now after three postwar decades of real housing-price decline? In addition to Thomas Piketty's (2014) hypothesis concerning the "Les Trois Glorieuses," we can add that for these same three decades, cities were able to escape the deleterious effects of land Rent by, in effect, creating a new frontier: the suburb.

URBAN LAND PRICE AND THE AMERICAN SUBURBAN FRONTIER AFTER THE SECOND WORLD WAR

Part of Henry George's argument resonates here. He said that new cities, such as his home of San Francisco, were less susceptible than older cities to the economic drain of land Rents. In older cities, he argued, land speculators had been afforded more time to capture ever-scarcer urban land and to collectively force up urban land value and thus more time to drain the productive efforts of capital and labour into Rents. This insight – that the natural equality that he found on the frontier gave way in time to the poverty of established cities – inspired his first and most important book, *Progress and Poverty* (1879). His thesis was that as the city progresses, it inevitably produces poverty. And for him, the cause of urban poverty was excessive land Rent:

> It is in the older and richer sections of the Union that pauperism and distress among the working classes are becoming most painfully apparent. If there is less deep poverty in San Francisco than in New York, is it not because San Francisco is yet behind New York in all that both cities are striving for? When San Francisco reaches the point where New York now is, who can doubt that there will also be ragged and barefooted children on her streets?
>
> This association of poverty with progress is the great enigma of our times. It is the central fact from which spring industrial, social, and political difficulties that perplex the world, and with which statesmanship and philanthropy and education grapple in vain ... So long as all the increased wealth which modern progress brings goes to build up great fortunes, to increase luxury and make sharper the contrast between the House of Have and the House of Want, progress is not real and cannot be permanent. (George 1879, 9)

George wrote well before the mass production of automobiles and likely could not have imagined how it would, for a time, help to undercut the monopoly power of urban Rent. But for the "three glorious decades," it did. In many countries, particularly the United States, with the encouragement of the oil and auto industry and with a massive program of taxpayer-funded highway construction, a vast new urban frontier was opened up surrounding the older walkable and transit-friendly streetcar suburbs and centre cities.

A half-hour drive on this new system of roads opened up over sixteen times the acreage contained within the old city limits. Such a vast new inventory of urbanizable lands kept the land prices in new subdivisions low and, for a time, made ownership of a single-family home and the newly necessary car an achievable goal for even grocery clerks.

Sadly, in time, once this new autocentric metropolitan landscape had reached its organic limits, and once the land within its reach had thus become scarcer and more precious (making it more susceptible to rent seeking), the housing-affordability progress of the second half of the twentieth century turned into the housing poverty of the twenty-first century.

With urban land Rent now pushing housing prices out of reach for millennials (or at least those without access to parental cash) and with highways now congested to the point that commutes sometimes take hours, not minutes, well-situated urban land is again at a premium. Now, this new generation finds itself victimized by excessive land Rents and suffering through the same levels of blatant urban inequality and homelessness that George decried in 1890. In order to grasp how land use and transportation currently impact health, inequality, and racial justice, it is helpful to look at this legacy of urban sprawl in the way that economists do.

THE ECONOMICS OF THE CENTRE AND THE EDGE

In Chapter 2, David Ricardo's (1817) law of rent was introduced (see Hawes 2010). This law is particularly relevant as a cause of urban sprawl. As land Rent in urban centres absorbs a higher and higher percentage of the productive value of capital and labour occurring thereon, the incentive to search farther afield for lower land Rent increases. The result is urban sprawl.

To illustrate, I return again to the three factors of production: land, capital, and labour. Let's imagine five sites for free-standing Starbucks coffee shops. The first one is located at the central crossroads of our imaginary city. The fifth one is out on the margin of the metroplex, where land Rent for urban purposes is next to nothing (or "worthless," in Ricardian terms). Between them stretch the other three at even increments. Starting with the one on the fringe of the city, the owner needs to sell only enough coffee to pay for the building and materials (or the capital) and to pay employees (or the labour) in order to be profitable. Land is not really a factor. So we might put numbers to these categories as follows: capital has 5 units of value, labour has 5, and land has 0. If the shop sells 15 units of value, the profit is 5 units, and the shop stays in business. At the other end of the scale, at the central site, the numbers look different. Here, the shop sells more product, so capital (including the coffee) might be 8 units of value, labour might be higher, too, at 8 units, but land (or Rent), as you might expect, is much higher, at 20 units. To earn a profit, the owner needs to sell 36 units worth of product just to break even and 41 units to get to a target of 5 units of profit. The other three sites pay successively less rent but also sell less coffee. Thus the profit level of each store is the same, and any increase in profits sensed by landlords leads to higher rents. What this simple example shows is that as you work closer to well-serviced and heavily populated central areas, more and more of the value of the capital and labour goes into Rent; in fact, Rent eventually gets most of the value while contributing nothing directly to the coffee business.[3]

Both David Ricardo and, earlier, Adam Smith understood that land Rent is unproductive in these terms, but it was left to Henry George to fully explain its significance for the emerging modern city. George explained that the law of rent ensures that land Rents will draw nearly all of the value that a favourable *urban* location provides and (in the most extreme cases) will leave only subsistence wages for labour and precarious profits for entrepreneurs. The idea is that wages and profit are barely adequate and always stay the same, with any advantage between one location and the next going to Rent.

What the concept of land Rent also explains is that the need to pay Rent affects your calculus about where to locate your business. The higher the Rent, the more likely you are to search for a more affordable site farther from the centre of economic activity. It also follows that, if not for the high Rent at the central location, you would be inclined to put your Starbucks across the street from the other one in order to poach your neighbour's customers or to attract new ones, adding economic activity at the centre. Absent the influence of Rent, there would also be more coffee to be had and likely at a lower price, too. The point to underline here is that, without Rent, activities would be more highly concentrated at a city centre than they are and more efficient as well. In sum, those who see land Rents as a major economic driver of urban inequality also blame land Rents for causing urban sprawl.

HOUSING AND LAND RENT

The same logic can be applied to the forces that locate housing. High land prices in city centres make it less likely that families will be able to afford appropriate housing near the conveniences of city centres or close to jobs – no matter their taste for high-density living. And when municipal-planning offices try to mitigate these effects by increasing allowable density, their rezoning efforts largely benefit landowners – who pocket windfall gains in land value while the price of homes stays high.[4]

So, as in the case of the Starbucks example above, the homebuyer (or the developer hoping to sell homes) searches for marginal sites that can be brought into use with tiny relative land costs. Again, the point to underline here is that if urban land prices were not a major factor, you could expect to see lands close to the centre used more intensively for housing – notwithstanding some degree of personal preference for detached or attached forms factoring into individual decisions, to be sure. And wage earners would not be forced by high Rent to seek affordable housing far from work – incrementally softening the burden on our taxpayer-funded transport systems as a result.

TRANSPORT AND LAND RENT

The land Rent issue described above has influenced metropolitan development in all advanced market-based economies, but in the United States it was quite pronounced after the Second World War for reasons that ranged from national defence to economic-development policy to encouraging the American Dream. As for national defence, it was argued that the more you sprawled, the harder it would be for the Russians to blow it all up (Dudley 2001).[5] With respect to policy, "What's good for General Motors is good for the country," argued Secretary of Defense Charles E. Wilson (quoted in US Department of Defense n.d.).[6] And for proof regarding the American Dream, see director Frank Capra's 1947 movie *It's a Wonderful Life* (discussed by Nero 2019).[7]

Building the network of interstate highways brought a flood of new formerly "worthless" lands inside the reach of the city, where, at least at first, the problem of land-price inflation was overcome by new supply and where the problem of traffic congestion was mitigated for a while by a new limited-access highway system. Cheap land, easy access by

FIGURE 4.1 Screen grab from the 1946 movie *It's a Wonderful Life*. For a brief few decades, Americans escaped the grip of high land Rents thanks to the car and the interstate highway system. A new "frontier" opened up – this time not in the west but in the American suburb. | From the film *It's a Wonderful Life*.

means of suddenly affordable cars,[8] and inducements like the GI Bill, tax deductions on mortgage-interest income, and the redlining[9] of medium-density neighbourhoods formerly served by streetcars pushed the urban fringes of American cities out much farther than in other countries. Over time, the average metropolitan density of older US cities dropped – often, as in the Boston metropolitan area, to less than one-fifth of their pre-war density levels (Condon 2010). This reduced density, of course, also undercut the price of land under older "streetcar suburb" residential zones (Jackson 1985, 136). In some US Rust Belt cities, those inner-city land prices are still low. But in the jobs-rich coastal cities, these former streetcar suburbs – at least those that escaped the ravages of so-called urban renewal from the 1950s to the 1980s – have recovered lost land value and then some.

Again, this issue varies only in degree of impact. The average density of American cities has trended lower than their counterparts in the

English-speaking world but not dramatically so. Thus these same land-price trends are identical and differ only in degree from one country to the next. Per square kilometre, the average density of major metropolitan areas is now 1,500 to 2,000 people in the United States, 2,000 to 3,000 in Canada, 1,500 to 2,500 in Australia, and 2,000 in New Zealand. These variations pale into insignificance compared with the world's densest metropolitan areas, such as Dhaka in Bangladesh, at 40,000 people per square kilometre, or even Istanbul in Turkey, at a middle-level density of 11,000 people per square kilometre (Demographia 2020).

5

Attempts to Provide Affordable Housing

AFFORDABLE HOUSING IN THE UNITED STATES:
A SHORT HISTORY

Americans, more so than other so-called Anglo-Saxon capitalist economies, have a powerful tradition (embedded in the Fifth Amendment
of the US Constitution)[1] of protecting individual rights to private property. This tradition has coloured government attempts to interfere with
urban land markets through both taxation and policy regulation. In
short, streaming land-value increases away from speculators and toward
housing support for citizens has proven difficult and rare. More commonly, government funds or tax benefits have flowed into private urban
land markets to compete for increasingly expensive urban lands, for
which suitors are forced to pay high market prices. This construct is
rooted in the fertile soil of Enlightenment thought, which permeates
America's constitutional structure, particularly John Locke's famous
declaration that government's only role with respect to the individual
should be "to preserve his property, that is, his Life, Liberty and Estate"

(Locke 1689, 305). Jefferson, ever the politician, changed Locke's phrasing to "life liberty and the pursuit of happiness" in his Declaration of Independence, but equating property with happiness is not much of a stretch for Americans.

Obviously, economic socialists, however few in number, have long had a problem with this Enlightenment point of view. Property law from a socialist perspective is the primary instrument by which the upper class perpetuates financial inequality – within and between generations. America's answer to this complaint has been a redistributive tax policy. Progressive taxes aimed at weakening the power of the wealthy have been the main device, especially inheritance taxes, which were 10 percent when first imposed in 1910 and rose to as high as 87 percent between 1940 and 1973. The US maximum inheritance tax is currently 40 percent, after having bounced up and down by 5 or 10 percent over the past twenty years ("Estate Tax" n.d.). Unfortunately, apart from relatively low municipal property taxes and modest capital-gains taxes at the time of sale, the Rent gains of urban lands have largely escaped an assault by redistributors, who have missed a chance to aggressively redirect land Rent toward social purpose.

EARLY STARTS

Prior to the twentieth century, US governments did not assume any responsibility for housing. Earlier government efforts took the form of building-code regulations aimed at preventing egregious fire and health hazards common to nineteenth-century tenements (Bauman, Biles, and Szylvian 2000).

Garden Homes Milwaukee

It was not until late in the Progressive Era that government got involved in providing housing. In 1916, Milwaukee voters elected socialist Daniel Haon as mayor, a position that he held until the 1930s. After campaigning on a platform of housing for workers, he delivered a complicated plan for what in essence would be a housing collective called Garden Homes, with land owned in common by residents. The utopian ambitions of the district and its more than 200 detached homes are still evident in the physical design of this unique community (Wisconsin Historical Society n.d.).

FIGURE 5.1 Garden Homes Historic District, Milwaukee, Wisconsin. | Courtesy Freekee via Wikimedia Commons and National Register of Historic Places.

Stein and Wright

In the 1920s and '30s, a number of more robust attempts were made to provide housing that was more affordable and of a higher quality than what the market provided. Most notable were the projects undertaken by Clarence Stein in partnership with Henry Wright (Stein 1957). Together, they developed numerous housing projects that became well known for their trend-setting innovations, particularly for adapting housing districts to the car and for providing immediate access to green space in front of every home by putting street access at the back instead of at the front. Their most famous project, Radburn in Fairlawn, New Jersey, is renowned for what is known as the Radburn Plan – a housing district set within a large plot of land bounded by a ring road (a configuration called a superblock) from which cul-de-sac roads extend to serve a group of individual houses.

Less well known, a point to emphasize in this volume, is that the land under the structures was and is collectively owned, with all residents taking ownership of individual shares of the land and claiming the property rights associated with their housing unit. In modern terms, housing units subject to this arrangement are known as "bare land condominiums." Although these detached buildings might be privately owned, the land under and around them is owned by a condominium association or a land trust. Stein's widely read book *Toward New Towns for America* (1957) captures his many successful housing-project collaborations with Wright.

FIGURE 5.2 Radburn, New Jersey, showing central car-free greenway street. |
Courtesy Creative Commons.

DEPRESSION-ERA PUBLIC HOUSING

Stein and Wright also worked on the design of a series of greenbelt communities during the Great Depression. The intent was to create complete suburban communities with jobs, housing, and civic infrastructure included in the plan. These plans were spatially generous like Radburn but departed to some extent from the Radburn design, with the fronts of homes turned decisively toward the street this time.[2]

Three greenbelt communities were eventually built: Greenbelt in Maryland, Greendale in Wisconsin, and Greenhills in Ohio. Unlike Garden Homes and Radburn, the land and structures of the new greenbelt towns were federally owned, with commercial and residential tenants paying rent to the government. The strongly collectivist structure of these new communities provoked political opposition from the start, leading to the discontinuation of the greenbelt program only a few years after it had begun (M.L. Williamson 1987). After the Second World War, the federal government privatized the greenbelt communities, selling residential units to former tenants.

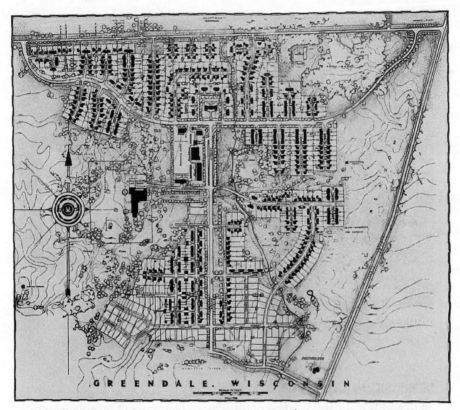

FIGURE 5.3 Greendale, Wisconsin, original plan, 1938. | Courtesy Wisconsin Historical Society and Creative Commons.

FIGURE 5.4 Greendale, Wisconsin, village centre today. | Courtesy Google Maps.

FIGURE 5.5 Techwood housing project in Atlanta, Georgia, which was America's first federally funded low-income housing. Shown in late 1930s but largely demolished in 1999. | Courtesy US Library of Congress.

THE FIRST HOUSING PROJECTS

Once the greenbelt program was killed, the federal government shifted to what was then a politically more palatable strategy: direct financial assistance to local authorities willing to build housing for the poor in buildings and on sites that would be city-owned. Funding was provided as a direct and universal subsidy of US$5,000 per unit (equivalent to US$94,000 dollars today). This low price frustrated housing advocates of the day and resulted in rather spartan designs that were located on less expensive sites in unfavourable locations (Radford 1996). Nevertheless, tens of thousands of new units were built prior to the outbreak of the Second World War, many of them close to war-production facilities in anticipation of the coming conflict.

The Techwood Homes project in Atlanta is credited as the first of these projects, completed in 1936. President Franklin D. Roosevelt dedicating it in person. It was built on the cleared site of a mixed-race community declared a slum. Although those displaced were both white and Black, only white families were rehoused therein. Assigning housing projects to either white or Black families was a practice that would officially last until the 1960s, leaving a legacy that endures to this day

(Gotham 2000). Like many such projects, it was unsuccessful as a neighbourhood and was largely demolished in 1996, to be replaced by the mixed-use and mixed-income community Centennial Place.

POSTWAR HOUSING PROJECTS
Hundreds of thousands of federally financed public-housing units were built after the Second World War for returning veterans, the officially poor, and elderly Americans of limited means (Hays 1995). Nearly all of these new housing projects employed urban design strategies that departed dramatically from tradition. Of greatest architectural influence was Swiss-French architect Le Corbusier's (1967) pre-war Radiant City project, which envisioned modernist tower blocks set in verdant parks, an idea enthusiastically taken up by postwar public-housing planners and designers.

The "tower in the park" pattern was later criticized by the likes of Jane Jacobs, author of *The Death and Life of Great American Cities* (1961), and Oscar Newman, author of *Defensible Space: Crime Prevention through*

FIGURE 5.6 Model of the Plan Voisin for Paris by Le Corbusier displayed at the Nouveau Esprit Pavilion, 1925. | Courtesy Amber Case via Creative Commons.

FIGURE 5.7 Single-loaded corridor with public space gallery at Pruitt–Igoe as imagined (top) and prior to demolition (bottom). | Courtesy US Department of Housing and Urban Development and Wikimedia Commons.

FIGURE 5.8 April 1972. The second widely televised demolition of a Pruitt–Igoe building that followed the March 16 demolition.
| Courtesy US Department of Housing and Urban Development.

Urban Design (1972), for exhibiting a flawed understanding of how people use and defend city spaces, a failure made paradigmatic in the notorious Pruitt–Igoe housing project in St. Louis – demolished by its own housing authority only twenty years after construction for irreparable flaws in the basic building and site concepts employed (Montgomery 1987).[3]

This failure and others caused planners, designers, and the public to question not only the formal strategies used in public-housing projects but also the need for and efficacy of public housing in general.

THE SHIFT FROM PUBLIC OWNERSHIP TO SUBSIDIES FOR THE MARKET AND FOR INDIVIDUALS

By the 1980s, the US government had largely abandoned the mission of directly housing the poor. Instead, it provided individuals with cash subsidies for use in the private rental market (discussed below) and provided private developers with tax credits in order to stimulate low- and moderate-income housing (also discussed below).

Still, it should be noted that these postwar efforts left the United States with over 1 million public-housing units sheltering 2.1 million Americans (Borderless Charity 2017). This total is less than 1 percent of all Americans, but the ratio is much higher in some cities, notably New York, where over 400,000 residents, or nearly 5 percent, are publicly housed (Bloom 2016).

These numbers, however, verge on pathetic in comparison to the numbers housed by other Western democracies. They provide nonmarket housing solutions ranging from 17 percent of all units in England (Gov. UK 2020)[4] to over 50 percent of all units in Vienna (Condon 2018).

HOPE VI

Centennial Place, mentioned above, represents a first in a second way. Involving the transformation of a publicly owned housing project into a largely privately owned community of mixed uses and mixed incomes, it was the first project to be funded by the HOPE VI program, an initiative of the US Department of Housing and Urban Development (HUD) (Turbov and Piper 2005).[5] As with many HOPE VI projects, the site was developed with a private corporate partner, the Integral Group LLC, which now owns and manages the site.

FIGURE 5.9 Centennial Place today with original main Techwood housing building in background. | Courtesy Google Maps.

The emergence of HOPE VI projects marked a shift in attitude about public housing. The social failures and stigma associated with living in "housing projects" could, it was thought, be overcome by more sensitive urban design strategies of a type recommended by American proponents of New Urbanism (Planning Tank 2018). These urban design principles included surveillance for safety, clarification of the distinctions between private and public space, a respect for the street as a crucial setting for civic life, a renewed respect for traditional (or nonmodernist) house forms, and a mix of residents, from the working class to the upper-middle class, without physical architectural distinctions associated with these economic class differences.

Close to forty distressed housing projects were selectively demolished, rehabilitated, and rebuilt throughout the United States under this program. Nearly US$7 billion in federal grants was dispensed, all between 1993 and 2009 (US HUD n.d. "About").

In October 2000, HOPE VI was honoured with national recognition as a recipient of an Innovations in American Government Award. HOPE VI was among ten winners chosen by the Innovations in American

Government Program, one of the nation's most prestigious programs focused on public-service awards.

It is also important to note that the HOPE VI program attracted its share of criticism, which tended to be grounded in concerns with policy, not design. For example, the National Housing Law Project and partners (2002) issued a scathing review with the following conclusion:

> HUD's failure to provide comprehensive and accurate information about HOPE VI has created an environment in which misimpressions about the program and its basic purposes and outcomes have flourished – often with encouragement from HUD. HOPE VI plays upon the public housing program's unfairly negative reputation and an exaggerated sense of crisis about the state of public housing in general to justify a drastic model of large-scale family displacement and housing redevelopment that increasingly appears to do more harm than good.

It should also be mentioned that the HOPE VI program returned scarce publicly owned urban land to the private sector, eliminating an available opportunity for future use of public land. Also important to note is that, according to estimates, far less than half of the occupants of HOPE VI projects nationwide were rehoused on the revived sites or provided housing vouchers to secure suitable alternative housing nearby.

THE CHOICE NEIGHBORHOODS PROGRAM

HUD later transformed the HOPE VI program into the Choice Neighborhoods program (US HUD n.d. "Choice"), which it designed to take HOPE VI to the next level by broadening the property types and activities at which resources can be targeted. The goal is for redevelopment to exceed the targeted benefits of HOPE VI, such that new investment in poor neighbourhoods will provide a robust anchor – one that spurs neighbourhood stability and elevated levels of investment. The hope is that this structure will help communities to implement strategies that are more comprehensive and better tailored to local context. This approach addresses the whole fabric of existing neighbourhoods and

FIGURE 5.10 Quincy Street in Boston, Massachusetts, locus for Choice Neighborhood project, as it is today. | Courtesy Boston Housing Authority.

seeks to strengthen connections to surrounding areas through mixed uses, mixed incomes, and revitalization (Tate 2007). In this way, the projects demonstrate a steep and laudable departure from earlier housing-project failures caused by intentionally separating public-housing projects from the organic fabric of surrounding urban districts.

This program builds new housing in poor neighbourhoods that may or may not contain housing projects owned by the local authority. It is distinct because it targets concentrations of poverty surgically, within the fabric of existing city blocks. Sponsors hope that the increasing separation of Americans by income can be reversed.

As mentioned in previous chapters, although urban America is becoming somewhat less segregated by race, it is becoming more and more segregated by income. As noted by program sponsors, the number of Americans living in designated "poor" districts climbed from 8 million in 2000 to nearly 11 million in 2007. The Choice Neighborhoods program seeks to halt or reverse this trend, but despite the local successes of the program, this trend is still accelerating.

JUST GIVE PEOPLE CASH: SECTION 8 VOUCHERS

In the late 1970s, due to the problems associated with concentrating the poor in housing projects and due to the fact that the housing problems of poor families had less to do with substandard housing and more to do with the high cost of acceptable housing, the US government started to supplement incomes so that the poor could afford market rentals. Currently, to help pay their rent, 1.1 million Americans receive Section 8 vouchers, named for the section in the housing legislation that enables them (Center on Budget and Policy Priorities 2019).[6] Vouchers are available to qualified applicants, but because there are far fewer vouchers available than renters who qualify, preference is given to families with children, the aged, and the disabled. Since the amount of the vouchers is tied to market rents, the federal government has become one more entity competing for a share of urban land and a player in propping up the asset value of urban land – or land Rent.

THE LOW-INCOME HOUSING TAX CREDIT (LIHTC) FOR AFFORDABLE HOUSING

As the US government turned away from public-housing projects, the United States increased its use of the Low-Income Housing Tax Credit (LIHTC) in order to supplement Section 8 vouchers, a tax credit designed to spur the construction of low-income housing by the private sector (US HUD n.d. "Low-Income"). In simple terms, tax credits for housing work as follows: private development firms are induced to build mixed-income housing in return for tax credits, which can then be sold to high-income individuals or to corporations for use in reducing their federal tax obligations. The credits are capped at a maximum of 70 percent of the total cost of the project. In return, project developers have to partner with a local housing agency to find low- and moderate-income households, which will pay only 30 percent of their pre-tax income in rent. After fifteen or thirty years (depending on the structure of the deal), the obligation to rent to low- and moderate-income residents ceases, and the project then reverts, without further obligation, to the owner. For over thirty years, these public-private partnerships have furnished the bulk of new federally subsidized units, providing more than US$6 billion per year in tax credits to produce over 50,000 housing units per year (US President's Economic Recovery Advisory Board 2010). The program has been criticized for costing on average 30 percent more per unit than similar private-market projects, as well as for fraud (Stamm and LaJoie

FIGURE 5.11 US Whip factory conversion in Westfield, Massachusetts. Financed with US tax credits for affordable housing during the author's tenure as Director of Community Development in Westfield. | Author's photo.

2020). Another criticism often raised is the loss of affordability in these units after the fifteen-year obligation to rent to low-income tenants lapses. Millions of units are approaching this point, and evidence suggests that rents are, predictably, spiking after the fifteen-year mark in high-rent districts – those where low-rent units are most needed (Khadduri et al. 2012).

As with Section 8 vouchers, the result of tax credits, in essence, has been the funnelling of taxpayer money into private hands – in the form of taxes never paid (or credits) – for the purchase of urban land. They are yet another tax-funded competitor for suitable urban land and a contributor to skyrocketing urban land Rent.

THE MORTGAGE INTEREST-RATE DEDUCTION FOR HOMEOWNERS

Of possibly subtler but even greater influence on urban land markets are those federal inducements for Americans to enter the housing market and become homeowners. Prior to the Great Recession of 2008, nearly 69 percent of all Americans lived in a home owned by a family member. The economic crash collapsed this homeownership share to 64 percent

(Huebl 2019). The crash was caused by the transformation of mortgages into an investment commodity, packaged and sold as mortgage-backed securities on global capital markets. Purchasers of mortgage-backed securities believed that they were shielded from risk, reassured by falsified triple-A credit ratings provided by complicit rating agencies (Lewis 2011).[7]

The crash vividly illustrates how the strength of the American economy, and even the world economy, is tied to the strength of the US housing market. The US housing market accounts for up to 18 percent of annual GDP and represents 71 percent of household debt held by Americans – or more accurately, by banks since the bank technically owns the house until the very last payment on the loan (Fontinelle 2019). Finally, over half of all wealth held by individuals (or their bankers) in the United States is in the form of land value – and as we saw in Chapter 1, the bulk of this value is in land that is urban, not rural (Kumhoff et al. 2021).

The mortgage interest-rate deduction primarily benefits Americans in the upper quartile of income and amounts to a huge annual loss in federal taxes. For instance, up until 2017, annual taxes forgone due to this deduction were in the range of US$60 billion annually, ten times

FIGURE 5.12 Urban land value in US as share of total

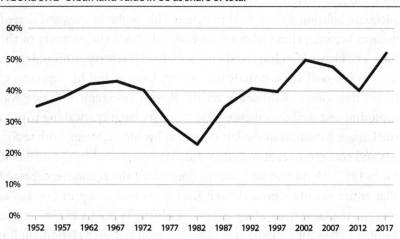

Based on data from Kumhoff 2021.

more than is lost to the tax credits for low-income housing discussed above.[8] Most economists suggest that the interest-rate deduction doesn't actually make housing more affordable either (Casselman 2015). Why? Because its value gets absorbed by higher housing prices or by excessively sprawling suburban development and/or higher land costs, with the main beneficiaries being, yet again, land speculators. Evidence to support this contention is found by comparing homeownership rates in the United States and those in Canada, where there are no mortgage interest-rate deductions and where the average density of the cities is substantially higher. US rates are almost identical to Canadian rates.[9]

AFFORDABLE HOUSING IN THE UNITED KINGDOM: AN EVEN SHORTER HISTORY

For the sake of simplicity, I speak to the housing issue in the United Kingdom as if it comprised one country. It does not. There are major differences between the member countries. But much of the policy discussed below is applied throughout the United Kingdom, and the differences are generally not relevant to our focus on land Rent.

The United Kingdom was the first nation to industrialize and thus the first to experience the metastatic growth of its industrial cities, including Belfast, Liverpool, Birmingham, and Manchester. In time, the social stresses of inadequate housing for urban wage earners became an issue too great to ignore. Usurious land Rent was the obvious barrier to adequate housing for the working class. This problem spawned heated debates between those who would make all lands the property of the state (i.e., Henry Hyndman and early socialists) (Flaherty 2020) and those who would only tax it heavily (i.e., Henry George and his supporters). In his day, George's influence on the British land-reform debate was profound and well documented. He made six lengthy speaking trips to the United Kingdom in the last decade of his life, debating both socialists and conservatives at well-attended events recorded by the media (P. Jones 1987). Hyndman and George dominated the economic debate of that entire decade – even though Karl Marx was living in London at roughly the same time, albeit in relative obscurity (ibid.). In time, it was George's ideas for a mixed economy that won out over Hyndman. But with a few notable exceptions discussed below (most dramatically in the "garden city" districts), his proposals for reducing land Rent were never fully implemented.

EBENEZER HOWARD AND HIS EQUITABLE PLANS
FOR INDUSTRIAL ENGLAND

In his book *To-morrow: A Peaceful Path to Real Reform* (1898) – retitled *Garden Cities of To-morrow* in 1902 – British town planner Ebenezer Howard described his revolutionary vision for the ideal industrial city, explicating a full systems approach to solving the problem of industrial-era housing squalor. Two garden cities were eventually built to Howard's plans in suburban London: Letchworth and Welwyn.

Letchworth, with construction starting in 1902, is the more complete of the two and has been much discussed in the urban design literature but with too little focus on the social motivations of its main proponent. Howard's main motive for dedicating his life to the political program of garden cities was not the garden aspect of his plans but his intention to avoid the damaging effects of urban land Rent. His plans introduced an urban development strategy that would permanently supply housing

FIGURE 5.13 A typical street scene in Letchworth, England. | Courtesy Stephen McKay via Wikimedia Commons.

to the wage-earning classes at a price that they could afford, but it would do so without treading into anti-capitalist notions of state-owned housing or state-owned urban land.

In this approach, Howard was inspired by the work of Henry George, who had a major impact on the thinking of the British at that time.[10] Keeping all of the land in the hands of the community was the strategy that he chose in this case, with individual land parcels not sold to homeowners but leased. In this way, equity gains would accrue only to the value of the structures, not to the land below. This approach left Letchworth housing far more affordable than homes in nearby communities, where freehold ownership of the parcel was the norm.

However, beginning in the 1960s, Parliament intervened to allow homeowners to purchase their own parcel through negotiations with the community corporation that owned the land, such that over time this cost advantage has eroded. Predictably, dramatic increases in home prices have been the result. To cite one example, at the time of this writing, a home at 16 North Avenue, Letchworth, is on the market for £347,000. The same home sold in 2000 for £85,000. Why the huge difference in price? In the intervening years, the dirt under this town-

FIGURE 5.14 Letchworth Garden City's original plan, by Barry Parker and Robert Unwin. Note that much of the plan was left sketched in. Letchworth was started in 1902 but not completed until the 1960s, indicating how slowly cities actually change. | Courtesy Creative Commons.

house had been released from leasehold and made freehold, illustrating just how much land value had been shifted from the commonwealth of the community to the individual freeholder.[11]

THE HISTORY OF GOVERNMENT-PROVIDED HOUSING IN THE UNITED KINGDOM

The British housing system as we know it today began in earnest following the First World War with the creation of homes "fit for heroes" (Colin Jones and Murie 2006, 9–10). Homes were built rapidly to accommodate the soldiers returning from war. The program ramped up further after the Second World War, with 4.4 million homes built in the following thirty-five years (Lupton et al. 2009). The rental sector for council housing – which was built and rented, hopefully at a profit, by municipal authorities – reached its peak in 1979, at 42 percent of all housing (Scanlon 2017). Since this peak, much of that stock has been sold off to tenants or transferred to nonprofit, independent housing corporations (ibid.). Now, only 8 percent of British housing is council housing (J. Harris 2016).

FIGURE 5.15 Example of "homes for heroes" public housing in Dagenham, England. | Courtesy Malc McDonald via Creative Commons.

FIGURE 5.16 Typical example of more modernist post-WWII housing in Wolverhampton, England. | Courtesy John M. via Wikimedia Commons.

Throughout the mid-twentieth century, council housing was seen as an integral part of the English housing and social welfare systems, providing homes of good quality for (mostly) working-class households. During this time, it was politically possible to support the growth of housing while also supporting the growth of individual homeownership at the expense of private landlords, who were widely seen as the cause of the substandard tenement conditions of the Industrial Revolution (Colin Jones and Murie 2006). Throughout the 1970s, housing finance, taxation, and organizational arrangements favouring homeownership changed the political environment, and the rental sector for social housing was increasingly seen to be at odds with individual homeownership (ibid.).

THE RIGHT TO BUY PROGRAM
The changing political attitudes were exacerbated as the public began to associate tenure in council housing with poverty, worklessness, and no-go estates – a story similar to the one told in the United States. This

view found political relevance with the election of neoliberal prime minister Margaret Thatcher, who ran on a campaign promoting a "property owning democracy" (Colin Jones and Murie 2006, 12).[12]

In its Housing Act of 1980, the Thatcher government introduced the Right to Buy program, which gave council tenants the ability to purchase the homes that they were renting at a discount of 30 to 50 percent depending on the location and year of the purchase. The program resulted in a mass sell-off of the council-housing units. Although it was seen as a positive step toward the promotion of Thatcher's "property-owning democracy" (R. Moore 2014), with it's supposed social and financial benefits, the program contributed to the decline of social housing in the United Kingdom. By 2015, approximately 2.5 million units had been sold to sitting tenants across the country, relegating local authorities to a much more marginal role in the provision of housing (Sprigings and Smith 2012).

Like many policies, the Right to Buy program had unintended consequences. Some households were living in estates and units that were much less desirable than others. Detached, semi-detached, and row homes were purchased by tenants at much higher rates than flats in multi-family apartment buildings. Those in apartments did not see the value of owning their unit and thus lost out on the benefits of the program. The homes were also sometimes seen as an opportunity to get out of undesirable council estates since the home could be resold on the market for a profit. This outcome was unexpected by policy makers, as they naively expected that tenants who purchased their rentals would feel more committed to them and their community (Sprigings and Smith 2012).

Private companies operated schemes in central London to accumulate a portfolio of poor-quality former council housing from Right to Buy purchasers who wanted to move. They purchased contracts to sell the property, which allowed them to avoid any restrictions attached to Right to Buy purchases and allowed purchasers to walk away from their council house with cash in hand (Colin Jones and Murie 2006). Although the scale of this scheme seems to have been contained to central London, it represents a larger trend in the marginalization of local authorities and in the growth and current dominance of private rental companies.

FIGURE 5.17 Photo-op during Thatcher administration showing former renters taking position of their council flat. | Courtesy National Archives and British Public Archives.

The Housing Act of 1988 removed the ability of local authorities to construct any new rental housing on their own. Instead, private nonprofit housing associations were created to construct and manage new afford-able housing (Monk 2010).[13] In recent decades, more units of social housing have been lost than housing associations could resupply.

By far the largest unintended consequence of the Right to Buy scheme was the promotion of the private rent sector. In 1979, private rentals accounted for about 10 percent of housing stock, most of which had regulated rents. By 1990, many of the homes that had been sold through the Right to Buy program began to enter the private market as private rentals. Geoffrey Meen (2018) of the UK Collaborative Centre for Housing Evidence explains that purchases for investment purposes increase both the level of house prices and their volatility – since accumulated equity in the form of existing homes is used to secure (or leverage) the purchase of additional properties. Moreover, first-time homebuyers are excluded, as they have no accumulated equity and are thus disadvantaged relative to investment buyers (ibid.). UK housing in the hands of private landlords is now 20 percent of all housing, and most of this privately owned housing is unregulated (Christiansen and Lewis 2019).

NATIONAL URBAN LAND PLANNING IN THE UNITED KINGDOM

On May 4, 1909, addressing the House of Commons as president of the Board of Trade, Winston Churchill said,

> Roads are made, streets are made, services are improved, electric light turns night into day, water is brought from reservoirs a hundred miles off in the mountains – and all the while the landlord sits still. Every one of those improvements is affected by the labour and cost of other people and the taxpayers. To not one of those improvements does the land monopolist, as a land monopolist, contribute, and yet by every one of them the value of his land is enhanced.

This statement reflects Churchill's admiration for the economic theories of Henry George and the mood not just of Churchill but also of many members of government in the early twentieth century. His argument reflects the growing public discomfort, felt in his time, with the monopolistic essence of urban land. His move to heavily tax urban land reached a peak with the passage in 1910 of the People's Budget (B.K. Murray 1973), whose central plank was a shift of taxes away from import duties, income, and capital and onto land (G. Lee 2008). However, the linked tragedies of the Great Depression and the two world wars gave the United Kingdom plenty of other things to worry about, so land reform languished. Thus it was not until 1947 that the new Labour government returned to the question of urban land value. It did so as part of a plan to rebuild a shattered economy. The Town and Country Planning Act of 1947, which was the first comprehensive planning legislation in the nation's history, set out planning guidelines from the national government that were to be mediated and negotiated at the local level. Crucially, it severed development rights from ownership rights nationwide. For the next seventy years, although the legislation was watered down in many other respects, British land-development rights still remain in the hands of the British state (Monk 2010). Crucially, the authors of the legislation acknowledged the probable windfall for landlords, who were to be granted development rights by the state. To prevent such unearned gains, the authors included a 100 percent tax on the difference between the value of the existing land and the value of the land as developable for residences. This tax would have achieved much the same effect as the ill-fated People's Budget, not through a direct tax on land value but through a capture of any land Rent increases due to any shift to a more lucrative land use. Since urban land is everywhere fantastically more valuable than rural land, the difference in price, and thus the tax, would be substantial. A shift from rural uses to urban uses, no matter where it occurs, increases land values by multiples.

These provisions meant that there would be no large profit made by landowners due to the change in land use catalyzed by government action. Profits, by this reckoning, could be made only through the construction and sale of homes. This approach aligns with classical economic thought, strategically placing the tax burdens on new land Rent, not on the buildings as capital (Bentley 2017, 42).

FIGURE 5.18 Monellan Crescent, Caldecotte, Milton Keynes. This new town with a current population of a quarter million was financed, in effect, by capturing the value of land improved by the larger civic "betterment" increment and recovering it from home sales. | Courtesy Cameraman @ Geograph via Wikimedia Commons.

The 100 percent tax, or betterment charge, was expected to bypass the private housing-development market entirely during these decades since private development was insignificant in scale. After the Second World War, large-scale housing development was mostly in the hands of government agencies, which after 1947 funded the New Towns program (Monk 2010).[14]

Among the most potent criticisms were the argument that a 100 percent betterment charge gave insufficient incentive for landowners to part with their land for development – an argument made by landowners who objected to any reduction in profits – and the possibility that the tax scheme would lead to land hoarding (Crook 2015). It was scrapped by the subsequent Conservative government in the Town and Country Planning Act of 1953. However, under this legislation, local authorities were still able to purchase land from private landowners at use value rather than market value – with these land sales being made compulsory, if necessary – because the purchases allowed local authorities to supply desperately needed public housing. Although in 1959 this portion of the legislation was scrapped as well, the eleven years between 1948 and 1959 mark the years when more than one-third of the 4.5 million social-housing units in England were constructed (Bentley 2017). This framework also allowed for the construction of many new towns. If not for the 1953 legislation, the cost of land in an unregulated market would have made the creation of a public-housing program on such a massive scale impossible (Crook 2015).

WEAK ATTEMPTS AT LAND-VALUE CAPTURE IN THE NEOLIBERAL DECADES

The UK government tried twice more to enact betterment fees, but neither attempt was successful. In 1967, the government, now in the hands of the Labour Party, set up the Land Commission, a body that would act as a land bank. It would assemble all developable land (purchased at its low value as rural land), put in the required infrastructure, and then sell plots to developers to be built on, thereby directing any land-value gains into the public purse. The commission was unsuccessful because it did not have a sufficient budget to purchase the land needed, even at its lower rural price, and was repealed in 1971. Within five years, both the Community Land Act of 1975 and the Development Land Tax Act of 1976 were passed. The Development Land Tax was largely ineffective at collecting any tax revenue from a betterment levy and was the last betterment tax ever enacted in England (Crook 2015). The Community Land Act gave local authorities, not a national body, a larger role in acquiring, servicing, and releasing development land to public and private developers. Informally, it gave local authorities the power to collect on betterment by negotiating planning obligations with developers within their own jurisdictions in lieu of a development charge (ibid.).

In short, the constant see-saw between Labour governments and Conservative governments, with the Conservatives backed by traditional landholding interests, impeded any consistency with regard to the issue of land Rent. In Chapter 7, where I discuss contemporary efforts to direct land Rent toward social purpose, we shall see where things stand today in the United Kingdom.

AFFORDABLE HOUSING IN CANADA: LIKE THE UNITED STATES BUT LESS SO

As in the United States, the federal government in Canada assumed very little responsibility over the market for housing prior to the Great Depression. With the financial difficulties that the Depression inflicted, the government was compelled to intervene. Its actions were relatively weak and not as inventive as, for example, the American initiative to build new greenbelt towns, discussed above. Contrary to its global reputation, Canada does not have a long or robust history of providing its citizens with housing supports in either built or financial form. Its weak federal system leaves many things, apart from national defence and the management of certain resources like fisheries, to the provinces. Thus responses to homelessness and family precarity due to the Depression were ad hoc and were undertaken with a parsimoniousness derived from a moral posture of blaming the victim (Steele 1998). In the national programs that did exist, government largess was concentrated largely on young employed families who needed a helping hand to join the ranks of homeowners, but these programs were of use only to those whose earnings were in the top quintile of family incomes (ibid.). With the advent of the Second World War, Canada ventured into the business of constructing housing itself via a 1942 housing co-op scheme overseen by Wartime Housing Limited. Roughly 24,000 rental units intended for wartime workers were built near armament plants under this scheme (Bacher 1993).

CANADIAN ATTEMPTS TO PROVIDE AFFORDABLE HOUSING AFTER THE SECOND WORLD WAR

Following the Second World War, in a burst of gratitude to returning veterans, the provincial and federal governments became more active. The scheme undertaken by Wartime Housing Limited was extended to help with the housing of returning veterans and their families. Prior to 1948, tens of thousands of new family-sized rental units were built and occupied. But a call to expand the national role in providing housing was crushed in favour of supports to the private housing-construction industry aimed at expanding the percentage of Canadians who owned their own home. The Canadian Mortgage and Housing Corporation

FIGURE 5.19 Lidar view of 1960s-era urban renewal housing project in the foreground, with the neighbourhood saved from demolition in the middle ground. Downtown Vancouver is seen in the background. | Courtesy Google Maps.

(CMHC) then dutifully sold off much of its publicly owned housing stock to residents wherever possible, shifting its function toward helping Canadians to buy new homes (Wade 1986).

This shift did not mean that no housing projects for the poor were built in Canada during the postwar decades, only that they were relatively fewer in number than in the nearby American states. Housing projects were built in many major Canadian cities in the then-fashionable urban renewal format of Le Corbusier's Radiant City project, with its "tower in the park" format. But by 1974, the social stigma associated with living in such starkly different housing projects became impossible to ignore, and the program was cancelled (Bacher 1993).

This postwar shift away from direct intervention in the housing market needs historical context. Like the United States, Canada emerged from the war physically unscathed, with an economy that had been wildly stimulated by wartime spending. This shift also marked the beginning of the unique period in the economic history of the West, as Thomas Piketty (2014, 140) points out, when the flow of capital to the top 1 to 10 percent was undercut. This weakened strength of capital in the context of growing GNP pushed the benefits of productivity gains toward wage earners, reversing previous trends and expanding what had been a much smaller middle class. Also, as mentioned with regard to the US circumstance, the new mobility provided by suddenly affordable automobiles (many manufactured in Canada) opened up vast formerly rural landscapes for suburban housing development.

Between what we might call the Piketty factor and the sprawl factor, both suburban housing and the automobile that was needed to reach it were, for the first time, available to grocery clerks and other service workers – those earning average wages, in other words. Given these circumstances, it is easier to forgive provincial and federal governments for taking the position that, for all but the elderly and those disadvantaged through no fault of their own, the market could do an excellent job of supplying housing – because it did. In 1950, in inflation-adjusted terms, the average cost of a detached home was Cdn$44,000 (E. Martin 2017a), and the average wage was Cdn$51,000. So homes in 1950 cost less than one year's average salary, compared to seven to twelve years today, depending on the Canadian city (Alini 2021).

THE CANADIAN HOUSING CO-OP MOVEMENT

More so than in other English-speaking countries, housing co-ops are an important element of the Canadian housing spectrum. Co-ops are not public housing or social housing but corporations held in common by their residents, who eschew the equity gains available to ordinary homeowners in return for long-term housing security and a style of communal living not available elsewhere. Most co-ops are thus not taxpayer-funded, even if governments, as discussed below, can assist in various ways. Although independent Canadian co-ops date back to the 1930s, the movement really took off in the 1970s when the CMHC launched, under the amended National Housing Act of 1973 (CMHC 1992), a program to provide mortgage funding that would enable co-op members to acquire land and build affordable-housing units. Between the start of the program in 1973 and the cancellation of funding in 1993, over 2,000 co-ops were built, housing more than 250,000 Canadians (Cole 2018). This total may seem to be a small proportion of Canada's 1993 population of almost 30 million people, and it is. But in cities like Vancouver where housing stress was and is greatest, the proportion is higher. About 3 percent of Vancouver's 300,000 housing units are in co-ops (City of Vancouver 2017).

One Vancouver housing co-op in particular has become world famous: False Creek South. Built in the 1970s near Vancouver's downtown, False Creek South has over 600 co-op units spread across 100 acres of city-owned land. The co-op units are mixed in with a nearly equal number of social-housing units for the poor and market-housing units for the better-off (False Creek South Neighbourhood Association 2016). Less prominent but probably even more significant is Champlain Heights, located in the southeast corner of the city. A planned community also built in the 1970s on city-owned land in the romantic style characteristic of that decade's community designs, Champlain Heights provides over 500 units of co-op housing in eleven co-op housing complexes (Champlain Heights Archive 2022; Hardwick 1994). As in False Creek South, the co-op units are provided in numbers equal to the number of units for both the poor and the well-off. Importantly, these three housing types are architecturally indistinguishable from each other.

For both of these projects, it is also worth mentioning that in addition

FIGURE 5.20 One of the many co-op buildings at the False Creek South development. This is a legacy of a particularly active period of Canadian co-op housing development. | Courtesy Google Maps.

to CMHC financing, the pro forma for the project included not only some cross-subsidy from the market products to defray the costs of site infrastructure but also a direct cash infusion from the city tax levy. These city-initiated projects with a focus on social betterment were highly unusual for their time and are almost unheard of in Canada today.

The late Walter Hardwick of Vancouver, who taught geography at the University of British Columbia, was one of the most influential promoters of both Vancouver projects. His writings show that, more than just providing affordable housing, these projects responded to the social foment of the 1960s, when ideas about the ideal social organization of the city, and about social organization generally, had been upended (Hardwick 1994). It was in this spirit of the city as tabula rasa that these unusual projects were designed and built, and those who visit these sites should always bear this motivation in mind.

One last thing to remember when considering co-op housing is that during the 1970s, when False Creek South and Champlain Heights were built, the price for urban land was relatively minor compared to the cost of site infrastructure and the cost of building construction. But now, in high-price cities such as Vancouver, the cost of the land per buildable square foot can be more than twice the price of constructing that same square footage of habitable space.[15] This cost per buildable square foot is yet again a manifestation of out of control land Rent. It is extremely difficult to build an affordable-housing co-op today in Vancouver, Sydney, San Francisco, or any other city that is now the victim of inflated land Rent. Making the numbers work is just as difficult for a housing co-op as it is for any market project – in fact, impossible if you want it to be affordable to average wage earners. Of course, if free land is available, making the numbers work *is* possible (M. Lee 2021), but free land in urban areas is as rare as hens' teeth. Higher levels of government can step in to purchase land, but sadly this intervention just adds one more player to the already overheated market for urban land and puts taxpayer money into the already overstuffed pockets of land speculators. In Chapters 7 and 8, I explore ways around this impasse – ways to control land Rent inflation in the context of affordable-housing development.

AFFORDABLE HOUSING IN NEW ZEALAND: LESS AND LESS OF A FAIR GO

New Zealand is a country where the influence of Henry George and his arguments about taxing land to wring passive wealth gain (or land Rent) out of the financial system can be traced. In 1890, George made a visit to Auckland on his way to Australia. There, he met with many supporters, including former New Zealand premier Sir George Grey (Anna George de Mille 1948). A decade earlier, in 1878, Grey had been influential in New Zealand's introduction of a nationwide land tax inspired by Henry George, the first national tax to be imposed in that country. It was a weak tax and thus inadequate to the task of stemming the power of landlords and the flow of productive capital into land Rent. As weak as it was, landowners fiercely fought every attempt to institutionalize the tax at levels adequate to its intent. It was finally repealed for good in 1991 in the midst of neoliberal enthusiasms for all things that benefited the landed class (Hobbs 2019). A correlation between the year of its repeal and the start of the unrelenting climb in home costs – which have increased at a faster pace and shot further away from the capacity of wage earners to pay for homes than in any other English-speaking country[16] – can be drawn, but given the weakness of the law, it is impossible to draw a direct causal link between the two.

PUBLIC HOUSING IN NEW ZEALAND

As in many English-speaking countries, public housing was largely unheard of prior to the 1930s, when the global Depression prompted its provision. Unique to New Zealand was the construction of State houses for the poor beginning in 1937. Mixed in with market housing, these modest detached homes in bungalow styles eventually numbered over 100,000. But support for a government role in housing waxed and waned as political power bounced between National and Labour governments. In an early burst of what became known as Thatcherism, the Labour government of 1949 promoted the sale of its state houses to tenants and in 1991 insisted on charging full rents for those that remained. The Labour government of 1999 reversed course, halting the sale of state houses and pegging rents to incomes rather than market rates. That is pretty much where things have stood for New Zealand public housing to this day.

A more significant and extensive government support for low-income citizens is provided in the form of rental vouchers. Almost 400,000 Kiwis,

FIGURE 5.21 New Zealand "state houses" built starting in the 1930s. Many of these are on very valuable land, which drives pressure to privatize these homes. | Courtesy New Zealand Archives and Wikimedia Commons.

or about 8 percent, receive some level of support to bridge the gap between their income and market rents. In recent years, as land Rents have surged, the cost to the taxpayers has increased dramatically – from NZ$27 million to NZ$37 million per week in just two years. Critics of the program maintain that the benefit of this support goes largely to landlords, not tenants, in the form of boosted land Rent because landlords can increase rents in the knowledge that the tenant's supplement will go up in order to match the rent and that the tenant can't or won't move to a cheaper apartment because the supplement will be immediately reduced. With every expectation that these costs will climb, the efficacy of this program is increasingly called into question. In the long run, it may be more cost-effective for the government to get back into the business of building public housing and, in the process, to return urban land to public ownership (Edmunds 2021).

AFFORDABLE-HOUSING EFFORTS IN AUSTRALIA: THE QUEST FOR UNIVERSAL HOMEOWNERSHIP

Briefly, Australia is a relatively loose federation of formerly independent colonies. It was not until 1901 that Australia's colonies agreed to federalize, but they did so under conditions that left most roles to the states, including housing. This weakness is revealed both by the lack of a federal housing ministry and by the lack of any housing responsibility in some other ministry that would be akin to the US Department of Housing and Urban Development. This hands-off relationship to housing issues extends to the states, only a few of which have a ministry of housing.

DACEYVILLE: A UTOPIAN VISION OF PUBLIC HOUSING

Australia is now, like the rest of the English-speaking world, in the grip of a housing crisis. In inflation-adjusted terms, the price of housing has increased by 400 percent since 1980, whereas wages have risen very little if at all (Australian Bureau of Statistics 2022). Since the cost of replacing structures has not risen dramatically, most of this housing-price inflation is attributable to land-value increases, boosting the price of urban land far above the value of the large majority of structures placed on it. Australia's long history of favouring plans to house the working class in privately owned homes has both fuelled this inflation and left the

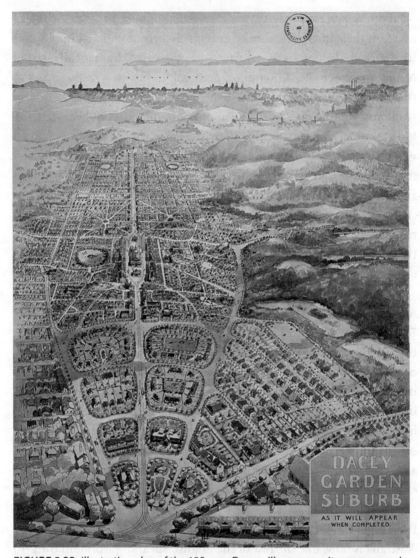

FIGURE 5.22 Illustrative plan of the 150-acre Daceyville community as proposed. Note the orientation of homes toward the centre of the block, akin to the much later Radburn plan in the United States. | Courtesy Photographic Collection from Australia and Wikimedia Commons.

country without any significant inventory of nonmarket housing. Public housing in Australia has never accounted for more than 4 percent of all homes and continues to fall. Another 2 percent of Australian households are currently on social-housing waiting lists.

One of the Australian government's earliest attempts to supply afford-able housing for wage earners was Daceyville (National Museum of Australia n.d.), a master-planned district of less than 200 acres in Sydney, New South Wales. The project was promoted by state legislator John Roland Dacey shortly before the turn of the twentieth century. This period saw rapid population increase in New South Wales, and the re-sulting housing stress was newly apparent.

Dacey was inspired by the British "garden city" proposals of Ebenezer Howard, and Dacey's plan bears physical resemblance to those com-munities, differing only in the fact that the land and buildings were owned by the state, not the collective. With the state owning Daceyville, it became subject to the ebb and flow of consistently weak Australian support for a public role in housing. Daceyville is thus an illustrative case study that mirrors the parallel trends occurring nationwide over these same decades.

Dacey was a believer in the power of community design to influence behaviour for the better. The original plan envisioned homes built not to face the streets but instead to address individual and community garden plots in mid-block areas.

During the 1970s, when Le Corbusier's Radiant City planning model was strongest, the state proposed tearing down Daceyville structures and replacing them with tower blocks. Daceyville residents initiated a resistance movement supported by the broader community, and the state had to abandon the plan.

However, as land values close to Sydney's city core continued to sky-rocket, the political appeal of extracting this land value continued to tempt. The centre-right Liberal-National Coalition, in power in New South Wales at the time of this writing, yielded to temptation and is in the process of auctioning off individual homes within the district (McGowan 2022) – at prices of about AU$1.5 million to AU$3 million.[17] They promise to use some of the proceeds to build more social-housing units than are lost – but in less favourable locations and with different types of buildings and sites. However, replacement housing is being built at a much slower pace than eviction actions, leading many to fear a political bait and switch.

The history of Daceyville strongly echoes the trajectory of social-housing policy in the rest of Australia and, indeed, throughout the English-speaking world, where governments are commonly encouraged to privatize public lands in order to extract an immediate and temporary cash infusion.

TAX ADVANTAGES AND DIRECT PAYMENTS FOR HOUSING

As in most other English-speaking countries, the local tax levy in Australia is largely on housing property, with generally separate assessments on land and improvements (i.e., structures). Also, as in other English-speaking countries, this tax does not rise to the level necessary to quell land Rent and rampant land-price speculation.

Federal influence over the housing market comes in the form of financial payments to the states drawn largely from national income tax. These returns come in two forms: tax breaks and direct payments to individuals. The most important tax break for individuals is the exemption from capital-gains taxes when owner-occupied homes are sold. The most important support for renters is the Commonwealth Rent Assistance program, which provides individuals with a direct cash grant to help them secure market-rate rental housing. The difference between the two is that all homeowners in the country benefit from the tax breaks. Nevertheless, as in the United States, rental subsidies fall far short of need.[18] Also, as in New Zealand, the program is criticized for adding to the inflationary pressures in the land market by incentivizing landlords to raise rents since this increase is passed along to the state, not to the renter (Monro 1997). Economist Cameron Murray (2022), a research fellow at the University of Sydney, is not alone in arguing that government's ever-increasing and ever-more-elaborate dependencies on the private market to house lower-income Australians only further inflates urban land Rents while missing an opportunity to use tax dollars to build public equity in these same land markets.

NEOLIBERAL STRATAGEMS

In 2008, in line with neoliberal strategies intended to induce housing markets to increase affordable rental supply, Australia's Labour government initiated the National Rental Affordability Scheme, which offered low-interest loans to private-sector developers in return for a measure of affordability. Much like similar Canadian schemes, the affordability measure was not based on income but on a 20 percent discount below market value, which might still be largely unaffordable in overheated rental markets. The program was killed by the Liberal government of Prime Minister Tony Abbot in 2014. The agreements for the units built under the scheme will run out in 2026, putting this inventory of units back on the market, likely at prices unaffordable for those of modest means (Convery 2021).

Because of steadily increasing land Rents, market-housing rents are now rising steeply (Bradbury 2023). This trend is reflected by a marked increase in the number of families in the bottom 40 percent of income earners who now find themselves spending more than 30 percent of income on housing and thus in a state of mild or severe housing stress. Most of this cohort is competing for rental housing, not homeownership. The proportion of this cohort experiencing stress has increased by about 15 percent per decade since 2000, and in 2016 it stood at about 60 percent of those in the bottom 40 percent of income earners (C. Martin, Pawson, and van den Nouwelant 2016).

Australia's already low percentage of publicly owned housing continues to shrink as more funding flows to private interests either directly through loans to private developers or indirectly through rent subsidies for individuals. Publicly owned housing stock, as a percentage of all housing, is still shrinking. Some of this shift in emphasis stems from the fact that public housing has a bad reputation in Australia (Monro 1997).

Relatively modest federal grants, occasionally combined with state funds, are sometimes provided to build government-owned housing, but as Australia's population has grown, the rate of social-housing construction has not kept up. The proportion of Australians living in social housing has fallen from about 6 percent in 1990 to just 4 percent today (Yates 2016).

MUCH SUPPORT FOR THE INVESTOR CLASS
In contrast to Australia's parsimonious support for social housing, its support for homeownership has been generous – as seen with the aforementioned exclusion from capital-gains taxes, homeowner exclusion from transfer taxes, and tax deductions for interest payments and other

losses associated with owning rental property (J.-F. Kelly 2013). Combine all of these factors with historic supports to ease the entry of first-time buyers into the marketplace through loan guarantees and financing assistance, and you have a perfect storm of financial forces combining to fuel the current surge in land-price speculation – a surge that has made Australian housing a great investment for storing wealth but impossibly expensive for those without the equity needed to acquire their first home.

In short, much as in other English-speaking countries but a bit more so, Australian public policy seems bent on guaranteeing the infinite increase of unearned land Rent gains. The potential inequities of such an approach were to be softened by state policies aimed at increasing the ability of the wage-earning class to share in this land wealth. The social upside of this approach was, at least for a time, an expanded pool of beneficiaries of policies meant to assist entry into the housing market for citizens with middle and lower-middle incomes. That was the case until relatively recently – when all of these stimuli inflated land Rents to the point where citizens of moderate means and younger households without access to the bank of Mom and Dad were left further and further behind.

What this outcome also means is that Australian policy has engineered a situation where household debt is the fifth highest among the twenty-seven OECD nations and the highest among English-speaking countries and where over two-thirds of the Australian finance industry has its money out in the form of housing mortgages. This alarming imbalance is causing many to fear that any shock to home values may very well threaten a quick banking collapse – one akin to that triggered by the United States in 2008.

WHERE IS HENRY GEORGE WHEN YOU NEED HIM?

These developments are disheartening, especially since Australia had a tradition of national land taxes. When the nation federated in 1901, it placed a tax on the unimproved value of land. The land tax was inspired by Henry George, who had an enthusiastic following in Australia and spent a month there on a speaking tour in 1890. During that decade, there was a raging debate over the desirability of confederation and its constitutional structure. Various plebiscites were placed before the voters that decade, each one based on various permutations of a draft constitution. Relevant to our topic in this volume were the debate on forms of taxation appropriate for this new federation and the question of who should pay the necessary taxes. Monied interests in Melbourne were violently opposed to land taxes, which would be levied against their holdings, and they argued for import duties instead, which would protect local industries and fall most heavily on wage earners. For George, his antagonism to import duties was grounded in his sense of social justice, as he feared that import duties would impoverish the working man while enriching the ownership classes. The land taxers eventually won the debate, and a national land tax was imposed, although not at a level sufficient to quell speculation or to replace the need for other taxes. Since the abolition of the federal land tax in 1952, various special task forces have recommended its reconsideration, motivated by concerns that land-price speculation increases inequality by limiting access to affordable housing and encumbers the economy by committing too large a share of GNP to unproductive land Rent. However, the political winds still blow strongly in favour of both demand-side and supply-side governmental supports for encouraging Aussies to commit to the asset economy by acquiring individual ownership of urban land, however much it might cost and however small a share each household might obtain.

6

The Vienna Model and Its Relevance Today

INTRODUCTION

Given the gravity of the systemic and linked crises explored in this volume, it is wise to look for successful models from other lands that our own jurisdictions might emulate. Sadly, after forty years of neoliberal-inspired privatizations, there are very few cities in the developed world that one can look to for equitable housing models that easily map over the form, economics, and culture of our own cities. Singapore is often mentioned as an attractive model, but the land of that city, and thus its Rents, are largely in public hands. Somehow moving trillions of dollars in urban land value from private to public hands in our English-speaking world seems highly unlikely absent political will.

The Netherlands is often mentioned in the same breath as Sweden, where housing production inspired by the Social Democrats after the Second World War gave rise to increases in publicly owned housing. However, more recent neoliberal enthusiasm for market-based approaches has led to a procrastinate decline in nonmarket housing units while the proportion of owner-occupied dwellings has doubled.

Germany, especially Berlin, was touted as a model until just a few years ago. There, most residents are renters who live in medium-density urban blocks that are presumably protected by unique housing laws, but staggering shifts of housing stock from public hands to private real estate investment trusts (REITs) and an associated 50 percent increase in monthly rents have provoked angry street demonstrations, with citizens demanding the return to public ownership of hundreds of housing blocks sold off during the recent privatization binge ("Berlin Spends" 2019).

So, although it is depressing to admit and does not bode well for our future efforts, only one advanced, liberal-democratic winner city seems to have largely solved the housing equity problem, providing a suitable model for so-called Anglo-Saxon capitalist countries in this the twenty-first century: Vienna.

THE VIENNA MODEL – HISTORY

Vienna, during the last days of the Hapsburgs, demonstrated its wealth in the form of impressive building facades. But behind the facades was a grimmer reality. Workers were crowded ten to a flat of 300 square feet. Many slept four to a bed. Some workers rented beds in shifts, sleeping during the day while the principal tenant was at work – all to pay the usurious rents. Are we heading this way again?

This Vienna was a city run by and for the landlords, wealthy owners of lands that had once been farms but now sprouted apartment buildings. Males of wealth, most of them landlords, were the only residents who could vote. Thus, in a city that at the dawn of the First World War contained over 2 million residents, fewer than 60,000 could vote. With control over public policy so heavily tipped to landlords, renters had no protection. One-month leases were common, and rents could be raised at any time, with no recourse for tenants. Evictions were immediate, coming without cause and without adjudication.

The gravity of this housing crisis and the plight of the people can be measured by the number of homeless. In 1913, there were 461,472 people living in asylums (or homeless shelters by another name), an astonishing one-quarter of the population. About 29,000 of these homeless were children (Reiss 2017).[1]

FIGURE 6.1 Typical lovely but overcrowded apartments such as these turn-of-the-20th-century examples were a source of great wealth for landlords but unaffordable for average wage earners. As a result, workers crowded into unsuitably small apartments to share the usurious market rents of the time. | Courtesy Wien Museum and Wikimedia Commons.

When Austria and its allies were defeated in the First World War, the Hapsburg monarchy collapsed. Universal suffrage followed; voting rights, previously extended to only 2 percent of the population, were now granted to all, regardless of income or gender. This change precipitated a dramatic leftward shift in Vienna's politics but in an unusual form.

The First World War was unkind to both the victors and the vanquished, destabilizing democracies and monarchies alike. The rise of Adolf Hitler as Germany's führer and the seventy-five-year reign by Russian communists are the most well-known consequences, but many other governments, both democracies and monarchies alike, were similarly destabilized.

For the next generation, citizens throughout Europe became separated into political camps, from Marxist class-focused internationalists on the far left to fascist nationalistic xenophobes on the far right, unleashing inevitable internal conflicts and the eventual conflagration of the

Second World War. Austria's political trajectory was somewhat different – but only at first.

With the fall of the Austro-Hungarian Empire, and with the universal suffrage that it made possible, the political left gained power – which it retained until the Depression and the rise of Italian and German fascism precipitated a right-wing takeover in 1934. The relatively short period between 1917 and 1934 is called the Red Vienna period for the socialist leanings of city leaders.

Significantly, elected and appointed officials during the Red Vienna period – unlike leftist parties in other parts of Europe – never set out to remove or even cripple capitalism by nationalizing property. Instead, they used a taxing strategy to meet their social ends – and the most important end was providing decent housing for every resident. In this undertaking, they succeeded. How?

FIGURE 6.2 The strongly set back central wing with its six monumental towers of the listed residential complex Karl-Marx-Hof of the municipality of Vienna. The building with 1,382 residential units was built during 1927–33 according to plans by the architect Karl Ehn (the official opening of the facility took place on October 12, 1930). It is not the most representative, but the best-known communal residential building in Vienna. It extends over 1,100 metres along Heiligenstädter Strasse. | Courtesy Thomas Ledl via Wikimedia Commons.

THE FINANCING

A number of development and taxing policies made Vienna's housing system possible. Even before the Red Vienna period, a key policy was imposed that was crucial to the city's later success: strict rent control. The government had imposed rent control to prevent war wives from being evicted while their husbands fought at the front. It has never been repealed. The government outlawed raising rents beyond a minimal amount yearly and thus, due to extreme currency inflation, made it less profitable to build new rental stock.[2]

Ordinarily, this approach would be a very bad thing for affordability since rental stock is usually less expensive per month (in the short term at least) than homeownership. Thus policies that impede the construction of rental housing are now generally frowned upon throughout the English-speaking world. Public officials often go to great lengths to induce the private market to produce new rental stock through subsidy, relaxed taxes, relaxed requirements, or density bonuses. That is certainly true in Vancouver, where city officials have offered substantial tax subsidies to induce the construction of new market-rate rental units. The effort has been successful in sparking production (City of Vancouver 2022b) but not successful in reducing living costs (Anderson 2022). Sadly, the monthly rents charged for these new market-rate units are unaffordable for all but the upper tier of renters. And despite the claims of proponents, these new high-priced units have produced little evidence of freeing up lower-priced units in a process that proponents refer to as housing-unit "filtering" (Condon 2023)[3] and that opponents pejoratively call "trickle-down housing" (McDonald 2021).[4] What evidence there is in support of the filtering idea suggests that its positive effects on affordability are minimal, take decades to achieve (Rosenthal 2014), and can in many cases result in fewer, rather than more, affordable-housing units (Nygaard, Galster, and Glackin 2022).

Vienna provides an interesting counterpoint. Because rent control disincentivized the private development of rental buildings, landlords were, for a time, removed from the market for urban land. Consequently, prices for development land went down, which allowed the city to buy land at a much reduced price, often with the city being the only buyer in the market. The reduced price was the consequence of falling land

FIGURE 6.3 Anton-Schmid-Hof public housing construction, 1964–66. The architects were Egon Fraundorfer, Robert Kotas, Eugenie Pippal-Kottnig, and Rudolf Hönig. | Courtesy Herzi Pinki via Wikimedia Commons.

Rents, which were lowered by the imposition of rent control. Rent control, in this case, advantageously limited the flow of labour and capital value into land Rents.

Although the theories of Henry George were well known in Vienna and made significant inroads in nearby Hungary, Austria's leaders shied away from the direct attack on land value that George had recommended, fearing a political backlash from small-parcel landowners. But their approach amounted to roughly the same thing. By progressively taxing the apartment unit rather than the land under it and by adhering to a strict rent-control policy, land Rents were lowered as an important consequence. The Vienna example thus provides a fruitful way of thinking more broadly about lowering land Rents than the purist single-tax position recommended by most of today's Georgists.

Given Vienna's newly powerful position in the land market, the city quickly became the dominant developer of new residential projects. Vienna had the wisdom to retain the city's best architects and developers to design and build this new housing, employing skills honed in service to the private sector to now build nonmarket housing (Förster and Menking 2016).[5]

One-fifth of this new housing was social housing intended for the poor and disabled. But the bulk of the new housing was for wage earners and their families, to be owned and managed by co-ops or nonprofit housing corporations. Vienna's nonprofit housing associations operate like market-rate housing corporations except that they are able to charge only cost-covering rents. They are exempt from corporate income tax, but in exchange, any profits that are made must be reinvested either in the purchase of more urban land or in refurbishment and construction (Marquardt and Glaser 2023). The interest paid on equity to owners and shareholders is limited (Mundt and Amann 2010). Now, about 25 percent of the city's residents live in publicly owned affordable housing, and another 18 percent live in homes owned cooperatively.

FIGURE 6.4 Somogyi-Hof at Hütteldorfer Strasse 150–158 in Vienna's XIV district. Designed by the architects Heinrich Schmid and Hermann Aichinger in 1927 as communal housing and named after the socialist writer Béla Somogyi (1868–1920). | Courtesy Haeferl via Wikimedia Commons.

FIGURE 6.5 The Holy-Hof in Hernals, Vienna, public housing project constructed by Rudolf Perco in 1928–29. | Courtesy Michael Kranewitter via Wikimedia Commons.

BUILDING BUILDINGS

Even though Vienna was able to keep land prices down, land and construction still cost money. In the late 1920s, approximately 30 percent of Vienna's annual budget was spent buying land and financing housing construction. Where did the money come from? Mostly from taxes on private property and land. Levied on apartment buildings, these taxes progressively increased with the assessed value of each unit, reducing the value of land under the building – its Rent. Very high taxes were also levied on vacant land, giving owners additional incentive to sell. These methods were clearly in keeping with the methods that Henry George had advanced two decades earlier.[6]

Of interest here is how these policy actions stripped land speculation, and thus out of control Rent, from the marketplace. Doubtless, any attempt to replicate this strategy in the English-speaking world, where faith in the free market remains strong, would provoke debate, but the gravity of the crisis that Vienna faced and the efficacy of its solution are beyond debate. The situation in jobs-rich global cities is now nearly as grave. As the housing crisis accelerates, many cities are strengthening rent-control legislation. Five US states – California, Oregon, New York,

New Jersey, and Maryland – have rent-control legislation authorizing cities to enact rent control. Oregon passed a law in 2019 making rent control the law state-wide. Controlling rents is a crucial way not only to protect tenants but also to quell the appetite of international REITs for a city's land.

In Vienna, taxes that support housing are broadly distributed, including a portion of income taxes now dedicated to housing. Residents support these taxes because in return they receive secure housing that is much more affordable than homes in most of the world's tier-one cities. Rents in Vienna are, at the time of this writing, less than half what is charged for similar units in Paris. This affordability seems to result in a lessening of the anxiety caused by the fear of missing out on the first rung of the housing ladder. According to one survey of European nations, Austrian homeowners and tenants were the only ones to enjoy equal levels of housing satisfaction (Elsinga 2005).

THE STATE OF THE VIENNA HOUSING MARKET TODAY

However, it is wise to avoid donning rose-coloured glasses when considering the Vienna model. Austria has not been entirely immune to the late-twentieth-century neoliberal enthusiasm for the privatization of housing. Nor are the Viennese entirely immune to the attractions of profit taking in the housing market. Vienna, like many other Western democracies, had essentially stopped building social housing for the poor by the early 2000s. This role has been handed over to limited-profit housing associations (LPHAs). Laws were changed to allow for the conversion of rental housing into condominiums in the 1990s. In the same decade, a rent to buy program was introduced in Vienna for new subsidized rental units, which could be purchased by residents after ten years of occupancy. Rent-control laws that governed all apartments built before 1945 were relaxed to let rents float closer to market rents. These shifts have altered the proportions of Viennese housed by tenure, with the biggest shift evident in the rate of homeownership, which increased from 16 percent of all housing to 21 percent in only seven years (Gutheil-Knopp-Kirchwald and Kadi 2017). Prices lower than the EU average for urban lands have attracted investors from other parts of the European

FIGURE 6.6 The semi-detached house of the Werkbundsiedlung, Vienna, in the 13th district of Hietzing. Semi-detached house built around 1930 by the architect Arthur Grünberger as part of a model estate of different house types built between 1929 and 1932. More than thirty architects took part in the planning of the individual houses. | Courtesy C.Stadler/Bwag via Wikimedia Commons

Union, leading authorities to ban REITs. Shifting to LPHA-produced housing, which depends on private financing, has led to higher entry fees and rents when measured against average wages, making it more difficult for low-wage workers and the young to gain entry than in previous decades (Kadi 2015).

Yet, despite these shifts, Vienna still builds far more cooperative nonprofit housing each year than any other European capital. The increase in homeownership can also be read as a positive shift since the price of homes in Vienna is much closer to average wages than in other European first-tier cities. Why? Because the dominance of the protected-housing market – where over 65 percent of residents are still shielded from housing precarity, with 26 percent living in pre-1945 rent-controlled apartments, 24 percent in social housing for the poor, and 18 percent in co-op housing – keeps market land Rents lower than in other European cities. Compared to Paris, for instance, market rentals and condominium purchases are over 30 percent less (Numbeo n.d.).

This systemic removal of over half of the housing market from the vagaries of urban land-price inflation also protects private-sector urban lands from the speculative pressures experienced in other cities like New York, London, Vancouver, and Sydney. In Vienna, speculative pressure on land price is mitigated by the market influence of such a large alternative urban land base, one specifically set aside to be affordable for people making average wages. Access to this affordable housing naturally mitigates the fear of missing out – the widely felt anxiety of those struggling to grab the first rung of the housing equity ladder – which is one factor in pushing urban land prices in other winner cities ever higher.

Obviously, in other winner cities, imagining an end to ever-elevating urban land-price inflation – a crash that might offer a corrective – is increasingly difficult. Why? Because after the global asset crash in 2008, largely triggered by the collapse of mortgage-backed securities in the United States, national governments can no longer afford such an outcome. To stop urban land values from collapsing, governments will now do whatever it takes – from quantitative easing to negative real interest rates – to ensure that such a crash can't happen again, as the unprecedented money printing during the COVID-19 pandemic made abundantly clear. At the time of this writing in 2023, global governments are reluctantly increasing interest rates to tame inflation. Why reluctantly? In part, because doing so might crash the housing market, leading to unacceptable social pain and threatening the stability of financial markets (Helman 2022).

Vienna thus offers a model of more than just a policy to provide affordable housing. It offers a strategy that can effectively steer rent seeking away not just from the nonmarket lands of the city but from all city land. With this much urban land protected from Rents, the tendency for private-market lands to inflate up to the maximum levels experienced in New York and other tier-one cities around the globe is mitigated. The Vienna example suggests that a balance between a private market for urban land and a protected one is possible and beneficial for both sectors.

FIGURE 6.7 Hundertwasser housing complex at the corner of Kegelgasse and Löwengasse of the Hundertwasserhaus in Vienna's 3rd district of Landstrasse. The complex with 50 residential units was built as an eco-house from 1983 to 1985. It was designed by the artist Friedensreich Hundertwasser, in collaboration with architects Josef Krawina and Peter Pelikan. | Courtesy Lucas7777 via Wikimedia Commons.

Although housing advocates in Vienna are worried (Prager 2018) about this neoliberal backsliding (Verlič 2015),[7] the millions of poor souls experiencing housing precarity in the English-speaking world should be so lucky.

THE DESIGN PROCESS

Vienna has also developed a system for working with nonprofit development corporations that compete with each other for the next city-sponsored project. The city acquires the land for a project, establishes the housing goals, and publishes the amount of any subsidy to be supplied. Stakeholder groups judge the proposals submitted in response and collectively decide which project team of architect, builder, developer, and management entity has the most intelligent one.

This competitive process ensures that projects are architecturally distinctive and varied – a dramatic departure from the process for building public housing in many other countries, where mediocrity seems to be the goal.

CONCLUSION

What can we learn from the Vienna example?

First, Vienna treats urban land like the precious public asset that it is. In light of trends in migration, demographics, and the global economy, it would seem crucial for cities to purchase much more land on behalf of the providers of nongovernmental housing, whether they be churches, co-ops, or charitable organizations. However, cities should, like Vienna, also tie land-acquisition strategies to policies like rent control that reduce land Rent. Without these coordinated strategies, cities run the risk of being just one more competitor in the already overheated market for urban land.

Second, when confronted with a situation in which the majority of its citizens could not find affordable homes, at least one Western capitalist city has solved the problem, demonstrating that it can be done.

And third, building housing only for the very poor while leaving wage earners to the maelstrom of the housing market will erode political support for government intervention in the housing market.

It's also important to mention that Viennese pay co-op rents that are not tied to income level. These rents cover the cost of upkeep and replacement but do not repay the original city subsidies. Thus these rental rates are below 30 percent of the average tenant income. In return for this cost break, citizens seem willing to pay housing taxes to support this housing system. These low rental rates are now part of the tradition of the city and unlikely to change without political disruption.

A housing program based on the Vienna model can also, in time, be self-supporting. If we assume that any city can manage to quell the fierce inflation in land Rent, whether through some combination of land-use controls, rent controls, and/or taxing policy, and if we assume that a local economy will produce enough middle-class jobs to ensure that renters have money to pay, there is no reason that nonmarket housing can't eventually repay all land, construction, and management costs to the city – and in the process remove an ever-increasing share of urban land from the ravages of the global market for urban land. Many cities already have a strong basis for doing so. In Vancouver, for example, 15 percent of all housing is already in the nonmarket category – co-ops, nonprofits, and social housing – and 30 percent would likely be free of socially destructive market forces if the government, in thrall to the neoliberal enthusiasms of the 1980s, hadn't eliminated support for housing during that decade.

After an initial period of subsidy, it is conceivable that, through intelligent management of policy and taxing levers, nonmarket housing could be provided for the majority of wage earners without draining the public coffers. A system can be built that would, over time, return to the city all of the capital and land-asset value that it supplied upfront. The problem is not construction costs but the price of urban land. If land prices can be reined in through public policy, broad-based housing affordability can be achieved without the need for perpetual taxpayer subsidy.

7

Policy Solutions and the Quest for Affordable Housing

WHAT POLICY CAN DO

Different countries around the English-speaking world have tried many strategies to expand access to affordable housing. Historically, they break into two different categories: strategies aimed at reducing impediments to market production of new housing and strategies using public funds to build affordable housing (often called social housing) outside of the private market. In this volume, I have tried to demonstrate how the first strategy has not met the hopes of its proponents due to the unique way that urban land holds and increases Rent beyond what new supply can fix. The second strategy is problematic, too, both because it adds one more competitor for the private parcels of land that fill the pockets of speculators and because it increases land Rents.

In the last quarter of the twentieth century, a third strategy emerged: the requirement that new market developments include a certain percentage of permanently affordable units as a condition of approval. In the United States, this shift was motivated, in part, by the tendency for municipalities to intentionally exclude residents not just for economic reasons but for racial reasons as well.[1] This strategy is a distinct variant because it is grounded in the notion that the housing problem is not solvable by loosening restrictions on the market for housing and because it assumes that the infusion of taxpayer dollars into the already hyper-inflated market for urban land will never be in the amounts necessary to solve the problem.

As the reader knows by now, the main point of this volume is to demonstrate that ever-inflating land Rent is really the root and branch of our current worldwide housing-affordability crisis. So the focus here is on strategies where the value that would otherwise go into land Rent is streamed into what we broadly call social benefit instead. And although land Rent can be streamed into many forms of social benefit (as is in the case of Vancouver, discussed below), I focus here largely on perma-nently affordable housing as the social benefit that most concerns us.

In this chapter, I provide very brief histories of affordable-housing policies throughout the English-speaking world, followed by a nontech-nical description of policy strategies now being tried. Housing policy can be gut-wrenchingly dull, so depth might be sacrificed in this effort.

Although variously named, all of these policies work either by with-holding authorization for new projects that do not include affordable units or by offering additional development value in return for affordable-housing concessions. In the end, both approaches take land Rent that would otherwise end up in the pockets of land speculators and stream it into affordability. The policies discussed have been tested by various courts and have survived challenges that, in most cases, have been based on the presumed illegality of a government action that reduces the value of a landholding without compensating the owner. As a rule, the courts have found that these policy actions do not constitute the taking of land but instead allow for its fair use and for a legitimate use of municipal "policing" powers, generally understood as necessary to ensure the health, safety, and welfare of the citizenry.

To put this perspective in practical terms, we can again turn to the case of Vienna, which resolved a housing crisis similar to the one that we now face. Taking a middle ground between the socialist policy of nationalizing the land and the laissez-faire policy of letting the market do its thing, the Viennese imposed a high tax on high-value housing units. This approach had a doubly beneficial result. First, the value of these properties was reduced because future owners knew that they would have to pay these high taxes; in other words, the tax lowered the land Rent values of all private-sector rental housing. Second, the proceeds from this new tax were used to buy urban land, whose prices had also been lowered by the imposed tax. So, with one policy, Vienna both lowered land price and provided funds to buy that same land.

Today, a policy like the one that Vienna used is still technically practical, but we must recognize that a huge tax increase on all urban land is very difficult to imagine as a political possibility. Nevertheless, we now have tools available that the Viennese did not, including many different forms of zoning and development controls respecting land use. Municipalities can now insist that a certain percentage of new housing stock approved by the city must be affordable. This stipulation is legal and avoids the political problems associated with a city-wide increase in property taxes across the board.

An important qualification here is that, in some jurisdictions, laws have been passed and have survived court challenge that allow city leaders to insist on affordability as an automatic condition of permit approval and to specify the percentages of affordable housing. This approach is generally called inclusionary housing or inclusionary zoning. More commonly, a different method is used by municipalities that do not choose to go this route or that are prohibited from doing so due to a lack of higher-level government authorization. Rather than insisting that projects conforming to existing zoning-density limits also include affordable housing, they allow projects to be built at existing density limits but offer additional density to those developers who agree to add affordable units at some negotiated ratio. This second process is typically called density bonusing.

A city's insistence that a certain percentage of new units be affordable does of course reduce the total project sale price that the developer can expect. This reduced profit leads many to assume either that the project won't get built (which is not good) or that the prices of the market units will need to be increased in compensation (which is also not good).

But neither assumption is true. Research shows that imposing these requirements eventually reduces the residual price of the land (Been 2005).[2] In lay terms, the residual value is the price that developers can afford to pay after figuring out their expenses. Adding affordable units to the list of project expenses reduces the residual value of the land – or the amount that developers can offer to landowners. This reduction, in effect, operates as a land tax on the development parcel by taking at least some of what would otherwise have been an inflated price for high-density land and streaming it away from the pockets of land speculators and into the social benefit of affordable housing. The resulting social benefit is why this process is generally not seen as the taking of land or value but as a legitimate way of ensuring the health, safety, and welfare of the community.

Controlling the land-value residual on the development parcel also has an off-site benefit. Having sold at the new noninflated residual value, adjacent parcels, when reassessed by the tax assessors, will not ratchet up in value. Elevating adjacent land values up to a new highest and best-use standard can fuel land-price inflation and unmerited tax increases on nearby commercial and residential properties.

This financial phenomenon is the basis for the many policy strategies listed below. Their proven success, limited at this time but fully capable of being expanded, can provide tools for citizens to use when grappling with this existential problem.

A TAX ON LAND: THE GEORGIST MODEL
This section begins with a return to Henry George and his idea of a single tax on land in order to see how it fared.

George promoted the single tax as a means of solving the affordable-housing problems described in this volume. Yet after his death, the movement that he had started failed politically and is virtually unknown today. Why? It fell victim to a pincer movement between the political left and right.

Those on the political right used their financial power to establish and finance an industry of academic economists hired specifically to argue that land was capital and that capital was land – all at the behest of the land barons (Gaffney 1994). Thus was the special toxicity of land Rent rendered invisible. We still live under their spell.

Those on the political left, the doctrinaire socialists of George's day (and still to this day), argued that he did not go far enough since clever strategies for treating only the land Rent pathology of urban capitalism were insufficient. Land Rent was just one of capitalisms many pathologies, all of which had to be excised root and branch, they said. All land needed to be nationalized. Nothing less would do (G. Miller 2000). Although the principles that George espoused remain valid today, the preconceptions of both the political left and right are still in place throughout the English-speaking world.

THE ONGOING LAND RENT BATTLE, NOW UNDER A DIFFERENT NAME

Most housing-policy responses in the English-speaking world can be read as ongoing attempts to navigate between these extremes. It is the contention of this volume that a focus on land Rent, in the spirit of Henry George, offers a robust and not well-understood third way out. The focus should not be on the market versus social housing but on how we can slow or stop the benefits of our collective industry from flowing solely into the pockets of urban land speculators – into land Rent.

Throughout the English-speaking world, local planning authorities are empowered to influence land value by either restricting or allowing development. It is unfortunate that under the present global conditions, both actions, ironically, tend to increase land value – the first by making land scarce and the second by inflating its price.

However, in most of the English-speaking world, taxes are already levied on property and, as discussed previously, now fall largely on the value of urban land. This commonplace taxing strategy can be used more wisely to direct land Rent to social purpose.

Unlike national and state governments, most municipalities in the English-speaking world have depended almost entirely on property taxes to fund local public services. For example, all US states but one, Oklahoma (Urban Institute n.d.), have authorized their cities to levy property taxes on real estate. But for better or worse, many US states also demand that municipalities not tax property beyond a certain rate – a trend that began in 1978 when California voters passed Proposition 13 ("1978 California" n.d.), which limited residential property taxes to no more than 1 percent of total assessed value annually. As property values have exploded in recent years, with states slow to lower these thresholds, American property tax caps based on market value have become less fiscally confining. However, the lack of public appetite for new taxes makes it politically difficult to levy steep new taxes on land in the way that George favoured. Any approach that attempted to tax urban land at anything close to its real Rent value would require property taxes closer to 10 percent of the full value annually – or over ten times higher than typical levels. Nevertheless, it is worth understanding how George's land-tax ideas might influence urban development, using an American example.

To operate in a way that drastically lowered Rents, as George proposed, the full value of a parcel of land should be subject to a land tax of 10 percent of the land's estimated total value each year, not to be paid all at once but in instalments like a mortgage. This may sound harsh, but in practice, if land taxes were this high, homeowners (and renters) would not spend more per month on housing. Why? Because the *purchase price* for the land itself would be driven way down by the tax liability. Thus the purchase price for a home would not be based largely on land value, as it is today, but on the replacement cost of the improvements (i.e., structures). Finally, the value of the structures would not be taxed at all.

Taxing just land would also have the salutary effect of favouring home types that are more efficient users of land – with a single parcel being occupied by a fourplex, for example, rather than by a single-family home.

True, the amount of equity built up by a homeowner over the course of a mortgage in *land value* would also be much reduced. The building would accrue most of the equity in this case. But this situation, too, provides homeowners with a strong rationale for improving the structure(s) on the land rather than depending primarily on land-value increases to build personal wealth.

THE PENNSYLVANIA LAND-TAX EXAMPLE

Twenty-nine US states assess property in a way that distinguishes land value from the value of improvements (M.E. Bell and Bowman 2006), a clear legacy of George's impact. However, most states tend to use the same tax rate (often called a mill rate) for both the structure and the land. Inspired by the single-tax argument, Pennsylvania authorizes its municipalities to tax urban land and improvements at different rates. Harrisburg and a number of other cities in the state have used differential tax rates on land to avoid disinvestments in their older districts consequent to urban sprawl[3] – disinvestments that still plague many other Rust Belt cities of a similar size.

Harrisburg, a medium-sized city and the state capital, was faced with Detroit-level property declines and abandonment in the 1980s. It responded by shifting taxes away from improvements and onto land. Today, land is taxed at five times the rate of improvements. When the city implemented this change, 90 percent of residential properties in its older, denser parts saw their tax bill go down – shoring up the value of smaller, older urban lots that are easier to service.

The city had 4,200 abandoned structures in 1985. By 2001, a decade and a half after shifting taxes to land, it had only 500. City coffers, near

FIGURE 7.1 Traditional "Old Town" street in Harrisburg, Pennsylvania. Property conditions stabilized through the use of disproportional tax on land at five times the rate of improvement. | Courtesy Google Maps.

bankruptcy in the 1980s, were in balance again by 2000, and legacy infrastructure, which had been wasting away, could be maintained anew (Vincent 2019).

Still, although the Harrisburg case is hopeful, the city's land tax is far from approaching the full Rent value of the land. Since George's time, advocates of land tax have been unsuccessful in implementing a true application of his tax on urban land in amounts equal to the land's annual Rent value (Hudson 2004).[4] The Pennsylvania example, although it offers tantalizing evidence that a land tax can work, is very far from George's original full tax on the Rent value of land.

Michael Hudson (2004) faults contemporary Georgists for being too timid in their ambitions, happy with a land-tax rate far below the land Rent value. Hudson and his co-authors (Goodhart et al. 2022) have proposed gradually increasing land taxes to as much as 6 percent of the full sale price per year, up from the more typical current rate of 1 percent, as a way to reduce the deadweight loss that resulted from the COVID-19 pandemic, a loss attributable to out of control land-price inflation.

Following Pennsylvania's lead, policy makers in states where differential rates on land and improvements are allowed should consider adding separate rates for land and improvements to their housing-affordability tool box. In doing so, states could lower taxes on income and capital gains to move the burden away from productive factors of the economy. For states, restricting these taxes would be a no-cost change worth proposing. If Harrisburg is any guide, this approach helps to prevent the decay of older neighbourhoods.

Viewed as pure policy, the separation of rates is an effective way to drive down land Rents and to fund nonmarket housing at the same time, with only the land speculators left worse off. However, the political problems associated with a city raising taxes on land, absent the ability to simultaneously reduce taxes on income, make the prospects for success admittedly daunting. Also a problem is that the prices paid for land are the result of low taxes on Rent. Although taxing the full value of Rent would eventually keep real estate from constituting a profound drag on the citizens, a clear majority of citizens throughout the English-speaking world own at least some small share of urban land and thus are now disinclined to support a 1,000 percent increase in their property tax. Getting from here to there, with recent owners forced to pay both high land prices and a huge new land tax, presents obvious political difficulties.

Finally, policy makers at the municipal level seldom recognize that, given their control of land-development policy and property tax, they are the only level of government that can control land Rents through policy controls. They typically have more power to alter geographic inequality than do state/provincial or federal officials. And property taxes are not their only tool. They also control zoning approvals and development taxes that can be used to the same effect – tools examined later in this volume.

AN EXAMPLE OF LAND TAX FROM TAIWAN

It's worth mentioning the case of Taiwan, one global example where the full value of land Rent was taxed.

Sun Yat-sen, Chinese physician, political economist, and the first president of a newly independent China after the 1911 revolution, formulated a revolutionary land-reform program that was eventually implemented in Taiwan. He did not call for nationalization of land, the strategy eventually adopted when the Communists took control of Mainland China after the Second World War. He called for a policy that would restrict annual land Rents to no more than 35 percent of the value of agricultural yield and that would tax land (but not improvements) at high rates to quell land speculation.

In this regard, he was following the economic principles of his contemporary, Henry George. Sun cited George extensively in his treatise *Memoirs of a Chinese Revolutionary: A Programme of National Reconstruction for China* (1918, 36–37):

> The industrial revolution in the European and American countries produced a sudden change in [people's] living conditions ... Its effect on society is exactly similar to that which Henry George described in his book: *Progress and Poverty*. He said that the progress of modern civilization is like a sharp wedge suddenly driven in between the upper and lower classes ... The rich become richer, while the poor

become ever poorer. The results of the industrial revolution bring happiness only to a few members of society, but inflict pain and suffering on the great part of the people.

Sun had a complicated life. Born in Hawaii and educated in British Hong Kong, he was fluent in English and had a deep familiarity with the West. In addition to the political economics of George, he read and absorbed the work of Karl Marx and the European socialist thinkers of his time. But it is significant in the context of this piece that he was, along with George, reluctant to agitate for state ownership of land like Marx and most socialists. Instead, in line with later liberal thinkers ("Milton

FIGURE 7.2 Sun Yat-sen, 1866–1925, the first president of the Republic of China.

Friedman" 2014), he saw the value of keeping land essentially private but opted to use taxing levers not only to quell speculation and to ensure that land was well used but also to direct the benefits of land to those who worked it.

Sun also had extensive relations with the Chinese diaspora in western Canada, capitalizing on his fame to make numerous speaking trips to British Columbia and Alberta, where he promoted and sought external funding for his revolution. In fact, it was during such a trip to Alberta in 1911 that his revolution broke out in his absence. He rushed back to China to lead and win it and for a short time served as China's first president, before being forced out by the warlord Yuan Shika. This unhappy event forced him into the first of a number of exiles that characterized his life until his untimely death from cancer in 1924 at the age of fifty-nine.

All of that history is too long and too complex for this short piece, so let us jump ahead to the end of the Second World War and the Communist takeover of China, which forced the Nationalist government under Chiang Kai-shek, with whom Sun Yat-sen had been aligned, to abandon China and retreat to the island of Taiwan ("Chiang Kai-shek" n.d.). At this juncture, we can return to our subject of land-value tax.

Despite his defeat on the mainland, Chiang Kai-shek had a few aces up his sleeve when it came to the problem of making a noncommunist government work on the island. Taiwan had been first a Dutch colony and then occupied by the Japanese, so the holdings of both the Dutch and the Japanese were largely up for grabs in the late 1940s. Nevertheless, landownership was still largely unregulated, with landlords extracting the maximum land Rents that they could from the tenant farmers who worked the land (Brown 1967).

This pattern reflected the dysfunction that both Sun and George had identified as the key factor holding back the economic and agricultural development of Mainland China. George spent many pages of his landmark book *Progress and Poverty* (1879) explaining why China's recurring famines were not caused by overpopulation. There was plenty of arable land, much of it fallow, he said. The problem was the ownership of this land by landlords and the crushing burden of land Rent that they extracted.

FIGURE 7.3 Rice terraces on a Taiwan mountain slope. | Courtesy berkeley_geography via Flickr Commons.

Chiang's government, rather than nationalizing Taiwan's land, implemented the program that Sun had formulated two decades earlier. Step one was land Rent control. Land would henceforth be rented for no more than 35 percent of the projected value of the crops that it would produce. This reduction lowered land value and slowed land speculation. Next would be a land tax fixed in relation to the remaining land value, the intention being to drive land Rent down even further. Finally, land would frequently be reassessed to document any increases in land value that accrued passively to landowners due to broader community development nearby. A progressive tax increase would capture this value gain. This progressive tax would both stabilize land values and provide funds for local betterment, such as irrigation.

The success of this program was dramatic. In just a few decades, the number of owner-farmers nearly doubled (Brown 1967), tenant farming almost disappeared, and crop yields also nearly doubled.

The above is all good news. This case is probably the world's best example in practice of using a land-value tax to quell land speculation and to make land available to those who wish to extract its productive, not speculative, value.

Now for the bad news. This model was never effectively applied to urban lands. During more recent decades, as urbanization attracted 80 percent of Taiwanese to urban centres, the mechanisms of privatization and the commodification of housing land reasserted themselves. The model that had worked so effectively on rural lands was watered down to the point that, as is the case in much of the rest of the world, the land tax was far too low to act as a disincentive for speculation. Thus in Taipei and other Taiwan municipalities, housing is now largely priced for its asset value (or Rent), not for its use value (La Grange, Chang, and Yip 2005).

If the rural model had been correctly calibrated to Taiwan's modern industrial cities as they expanded, we have every reason to expect that it would have been possible for public services and a social safety net to have been funded by land value without the exchange value of urban land getting out of control.

Now, urban Taiwan is ravaged by the same global housing crisis that rages throughout the world, with governments being largely aligned with real estate interests and politically supported by the upper-middle-class baby boom generation, who have their own share of unearned land wealth to protect, making any near-term solution to this grave problem hard to imagine (La Grange, Chang, and Yip 2005).

POLICIES IN USE IN THE UNITED STATES – AND OFTEN ELSEWHERE

Generally, there are two types of public-policy tools used to secure affordable housing in the United States: exactions and bonuses. Exactions are basically a tax on development, with funds used to secure nonmarket-housing units. Bonuses are approvals for additional saleable value beyond "as of right" limits in return for nonmarket-housing units. "As of right" refers to a zoning limit already stipulated in ordinances. Giving bonuses is a special permitting process that grants more intense land use than an ordinance authorizes in return for a negotiated or fixed number of nonmarket-housing units.

These basic strategies have survived constitutional challenges in the United States many times. Cities have well-established powers to use zoning as a means to limit private-property rights and to protect the health, safety, and welfare of the general population. Supreme Court challenges dating back a hundred years support these powers (Simpson 1969). More recent court cases specific to affordable-housing requirements have reinforced this public right, although challenges have come before the Supreme Court as recently as 2019.[5] City officials are thus not obligated to ensure the highest and best use (or maximum profits) for privately held parcels if health, safety, and welfare can be established as the basis. In terms that Henry George might have used, cities are not required to ensure that the owners of development parcels must be rewarded, to the penny, for the value of improvements made by citizens on lands that surround their parcel. This limit on property rights is no small thing since it provides policy makers with a tool to ensure that social benefits accrue from the urban developments that they authorize. This power is already widely used but at a scale that only weakly influences land Rents.

EXACTIONS AND THE APPROVAL PROCESS

Negotiating exactions on a project-by-project basis is particularly unsettling for proponents, as project pro formas and residual land-value calculations are difficult to ensure in such circumstances. Developers may have already purchased or optioned[6] development parcels years in advance based on predictions of what will be exacted. And since land must be secured well in advance of permit approvals, a faulty guess can be very costly. This situation likely explains why many American municipalities have been too timid to admit that driving down land price might be the point! The following sections of this chapter offer a representative sampling of policy strategies (in lay terms) now used as opposed to direct government funding of social housing projects. All of these policy strategies can be viewed through a Georgist lens as a means to take the wealth that would otherwise have increased land Rents, thus enriching only land speculators, and stream it into permanently affordable housing.

IMPACT FEES

The most common form of exaction, the one most widely used, is the impact fee, which is imposed when land parcels are proposed for a more intensive (and lucrative) use. Although impact fees are still most commonly used to pay for off-site infrastructure, such as upgrading a sewer interceptor or resignalizing a nearby traffic intersection, they are increasingly used to fund affordable housing. Impact fees for affordable housing, used in California, New Jersey, Massachusetts, Colorado, and Florida, are typically levied at modest levels, but no court finding prevents cities from requiring fees at a level adequate to produce one permanently affordable unit for every market-rate unit – fees coincident, say, with a doubling of allowable density. Given the current affordability crisis, a nexus (or social-impact) study would surely support this rate.

California's municipalities, likely because of the severity of its housing crisis, have been less timid than most states in imposing affordable-housing impact fees. Over sixteen California cities have used impact fees to fund affordable housing directly – fees that must necessarily shift value from land Rent to public purpose. As expected, landowners have challenged these exactions on more than one occasion. Courts in California and other states have responded by allowing fees for affordable housing if a nexus study shows that a project will generate an identifiable need for affordable housing (Preiss 2017). Municipalities have successfully shown that the production of market-rate housing produces a need for homes for low- and moderate-wage service workers in some proportion to high-wage earners and that requiring the production of these homes is a proper use of their "policing" power. In California especially, commercial linkage fees are assessed on commercial and office projects to determine the impacts of new jobs-rich centres on housing supply and price (Inclusionary Housing 2019a). For example, one such nexus study, conducted for the City of Albany in California, has provided evidence that market-housing projects generate a need for affordable units at a typical ratio of one affordable-housing unit to every three market-rate units (Keyser Marston Associates 2016). As housing inequality becomes more extreme, with housing costs for wage earners more and more out of reach, it follows that newer nexus studies will show an increasing need for affordable units, likely in the rage of one to two or even one to one. This increase in affordable housing would mitigate the tendency for land prices to inflate in proportion to new density allowances and thus redirect land-value increases toward socially crucial ends.

Currently, approximately 60 percent of US cities with more than 25,000 residents impose impact fees to fund the infrastructure needed to service new housing (US General Accounting Office 2000). A far smaller number impose impact fees to fund affordable housing. In California, these impact fees were added to fees for off-site infrastructure relatively recently, partly in response to a court case that limited inclusionary-zoning policies in that state (Inclusionary Housing 2019b).

An informal analysis by the Non-Profit Housing Association of Northern California found that among Bay Area jurisdictions that replaced inclusionary-zoning requirements with affordable-housing impact fees, all of the adopted impact fees were less than the "cash in lieu" fees of their prior inclusionary-zoning program. Whereas the in-lieu fees had been based on the cost of providing an affordable-housing unit, the impact fees were based on a nexus study. Sadly, most cities chose to set their impact fee well below the maximum fee suggested by their nexus studies.

DO EXACTIONS ADD TO HOME PRICE?
Evidence indicates that, over the long term, the final sale prices paid by new home purchasers are not elevated by imposed development fees, as final home purchase prices are set by the strength of the regional housing market and by the advantages that city living provides for residents.[7] The fee levels ultimately affect and reduce the residual value of land. This is the case because the upside price limit for new homes (usually based on the price per interior square foot) is capped by the strength of the housing market in the city and across the region. Development taxes imposed on a single parcel or zone will not change this cap. However, a development tax imposed late in the approval process *may* make the business case for a project unworkable. At that point, either the project will be cancelled or the price for the land will be renegotiated down. Municipalities are therefore in a position to moderate or eliminate land-price inflation by signalling their intention, years ahead of time, to impose a development tax. One might call this process disciplining the land market.

The point to emphasize here is that, in most US states, municipalities are the only level of government that has the power to control the speculative value of urban land with the stroke of a pen. Insisting that financial exactions drawn from project proponents be used for affordable housing has been ruled a legitimate use of municipal "policing" power by the courts. It is thus both legal and increasingly necessary to use these policy and taxing tools to drive down land Rents and to increase afford- able housing at the same time. To understand this strategy a bit better, it's worth learning about what developers call residual value.

RESIDUAL VALUE
Purchase prices for development parcels are determined by the residual value – or land value that remains ("Residual Techniques" 2019) – after all costs of construction, profits, and fees are deducted from the expected total sales price. Residual value, which drops as development costs rise, is the left-over amount that can be offered to a landowner after expenses. Development fees are part of the list of expenses. As development fees go up, land prices go down. Theoretically, municipalities can elevate fees to the point where land prices drop to zero. Doing so would, again in theory, reduce land Rents to zero, as Henry George recommended. But exactions equal to or just below the *increase* in land-lift value that results from a higher-density authorization will dampen the tendency for land prices to inflate, leaving original land prices much less affected by plans proposed for new areas of the city and/or by project approvals. In jobs- rich coastal cities, where land Rents are already far out of control, it would be more than sensible to calibrate a suite of exactions and bonuses aimed at keeping land Rents stable. It would even be appropriate to use these policies to nudge land prices lower over time.

WHY DIDN'T HENRY GEORGE PROPOSE THESE STRATEGIES?
During his short life, Henry George did not propose zoning policies and development taxes as a potential solution to the problem of urban land Rents because when he wrote *Progress and Poverty* (1879), zoning ordin- ances and development fees did not exist. The United States did not even have a national income or business tax at that time but depended almost entirely on import duties and excise taxes to finance the federal budget. A federal income tax would not become a fact of life until 1909, and zoning would not pass constitutional muster until 1926.[8] Yet during George's life, the tenuous status of the United States on the world stage as other nations began to concentrate power at the federal level forced

the United States to find a more robust source of federal tax dollars. It was in this context that George proposed his national land tax. After his death and after two decades of debate in Congress, the nation chose to pursue a national income tax rather than a national land tax – much to the dismay of his son Henry George Jr., who was serving in Congress at the time.[9]

INCLUSIONARY-HOUSING REQUIREMENTS

Inclusionary zoning refers to measures that require or incentivize the creation of affordable housing as part of new development. Inclusionary-housing ordinances have been shown not to increase the prices of market units in the same project but to lower the prices of developable parcels (Kautz 2002).[10]

A 2016 study by the Lincoln Institute for Land Policy identified 886 US jurisdictions with inclusionary-housing programs located in twenty-five states and the District of Columbia. About 80 percent of all municipally administered inclusionary-housing programs are located in just three states: New Jersey (45%), Massachusetts (27%), and California (17%). These states have either state incentives for local policy adoption or state-wide inclusionary-housing policies. A total of 1,379 policies were found in 791 jurisdictions. The study reported that 373 jurisdictions had created a total of 173,707 units of affordable housing and that an additional US$1.7 billion had been spent on impact or in-lieu fees for the creation of affordable housing (Thaden and Wang 2017, Abstract, 1). This achievement is laudable, but it's worth remembering that the true need for affordable housing nationwide is in the range of many hundreds of billions of dollars.

The study found that mandatory policies applying to all types of residential development were the most prevalent type of inclusionary-housing policy, followed by voluntary policies on residential development. The most common option for developers to fulfill their contribution to affordable housing under the inclusionary-housing policies was to build on site, and the second most prevalent option was to pay an in-lieu fee. In-lieu fees are often set lower than the cost of producing an affordable unit in the area where a new development is located, a process that works against income mixing in a single project.

The study also found that, depending on the jurisdiction, anywhere from 6 to 20 percent of the newly developed units needed to be affordable. Formulas for how affordability is determined vary from place to place, based on the gaps identified in housing access. It is financially easier to provide housing for families who earn 80 percent of area median income than for those who earn sixty percent since their rents must of necessity be lower, feeding less monthly income to the project. The result is that the deeper the desired affordability, the greater the strain on the project finances. Ultimately, the proportion of affordable housing that is required depends on the economic feasibility of an inclusionary-housing policy and on local political will (Thaden and Wang 2017), which can be fortified to the extent that project stakeholders understand the mechanics of land Rent and the power that a municipality has over land price.

A study of the inclusionary-housing program in Santa Monica shows how land-value capture (or siphoning off land Rents) to incentivize inclusionary housing can lead to a relatable number of affordable units to market-rate units. These numbers are stagnant in places like Los Angeles and San Diego, where dramatically increased land Rent has apparently gone largely to land speculators (Nzau and Trillo 2020). Although Santa Monica has been criticized for not building much new housing, the proportion of affordable housing that it did allow was much higher than in adjacent Los Angeles.

HOUSING OR CASH IN LIEU OF HOUSING

The approach of charging developers in-lieu fees allows them to contribute cash to the jurisdiction, to its housing trust fund, or sometimes to a designated nonprofit organization instead of building affordable units. The fee is pegged to the construction cost for a developer to add one market-rate unit to a proposed development. In general, the fee does not include land Rent cost, which is a major weakness of most in-lieu payments.

Developers often choose to produce affordable units in other areas of the jurisdiction that have lower land Rents, more compatible housing characteristics, or existing and available improved lots, city-owned properties, or housing suitable for renovation. The programs may require that the locations of the off-site developments be near the proposed market-rate developments (Porter and Davison 2009).

Most studies suggest that in-lieu fees are typically set far lower than the cost of producing an affordable unit in an area where the new development is located. This reticence on the part of cities to charge proportionate in-lieu fees is yet another example of how the value of these taxing tools has been limited by a lack of focus on land Rent and by a political reluctance to explicitly embrace the goal of driving down the cost of urban land (Thaden and Wang 2017).

The larger point here is that legal tools exist to divert land Rent increases into affordable-housing options, but municipalities remain reluctant to use these tools to drive down land Rents. This may be the case, as this volume contends, because land speculators exert disproportionate influence on local officials and have deep enough pockets for expensive court challenges.

Table 1 shows a comparison of the different US cities that have adopted in-lieu fees. The money is nice, but one can see that these funds don't go far in their housing markets, and there are many cities where the market price for housing is over US$1,000 per square foot of interior space.

TABLE 1: In-lieu fees charged in US cities

Location	Started	Population	Charged On	Amount ($US)
Boston, MA	1987	673,184	Commercial over 100,000 square feet	$10.01 per sq. ft. after the first 100,000 square feet (or $8.34 for housing and $1.67 for job training)
Denver, CO	2017	693,060	All new developments	$1.55 per sq. ft. for multi-units and $1.75 for single units
Winter Park, FL	1990	30,208	Commercial and residential	$0.50 per sq. ft.

Location	Started	Population	Charged On	Amount ($US)
Jupiter, FL	2015		Commercial and industrial over 2,000 square feet	$1 per sq. ft. after 2,000 square feet
Arlington County, VA	2006	230,000	Commercial only	$1.77 per sq. ft. (with increase subject annually to the Consumer Price Index)
Seattle, WA	2014	744,955	Commercial and multi-family residential	$5 to $22 per sq. ft.
Boston, MA		694,583	Commercial over 100,000 square feet	$9.03 per sq. ft. for housing
Boulder, CO	2015	107,353	New market-rate	$30 per sq. ft. (second highest in the United States)
San Jose, CA	2015	1.03 million	New market-rate	$17.00 per sq. ft.
Palo Alto, CA		66,666	Large commercial and industrial	$19.31 per sq. ft.
San Bruno, CA	2016	43,047	Net new residential floor area for apartments and condos	$25 per sq. ft. of net new residential floor area
			Single-family detached homes	$27 per sq. ft.
			Retail, restaurants, and services	$6.25 per sq. ft. of net new gross floor area
			Hotels, offices, and medical offices	$12.50 per sq. ft.

Location	Started	Population	Charged On	Amount ($US)
Cambridge, MA	2010	118,977	New nonresidential of more than 30,000 square feet of gross floor area	$20.10 per sq. ft. of gross floor area
San Diego, CA	1990	1.426 million	New market-rate nonresidential	$99 per 100 sq. ft.

Source: Author's research conducted with guidance from Malach 2010.

CALIFORNIA, THE FIRST US STATE TO BLOW UP LOCAL
ZONING CONTROL

No overview of affordable housing in the United States would be complete without an account of the influence of zoning on housing price. American housing advocates are currently engaged in a fierce debate. On one side are the disparate advocates of neighbourhood control, who, in the worst case, are labelled NIMBYs for their "not in my backyard" sentiment or, in more forgiving terms, are regarded as citizens opposed to the degradation and gentrification of their neighbourhoods. On the other side are those labelled YIMBYs for their "yes in my backyard" stance, who advocate for the removal of zoning restrictions on all neighbourhoods in the belief that their removal will enhance affordability.

As with most things American, this reaction against local restrictions on housing construction began first in California, which is no surprise since housing costs in California are, on average, more than double the price per square foot that is charged in the rest of the country. In some California metro areas, such as Los Angeles and the Bay Area, the gap is even more alarming, being much more than four times higher. In response, over the past few years, California has tabled legislation meant to overrule local zoning ordinances. After a few failed attempts, it finally succeeded when the California HOME Act of 2021 was signed into law (Government of California 2021; see also Kwok and Lim 2021).

The protracted debate and various failed attempts are instructive and highly relevant to the land Rent theme of this text. Opponents argued (as they still do) that if the purpose of this legislation is to make housing more affordable, it will fail – with only land speculators benefiting – and that those in need of housing will still end up unable to afford the new denser housing.

In the hope of mitigating this unwelcome result, the California HOME Act includes a few unique features. Most importantly, it authorizes only resident homeowners to split their parcel, and these owners must stay on the property for at least one year. This requirement is meant to encourage older owners to split their holdings and to transfer some of their accrued land wealth to their children in the form of a new home on the same lot – all while keeping the forces of land speculation at bay, at least for a time. Also excluded are single-family homes owned by landlords where tenants have resided for more than three years (Government of California 2021).

These amendments, added during the legislative process, are more than interesting since they indicate a sophistication of analysis often lacking when blanket upzonings are proposed. Here, the amendments constitute policy acknowledgments that land Rent and land speculation are drivers of the affordability crisis and that this crisis is not caused primarily by zoning restrictions placed in the way of the free market. A more complex phenomenon seems to be at play.

It remains to be seen how efficacious this legislation will be at matching outcomes with ambitions. This author has doubts, but it will be an important precedent to watch.

CONTEMPORARY AFFORDABLE HOUSING EFFORTS IN THE UNITED KINGDOM

The issue of providing affordable housing in the United Kingdom remains unsettled, with neoliberal policies that favour letting the market fix the problem pitted against proposals for the government to reinvigorate the tradition of managing the land markets by imposing betterment charges.

Unlike in the United States, where housing rules are set at the state and local levels, housing policy in the United Kingdom is administered at the national level. In this way, the jurisdiction of the planning authority responsible for local-area land use differs from more local jurisdiction in Canada, the United States, New Zealand, and Australia. Yet despite this centralization of authority, decisions end up being made largely at the local level and are overseen by local actors.

The first modern-era government response to the housing issue was the passing of the Town and Country Planning Act of 1990. To this day, Section 106 of this legislation remains the primary way for local authorities to capture increases in land values consequent to the urbanization of land (Bentley 2017). Section 106 gives local authorities the power to negotiate contributions to transport, education, and other social infrastructure in exchange for development rights. Contributions by developers are negotiated with the local authority, with a majority of these contributions expected to be in the form of the on-site provision of affordable housing. In this way, Section 106 is partially successful in streaming what would otherwise be unearned land Rent into social benefit. Under this legislation, affordable housing can be interpreted either as social rented housing (owned by a private nonprofit housing association) or as lower-cost homeownership. Ideally, the regulatory framework can be used to enforce the provision of affordable housing and to reduce the price of land overall. The price paid by the developer for the land will likely be reflected in a reduced land-price residual that is proportionate to the value of the social benefits demanded (Whitehead 2007). As Sarah Monk (2010, 124) puts it,

> S106 aims to ensure the transfer of planning gain, or betterment, from the landowner to the local authority via the developer. Because the developer anticipates a major S106 commitment, the price paid for the land is enhanced by planning permission, but only the amount of the increased value less the anticipated cost of S106 agreements. While the market development value decreases, the cost is passed on entirely to the landowner, who still receives a higher price for the land because of the planning permission.

So, in short, this is a land-value tax targeted to capture some of the new land Rent value triggered by rezoning – a tax to manage land Rent.

A recession in the early 1990s slowed the UK housing market in the years after the Town and Country Planning Act was passed, recovering only in the 2000s. By then, the consensus favouring free-market Thatcherism and austerity politics was eroding, and the failure of the housing system to provide affordable dwellings for the middle class was glaringly obvious once again. In accordance with Section 106, plans were finally authorized to make explicit demands for affordable housing a part of required betterments (Monk 2010, 132). Prior to this time, affordability was thought to be best achieved with smaller, more densely configured buildings sold at market price since a smaller house and no yard meant a lower price (Whitehead 2007).

Sadly, most local authorities still fail to achieve their target proportions of affordable housing due to a lack of skilled staff or effective negotiations with development corporations. The emphasis on local delivery has frequently allowed local politicians to undermine national policy goals (K. Barker 2006; Monk 2010).

The agreements under Section 106 are also subject to viability assessments by developers, who are able to undertake an analysis of the costs of their contributions in order to ensure that they are still able to make a profit. In some circumstances, developers will pay a premium price for their land and then appeal their obligations under Section 106 because the obligations make the project unviable. Although these appeals are not always successful, they have the overall effect of driving up land Rent, making landowners the only real winners. This outcome has led to land values that continue to rise while developer contributions drop. It also signals a shift of negotiating power from local authorities to developers (Bentley 2017), limiting the efficiency of Section 106 to capture the land Rent gains that flow into landowner pockets.

Section 106 is used across the country but seems particularly crucial for housing equity in London, where over 65 percent of households are not able to afford market housing, meaning that house prices and rents have become out of reach for both low- and middle-income residents (Marom 2015). Previous policy has emphasized new housing provision due to the acute shortage and high demand while targeting 50 percent of new construction for affordable housing. Unfortunately, as in most English-speaking counties, the term "affordable" is tied to the market value of the unit. Units are deemed affordable at relatively modest reductions below largely unaffordable market rents. Thus affordable units are *not* affordable for those earning median household incomes (ibid.).

As in other English-speaking countries, the UK government subsidizes income-qualified individuals to compete for market-rate rentals through its Housing Benefit Program – which pays private landlords a portion of otherwise unaffordable rent (Bentley 2017). As in the United States, Australia, Canada, and New Zealand, these rent subsidies are not sufficient to meet the growing need and have the unintended consequence of adding upward pressure on land Rents. As a result, most areas of London are still deeply unaffordable for wage earners making average salaries while land Rents skyrocket (Marom 2015).

THE ONGOING LONDON HOUSING CRISIS

As mentioned above, land use in the United Kingdom is adjudicated at the national level. However, the observable results of its affordable-housing efforts seem no more successful for it. London is a particularly heartbreaking example. To address the affordability issues discussed above and to capture some of the planning gains from new development, the Office of the Mayor of London has released a plan that prioritizes the on-site delivery of affordable units – as opposed to the "cash in lieu of housing" payments that prevailed previously. The threshold approach was introduced in a 2017 report as a supplementary document to the London City Plan. This plan streamlines the development-permit process for proposals with 35 percent affordability in order to incentivize developers to build more affordable units as part of market projects. This fast-track route allows developers to skip the viability-plan application with the expectation that they will also seek government grants to help them hit the city's 50 percent target for affordable units. At 35 percent of affordable units, there is also a possibility for density bonuses to increase the number to 50 percent (Mayor of London 2017). Although laudable, and even if every bit helps, this program and others have not significantly altered the larger trend of ever-worsening overall housing affordability in the London region.

Although a London land-value tax has recently been proposed to deal with the underlying systemic problem of skyrocketing land Rent, a specific and higher tax on the land Rent component of property has yet to be imposed at the time of this writing (Barnaby and Pearce 2017; Gavron et al. 2016).

Meanwhile, London scrambles to supply housing for a backlog of over 250,000 residents who qualify for, but cannot get, council housing. Part of the city's desperate attempt to deal with the crisis, a measure that is both ironic and a vivid metaphor for our times, is its Right to Buy-Back program, in which the city's boroughs buy back council-housing units from private owners – units that had gone to private hands during Thatcher's Right to Buy privatization program of the 1980s (Talora 2021).

CONTEMPORARY AFFORDABLE HOUSING EFFORTS IN NEW ZEALAND

New Zealand depends on land tax for public revenues far less than the OECD average. That is no surprise given that New Zealand remains one of the only countries that does not have a capital-gains tax to capture some of the rise in land value accrued at the point of sale. New Zealand repealed its long-standing national land tax in 1992 as part of its neo-liberal enthusiasms (Barrett 2012). Regrets ensued. In response to the severity of the nation's housing crisis, the government has remediated this lack partly by means of what it calls a land tax, which is really a speculation tax (G. Harris 2014). This tax captures a portion of the capital gains accrued by speculators who buy, hold, and sell land for profit. Homeowners are exempt. New Zealand's demand-side measures also include a ban on foreign investment in housing (N. Perry 2018). None of these policies has moderated New Zealand's out of control land-price inflation (Samarasinghe 2020). Although land prices *are* being driven down at the time of this writing, this decrease is not caused by new supply but by the rise in interest rates, which is lowering the dollar amounts that real estate investors can leverage.

In desperation, various supply-side interventions have been attempted, most notoriously the KiwiBuild program, which is a government-sponsored initiative to build 100,000 affordable homes in ten years. It is well behind schedule (Small 2019), with speculation rife that this failure helped to bring down Prime Minister Jacinda Ardern in 2023 (Cohen 2022).

The thought seems to have been that it was construction costs and permitting inefficiencies that stood in the way of affordability. This complaint is voiced worldwide, not only in New Zealand. The other idea was that a massive increase in housing supply would lower costs in conformance with the laws of supply and demand – also a presumption voiced worldwide. Despite the government's heroic attempts to smooth the permitting process, prices sadly continued their inexorable rise, and construction starts did not noticeably increase. Among the criticisms of the program was that the price of land was never considered a factor. Real estate interests suggest that the land problem could be mitigated if more land was opened up for urban development on the fringes of urban regions, the idea being to sprawl till we hit affordability (Ryan-Collins and Murray 2021) – a new version of the "drive till you qualify" strategy, which entails moving far enough from the city centre to qualify for a mortgage.

THE STRUGGLE TO GET INCLUSIONARY ZONING IN NEW ZEALAND

Although inclusionary zoning is not unknown in New Zealand, its use remains contentious and is strongly opposed by the building trades and by their land-speculating allies. As mentioned above, land-use law is managed at the national level and implemented locally. Certain municipalities, most notably Queenstown, have tried with some success to use the Resource Management Act of 1991 –which mentions "the social, economic, aesthetic, and cultural conditions" that shape communities – as the basis for nexus-type (Mallach 2010) requirements to provide a legal foundation for insisting on the provision of affordable units as a condition of project approval. The Queenstown model is anything but aggressive, as it requires setting aside only around 5 per cent of a project for affordable housing, which makes its opposition by real estate interests[11] and its failure to extend into other New Zealand municipalities especially depressing. To reiterate, inclusionary-zoning ordinances are a practical and precedented way to stream at least some portion of land Rents away from the pockets of speculators and into the social benefit of providing housing that average wage earners might be able to afford.

LET'S JUST GET RID OF ZONING, SHALL WE?

In 2021, New Zealand made waves worldwide when, by government fiat, it outlawed single-family zoning nationwide (New Zealand Legislation 2021; see also Corlett and Cassidy 2021). Now, any formerly single-family parcel can be rebuilt or modified to include up to three separately owned dwelling units and can be build up to a height of three storeys "by right" – no rezoning required. The legislation, in effect, repealed many features of the Resource Management Act of 1991 (mentioned above), which had been criticized for elevating the values of environment over the values of housing and infrastructure (Greenaway-McGrevy 2022). Both inspired by and inspiring similar decisions in other parts of the world, this proposal is of course motivated by a conviction that zoning by its nature pushes up price because it stands in the way of the housing market's capacity to respond to demand. Although this idea is intuitively appealing, it is extremely hard to find evidence of any downward pressure on home prices per interior square foot as a result of eliminating single-family zoning in New Zealand.[12]

But perhaps such a massive increase in zoned capacity will overwhelm other influences on home price. We shall see. Perhaps New Zealand's nationwide removal of single-family zoning will overwhelm the influence of global investment trends. Perhaps New Zealand will finally provide the example where new zoning lowers prices. Perhaps removing single-family zoning will undercut the rampaging forces that are fuelling the global financialization of housing that has been spawned by near negative real interest rates during the first decades of the twenty-first century and by the glut of securities gushing from pandemic-panicked central banks worldwide – a glut that has inflated all asset prices globally, especially for housing.

However, there are many reasons to doubt New Zealand's prospects of success. Many cities already have zoned capacity far in excess of demand. Vancouver, for example, has zoned capacity for at least double its present population (Bertolet 2016; Larsen 2018). Still others, most famously Houston, have no zoning at all but are now similarly afflicted with spiking home prices, which have risen by nearly 50 percent in five years (Rohde 2022). If nationwide upzoning succeeds in quelling out of control land-price inflation, we will have to junk the economic canons of Adam

Smith, John Stuart Mill, David Ricardo, and Joseph Stiglitz, all of whom decry the tendency of land to absorb, up to the last nickel, every bit of value created by a region's wage earners and entrepreneurs. Viewed from this perspective, the benefits of adding new allowable density without insisting on affordability accrue to land owners, not to renters and not to first time home buyers.

CONTEMPORARY AFFORDABLE-HOUSING EFFORTS IN AUSTRALIA

Sydney now holds the dubious honour of having the second most expensive housing in the world when measured against the average wages of the Sydney area. Hong Kong is number one, and Vancouver is number three (Demographia 2021). Other Australian cities are not far behind. Capital cities in each Australian state made the list of the world's top twenty least affordable cities (Collins and Johnson 2022), which is strange because housing construction during the COVID-19 pandemic hit an all-time high of 192,636 starts in Australia, up by 17.4 percent in annual terms year over year, strongly suggesting that the problem was not one of blocked supply (Mawby 2021).

The thesis of this volume, one that the Australia experience reinforces, is that the housing crisis is not caused by an impeded supply of homes but by the asset value of the land below them. This Rent value is inflated when higher-density homes are authorized, much to the disappointment of those who argue that the housing-affordability problem is caused by constrained supply. This hypothesis is backed up by the extreme urban land-price inflation seen there in the past two decades. Australian urban land-price inflation in 2021 amounted to AU$600 billion, which was thirty times the size of total banking profits that year (Fitzgerald 2021).

LAND-VALUE CAPTURE MAKES A RETURN – AND DOESN'T

It's regrettable to many Australians that the national land tax was repealed in 1952, just when it could have started to moderate urban land Rent inflation. It's a lot more difficult to reinstate a tax after its repeal, especially when all those urban landowners (who are also voters) paid a high price for the land based on the assumption that it's land Rent was theirs to keep. Yet, when the Australian home-price crisis spiralled out of control, when the ratio of household debt to GDP went more and more into the red zone, and when over two-thirds of national wealth was devoted to urban land value (an asset class that is, in economic terms, a deadweight loss), wiser heads increasingly looked for correctives. One such attempt was the Henry Report, which resulted from a review initiated in 2008 under the government of Prime Minister Kevin Rudd. Chaired by Ken Henry, senior policy advisor to the Australian Treasury, the review produced 138 recommendations grouped under nine themes, the first of which reads, "Concentrating revenue raising on four efficient tax bases: personal income, business income, private consumption, and economic rents from natural resources and land ... Taxes fitting into none of these categories should eventually be abolished" ("Henry Tax Review" n.d., citing Australian Treasury 2009).

For housing, it was the inclusion of economic rents that held the most promise, as this change envisioned a shift away from various income, transfer, and stamp-duty taxes that have modest to no effect on land prices in favour of taxes on nonproductive urban land wealth. Rudd attempted to implement only 3 of the 138 recommendations, and none of these three had anything to do with economic rent. His efforts, modest as they were, contributed to his defeat in 2010. Sadly, no other major effort to moderate land-price inflation through taxation has been made since that time. The exception is within the Australian Capital Territory, home to the nation's capital city, Canberra. Here, in line with the Henry Report, the stamp-duty tax is being phased out and replaced with a land-value tax – an easier revenue draw for the capital district since, unlike in the Australian states, the urban land in this district is largely owned by the federal government and leased to homeowners (Helm 2019).

INCLUSIVE-ZONING EFFORTS IN AUSTRALIA

As already mentioned, Australia is a relatively loose confederation of largely independent states. The positive side of this arrangement is that, in most respects, states are free to make their own laws and policies governing affordable housing. As has also been touched on many times in this volume, in the absence of true and substantial taxes on land Rent, the policy tool that best achieves this same effect is inclusionary zoning. Two of Australia's states have successfully incorporated inclusionary-zoning requirements into their development policies: South Australia and New South Wales, where the Australian Capital Territory is located. Housing advocates in other parts of Australia, notably nearby Victoria, where inclusionary zoning does not exist, look jealously at the relative success of both states, especially that of South Australia.

In South Australia's Adelaide metro area, 15 percent of any project must be comprised of affordable-housing units (Government of South Australia 2017, 66). Projects are approved through negotiations between developers and planners according to rules that link approval to a project's social impact. In this regard, the process is similar to the approach taken in California, where nexus studies are used to assess the degree of social impact consequent to a project, with affordability remediations being demanded on the basis of this nexus connection. Thus these policies do not explicitly express an intent to capture the newly elevated land Rent increment due to rezonings. Rather, the policy demands are grounded in an assessment of project impacts on access to housing for a wider range of incomes than might otherwise result if the market were left to its own devices.

The density that builders can assume "by right" is not specified by policies but must be negotiated. Consequently, the residual value of the land is influenced. The greater the requirement for affordable housing, the lower the land-price residual will be. And the higher the density allowed, the higher the land-price residual will be.

The Australian Capital Territory, with the Canberra metropolitan area at its centre, has done slightly better than South Australia, at times insisting that up to 20 percent of all greenfield developments be comprised of affordable-housing units (National Shelter 2019, 18). However, this proportion is admittedly much easier to ask for given that all housing land in the capital area is uniquely state-owned and is provided to homeowners only as leasehold land in the form of ninety-nine-year leases (Bladen 2019). With land Rent effectively in the control of the state, making it similar to Singapore in this respect, a higher threshold than the 20 percent benchmark could certainly be reached.

Finally, and sadly, real estate interests in Australia are generally very hostile to inclusionary zoning, arguing that it interferes with the free operation of the housing market. This effect explains why the most expensive cities in Australia – Sydney and Melbourne – have no inclusionary-zoning requirements whatsoever at this time (Shaw 2022).

CONTEMPORARY AFFORDABLE HOUSING EFFORTS IN CANADA

Canada is a federation of highly independent provinces. This arrangement makes housing policy (and in many cases, the lack of one) a creature of the provinces. As discussed earlier, the federal government has intervened with housing funding from time to time over the past century, but the execution of this policy, supplemented by provincial and local resources, has been spotty and largely a local affair. Thus it is impossible to say anything universal about the country's housing policies. Instead, I look at one little corner of this cross-continental land mass that has attempted the most: Vancouver.

The Vancouver metropolitan area, with the city at its core, has without question done more than any other metro area in North America to capitalize on the engine of its rapid development in order to deliver social benefits. What this undertaking means, in the context of this volume, is that Vancouver has streamed a significant share of land Rent increases consequent to development away from the pockets of land speculators and into socially beneficial expenditures through a planning process colloquially called conditional zoning.[13]

CONDITIONAL ZONING IN VANCOUVER, A SHORT HISTORY

In the 1980s, Vancouver grew up. This sleepy resource town was discovered by international investors. Hong Kong emigres were the first to spot the potential of a city set in a landscape so stunning that it brought tears to one's eyes. Luckily for Vancouver, it had city officials who knew an exciting opportunity when they saw one. Uniquely, they set up a system to capture as much of this influx of new capital value for public benefit as seemed possible. Derelict industrial sites blessed with incredible water views were rezoned for homes (L. Baker 2005).

With some sage advice from Hong Kong investment experts (Douay 2015), city officials zoned these areas for very high-density housing, depending on towers to deliver the bulk of this new density.[14] This approach was the secret to their success. Because British Columbia's laws allowed it, city staff and other stakeholders could, in effect, bargain with developers for amenity payments as a condition of project approval (Government of British Columbia 2014).[15] The payments were to be negotiated, not imposed.

This model will get a city into trouble in many parts of the world and often for good reason (Hein 2022). In some places, this process, pejoratively called paying for zoning, is illegal. Below, I discuss how decades later this strategy got Vancouver into trouble – even if, for a few decades, it all worked out (City of Vancouver 2009).

In the 1980s and '90s, city staff and political leaders collaborated with talented designers and accommodating developers to evolve what became known worldwide as Vancouverism (Beasley 2019). When it emerged, Vancouverism was unique, an unprecedented model of high-density living in the midst of an amenity-rich urban environment where all the lessons of urban-planning theorist Jane Jacobs (1961) and other late-twentieth-century urbanists could be executed. And it was all paid for with captured land Rent, as explained below.

A TAX ON LAND LIFT

As in any revolution, a new vocabulary was needed. Most important here was the term "land lift."[16] When developers negotiated with the city for how many millions they would contribute to the city in return for a new high-density zoning allowance, the yardstick was expressed in percentage terms. The city was explicit in suggesting that 80 percent of land lift should go to the city, with 20 percent left for the landowner in order to motivate the sale. Land lift was (and is) the difference between the value of the land – its land price, or Rent – before and after rezoning. In the Vancouver example, the difference between its value when authorized for a two-storey building and its increased value when reauthorized for a twenty-storey building was immense. For our purposes, we can assume that there was a one-to-one increase in value as allowable density increased. Doubling the allowable density doubled the land value, which in Vancouver was under Cdn$100 dollars per buildable square foot at the time and is over Cdn$600 today.[17] So, using 1990 figures, a developer that starts off with an "as of right"[18] allowance to erect a building on a parcel of 10,000 square feet, for which the "as of right" zoning might allow for a two-storey construction – that is, a building with twice as many interior square feet as the site, or a floor surface ratio of two (FSR 2)[19] – would be worth Cdn$1 million at the outset of the project. If the construction is allowed to go to twenty storeys, with an interior floor space of 100,000 square feet, the value of the parcel can shoot up to Cdn$10 million. If the city negotiates for 80 percent of the land lift, it will net Cdn$8 million from this one tower project.

The use of land lift was (and is) a bit more complicated than this account might suggest, especially when the new allowable density is calculated,[20] but this type of revenue gain was the idea. You can now understand how such an accrual of Cdn$8 million was really a tax on land, not a tax on the building itself. Thus it captured the bulk of the post-development increase in land Rent, providing the city with funds to be used for civic purposes.

This captured land Rent was more than enough to create an urban design balance between density and amenities. Community Amenity Contributions (CACs), the politically more palatable name for the land-lift tax (City of Vancouver 2022a), paid for the generously provided open spaces and waterfront promenades that became a part of the city's fame. CACs paid for community centres and daycare facilities. They paid for broad, well-landscaped boulevards. Portions of land to be used for af-

FIGURE 7.4 View of waterfront improvements all paid for with "community amenity contributions." | Author's photo.

fordable housing (assuming that construction money was forthcoming from the province) were handed over by developers in their negotiations with the city for future development.[21] Based on the model of False Creek South (discussed in Chapter 5), the original aim was the construction of an equal number of low-income, medium-income, and upper-income units, and for a time these targets were nearly met – that is, until global land Rent inflation caught up with Vancouver, making it one of the world's most unaffordable cities (Ang 2022).

VANCOUVER LOSES THE PLOT AS GLOBAL LAND RENTS GET OUT OF CONTROL

Sometime in the first decade of the twenty-first century, Vancouver lost the synergy that had existed between the civic ambitions of city stakeholders, on the one hand, and the demands of capital (or rent-seeking interests), on the other. It was around this time that Vancouverism became a world-famous model for density done right. This reputation did it no harm when large financial institutions like sovereign wealth funds, pension funds, and real estate investment trusts (REITs) were making investment decisions. There was no contest between beautiful coastal Vancouver and prairie-town Regina. Furthermore, by this time, Vancouver had proven the viability of tall residential towers, unheard of in any other North American city – even New York, where towers were largely for office uses, which is not the case any longer. Eventually, land Rent inflation would play a part when new high-density housing supply tragically failed to remain affordable. The problem was land Rent inflation.

LAND RENT INFLATION KILLS THE GOOSE THAT LAYS THE GOLDEN EGG

When the first tower districts were built in Vancouver, land Rent was a relatively small portion of the final cost of high-rise projects. A tower can have over 100,000 square feet of interior space, and with the cost of construction at Cdn$200 per square foot in the mid-1990s, that was Cdn$20 million. But the Vancouver land market was much different in 1990. Land was cheap compared to today. Even though local landowners were aware that fantastic new density was proposed for their sites, they were happy to get a 100 percent bump in price above the land's previous assessed value, which represented 20 percent of the land lift, as discussed above. The 80 percent of the land-value increase that went to the city was no great burden for landowners, who still doubled their investment. Thus, when the first residential towers were sold in the late 1980s and early '90s, nearly all of the new investment ended up being spent on urban improvements in the form of either buildings or civic infrastructure. Vancouver, then, is a textbook example of how, in the spirit of Adam Smith, Henry George, and Joseph Stiglitz, you can tax (nearly) the full value of the land lift and use the money for civic betterment while hardly taxing the improvements to your city – in this case, the buildings. Not only that, but this new density was affordable to ordinary wage earners. Purchase prices in the 1990s were about Cdn$300 to Cdn$400 per square foot for an apartment in a new Vancouver high rise – affordable for a family with an income of around Cdn$70,000 per year.

New residents were able to move into attractive urban areas whose purchase price nearly matched local salaries, with a two-bedroom unit selling for approximately Cdn$250,000. Now, newly built high-density homes cost between Cdn$1,300 and Cdn$2,500 per square foot (Livabl n.d.),[22] putting the cost of the same home at over Cdn$1.2 million or more – often much more. And, as should be no surprise, the difference in price between then and now is mostly attributable to land Rent inflation, not to construction-price inflation. Since 1990, land prices (inclusive of any land-lift tax) as a percentage of the total price have risen from under 20 percent of the total cost per buildable square foot to over more than 60 percent in most cases. In other words, the cost of land is now twice the cost of construction.[23] These days, homebuyers more than ever are really buying their share of city dirt, not homes.

Counterintuitively, in Vancouver, where the ever-rising land price per buildable square foot is residual to the market price per interior square foot, the land price per interior square foot does not vary much between higher-density condominiums and lower-density townhouses and detached homes. Vancouver's housing prices are set by the global market's appetite for its floor space across varied housing types and density configurations, with only modest differences in the price per interior square

FIGURE 7.5 View down the Pacific Boulevard main spine of the Yaletown district in Vancouver. A combination of the urban vision of both Corbusier and Jane Jacobs can be traced in this view where both towers and active streets form the basic structure of the space. | Author's photo.

foot between detached, townhouses, and apartment products. Of course, detached Vancouver homes *do* cost more, on average, than condominium units because lots for detached homes typically allow more interior square feet than are common in condominiums. But that is not necessarily because detached homes are inherently more valuable per interior square foot. Often, they are not.

The increase in the price of a square foot of built space by over 400 percent in one decade has been felt mostly in the increase of over 500 percent in the residual price for urban land over the same period (MountainMath Software and Analytics 2021a). As urban land prices rose and the entry fee for a starter home moved inexorably away from wage-earner capacity to finance it, the city began to devote more and more of the CAC bounty to affordable housing – either in the form of negotiated affordable units in lieu of CACs or in the form of cash in lieu of units, with the latter approach also reducing CAC taxes. But by the second decade of the twenty-first century, CAC taxes had begun to decline as a share of total project costs. I explain why below.

THE GOLDEN GOOSE IS COOKED

Unfortunately, the discretionary essence of this process proved to be its undoing. Over time, global capital markets began to take notice, and land prices started to inflate long before new projects were proposed. This run-up in land value paralleled the increases in land value afflicting other so-called global cities (American Enterprise Institute n.d.), but Vancouver led the pack in this regard (D. Wong 2018). The tragedy for Vancouver was that the run-up in land values was violently at odds not only with any of the real estate fundamentals of local economic vitality (e.g., high-paying jobs) but also with the ability of the average family to afford housing (i.e., income). Land Rents city-wide increased by over 500 percent between 2006 and 2016, with an increase in city-wide land values of over Cdn$100 billion in 2016 alone (MountainMath Software and Analytics 2021a). And to repeat, this run-up in land value could not have been for lack of trying to add new supply since the number of housing units built within city limits had tripled since 1960, all through infill.

Charting the assessed values for these years shows that land Rents for likely development parcels were governed not by the present value as currently zoned but by the speculative value of developable locations, with assumptions of new density allowances baked into the land price years ahead of time. And as urban land prices rose, developers meekly paid the price.

The simple point is that the land lift successfully captured by the city during the early years of the Vancouverism revolution had, by 2010, already been largely squeezed out of the land by speculation and by its influence on the new higher assessed values of parcels located near new higher-density development. By the time more recent projects began, the value of most of the new density negotiated discretionally with city staff had already factored into the land price.

As a result, in comparison to land-price inflation, construction cost, and final purchase price, the proportion of city-gained CACs shrank dramatically, weakening what had for a short time been a successful strategy to keep most development value above ground in the form of new structures for the middle class, complete with the necessary civic amenities. The deleterious effects of Land Rent came back with a vengeance, and city staff lost the tradition of effectively negotiating the public's due share of land lift. That is why the discretionary magic that gave us Vancouverism eventually became a curse. Because the CACs and other contributions were negotiated rather than required, there was a natural tendency to be forgiving during CAC negotiations due to exogenous factors such as the worldwide land-value appreciation mentioned above and the loss of institutional memory as staff turned over. Developers who overpaid for land insisted that the price was just the price, arguing that there was no land lift left in their projects.[24] Absent a fixed CAC tax, newer staff tended to agree.

An alternative might have proven more useful. A fixed, very high CAC established years ahead of time would have influenced the land market, helping to wring out the speculative forces that had, in effect, stolen the civic share of future land lift. Vancouver tried to rectify its mistake by implementing a Development Contribution Expectations charge of Cdn$340 per square foot of interior space on its next transit-corridor rezoning (City of Vancouver n.d.). Municipalities with similar powers might consider being more forceful than Vancouver was in disciplining the land market in this way for future civic benefit.

8

City-Wide Zoning Approaches and a Modern Tax on Rent

Land-use zoning has been implemented for more than a century and is deeply supported by case law in all English-speaking countries. However, only recently has zoning been clearly understood as a means to influence land Rent for social purpose. The reasons for this turn to zoning are complex, but the combination of neoliberal austerity policies with the simultaneous (and likely causally linked) inflation in urban land Rent has left city leaders to seek local solutions to this always local problem. Here, I focus on two US cities that were early adopters of city-wide strategies. These policies could be adapted for other cities in the English-speaking world since land use and property laws are largely consistent. Two basic approaches are now being applied in the United States. The first involves the retooling of a city's basic residential-area zoning codes to incentivize the production of affordable units, as seen in Portland, Oregon. The second involves the imposition of an overlay district across an entire city, which does not replace existing city-wide zoning but instead provides an alternative approval path in return for affordable housing, as seen in Cambridge, Massachusetts. Each model is discussed in turn below.

PORTLAND, OREGON: ADDING SUPPLY
AND AFFORDABLE UNITS CITY-WIDE

In the summer of 2020, Portland City Council voted three to one in favour of its Residential Infill Project after four years of debate (City of Portland 2020a). The new zoning ordinance brought a raft of changes to the city's residential zones, including reducing the limit on new single-family homes from 6,500 square feet to 2,500 square feet, encouraging multiple units on most lots, and slashing requirements for off-street parking (City of Portland 2020b).

But the real and lasting boost to affordability may come from a provision allowing for up to six dwelling units on all residentially zoned lots in the city – including the more than 50 percent of lots with single-family zoning[1] – in return for half of these new units being permanently affordable.

FIGURE 8.1 Downtown Portland, Oregon, and environs viewed from the north. | Courtesy Sam Beebe, Ecotrust, via Wikimedia Commons.

This measure offers a way to achieve permanently affordable housing in every Portland neighbourhood – at no cost to the taxpayer. This absence of reliance on taxpayer funding is a crucial point. Most historic discussion of affordable housing still presumes that such funding is a necessary element. Although this funding is welcome, one very large negative effect of government funding is that it adds one more competitor to the marketplace for already overpriced urban land and fills the already overstuffed pockets of land speculators. The Portland strategy streams the increases in land Rent value provided by newly approved density away from the pockets of land speculators and into social benefit instead. The density bonus is effectively a tax on future land Rent imposed at the point of its increase – that is, when the new density is allowed. This obligation to ensure affordability in return for density reduces what would otherwise be the residual value of the parcel, thus controlling land Rent inflation.[2]

Portland's stated goals are to "provide opportunities for a wider variety of housing options" and to "reduce the cost of a single unit by roughly half the cost of a single new house" (quoted in Condon 2020b).

Adding density without requiring affordability, as this volume contends, leads to land-price inflation and no net gain in affordability. In the end, you get bigger buildings but no decrease in the per-square-foot price of the units. As mentioned before in this text, adding new density to existing districts is good for many reasons: more efficient transit, commercial services within walking distance, more efficient infrastructure, and lower greenhouse gas emissions. But if affordability is your number one objective for making this change, there are better ways to achieve it.

As I have noted elsewhere,

> Portland has set a strict definition of affordability. Units in six-unit buildings must be affordable for families with 60 per cent or less of the city's median income.
>
> It took four years worth of meetings and 38,000 individual mailings to mitigate fears and incorporate important neighbourhood residents' views into the final plan.

It requires new buildings to respect a neighbourhood's character (often a difficult concern to satisfy, and even harder to define) by not overshadowing neighbours.

Importantly, the city eliminated on-site parking requirements for affordable units, freeing up lot space for gardens and structures. This is always a contentious issue and not everyone in the city agreed. But in the end councillors understood that affordability objectives could not be met if much of a redeveloped site was used up for car storage.

Also critical, the city will require the preservation of character homes as part of any plans. (Condon 2020b)

Portland city councillor Chloe Eudaly, a tenants' rights activist, said that social and racial justice issues drove the initiative:

For over 100 years, exclusionary zoning laws have kept certain types of housing, and therefore certain classes and races of people, out of single-family neighborhoods. Simple upzoning will not remedy past harms or guarantee more affordable housing and diverse neighbor-hoods. That is why I've worked so hard to ensure that we included incentives for affordable housing, commit to developing and imple-menting anti-displacement measures, and encourage the preservation of existing housing. (Quoted in KATU Staff 2020)

Housing advocate and architect Sean McEwen noted that "a low-rise scale is kept in existing neighbourhoods, with a wide range of housing options that promote housing affordability and compatible housing forms. No land assembly is required to densify ... And the approvals process is significantly simplified." He explained that the ordinance cre-ates new opportunities for "existing homeowners to contemplate adding density on their properties to better accommodate aging in place." It also enables them to free up equity when they need it without selling and moving away. Furthermore, the strategy allows for "separate hous-ing units for grown-up children who can't afford to buy back into the neighborhoods they grew up in" (quoted in Condon 2020b).

As I have written,

> There are legitimate criticisms of the changes. The requirement for affordability only kicks in when six units are planned. If developers choose, they can build four units, and those four can be sold or rented at market rates. There is a fear most projects may just add expensive units, displacing families with no social benefits realized.
>
> And the bylaw does not specify the size of the affordable units, so there is an incentive to make them very small and unsuitable for families. (Condon 2020b)

These concerns illuminate the necessity of carefully calibrating the requirements of such an ordinance. Not mentioned since Chapter 2, but still relevant, is that wage rates across the English-speaking world have not kept up with home costs. In jobs-rich global cities, this gap is yawing. The higher the gap, the harder it is to make projects work without demanding rents too high for median-income earners. The wider the gap between current wages and current land prices, the fewer the social benefits that can be demanded without rendering projects unprofitable in the absence of a subsidy.

Given the current land and wage rates in Portland, one fears that the city could have insisted that at least 50 percent of the floor space of six-unit projects be affordable and could have required that at least one unit in the new fourplexes be affordable.

In the end, the Portland ordinance seems to reveal a mixture of a belief in the power of new supply to lower prices by adding more market units and a recognition that land Rent is the problem and must be stopped in its tracks. The ordinance's dual approach may be an uncomfortable compromise between two opposed interpretations of the problem.

CAMBRIDGE, MASSACHUSETTS: IMPLEMENTING AN AFFORDABLE-HOUSING OVERLAY DISTRICT

Citizens and policy makers in Cambridge, Massachusetts, have discovered a powerful new way to stem the seemingly inexorable rise in city land Rents: an ordinance that authorizes a doubling of allowable density,

FIGURE 8.2 Typical simple housing in Cambridge, Massachusetts. This form of density would be encouraged by the city for affordable housing in the city. The market has pushed the market price of homes like this to close to one million dollars per unit. | Courtesy Jack E. Boucher via US Department of Housing and Urban Development.

anywhere in the city, but only in return for 100 percent of the housing units being permanently affordable.

Cambridge City Council adopted its Affordable Housing Overlay (AHO) district in the fall of 2020 (City of Cambridge 2020). The new zoning district is called an overlay district because it does not change the base zoning of any parcel in the city but overlays city districts with an optional set of more generous rules to which developers may choose to conform instead. Overlay districts are not a new thing. Similar ordinances have been in use in the United States since the 1970s, especially in New Jersey and California, but never before has an ordinance been adopted that covers an entire city while also requiring that 100 percent of all the new units built according to these new overlay rules be affordable to the area's average wage earners.

Nonprofit housing-development corporations are especially favoured by this model, as they are institutionally equipped to both build and manage this kind of housing.

The Cambridge AHO is subject to court challenges less than some of the strategies discussed in Chapter 7 because it does not exact concessions as a condition of development approval. On the contrary, landowners in AHO zones remain perfectly free to adhere to the existing base zoning if they wish. An overlay zone of this type is safe from the kinds of court challenges that tripped up more than one California inclusionary-zoning ordinance because the AHO cannot be deemed an uncompensated taking of land value. It is entirely a bonusing policy with no adverse effects on the market price of existing parcels under base zoning. However, if owner-developers opt to conform to the affordability constraints of the overlay district, they can add more density (and gain planning concessions on things like parking requirements) than the underlying zoning allows. Why does that matter? By not changing the underlying zoning, the city does not send a signal to the land markets that there may be speculative land-value increases consequent to any density increases that it grants.

The Cambridge AHO authorizes a doubling of the allowable density, expressed as a doubling of the allowed floor surface ratio (FSR),[3] in order to double what the base zoning allows. To qualify for a permit under the standards set forth in the ordinance, proponents must agree that all

FIGURE 8.3 Former rectory, school, and convent of the Cambridge Catholic Sacred Heart parish church at 49 6th Street. It is to be converted into affordable housing under the Cambridge, Massachusetts, Affordable Housing Overlay option. | Courtesy Google Maps.

new units will be permanently affordable.[4] Affordability thresholds are set in the ordinance so that rent can be no more than 30 percent of a resident's gross income. Eighty percent of the units must be available to households with incomes at 30 to 80 percent of the area median income, with some of these units going to residents whose incomes are below 30 percent but who have Section 8 housing vouchers that help them to pay their rent, as discussed in Chapter 4.

These numbers may seem arcane to those not familiar with this American policy parlance, but they are crucial to understand. In jobs-rich global cities like Cambridge – which is functionally a part of Boston proper, even if Cambridge residents might suggest that the reverse is more true – the average wages are too low relative to the exploding cost of housing. Pegging housing payments to 30 percent of median wages rectifies this disparity.

What does all this planner speak have to do with land Rents? It's worth illustrating why this is relevant, using Cambridge as the example.

As shown throughout this volume, if you simply increase allowable density without requiring affordability, the land value (or land Rent) is pushed up. Imagine a parcel of 4,000 square feet with an allowable floor surface ratio of one (FSR 1) that sells for $2 million dollars prior to rezoning. If the allowable density is doubled to a floor surface ratio of two (FSR 2), the redevelopment value increases in kind, forcing a near doubling in the value of the land to $4 million.

Why?

When the city authorizes a doubling of market density without requiring affordability, the residual land price goes up in response. The city gets more efficient use of the land with the new density – all good – but no substantial decrease in the cost per square foot of new housing. That is because the housing market, as it presently operates, does not price housing based on any fixed idea of the cost of a square foot of dirt but instead on the market's established sale price of a square foot of finished interior space. As allowed density goes up, so too does land price.

Land-price residual is the price a developer can afford to pay for land after all construction costs, soft costs, profits, and fees are deducted from the hoped-for market price per interior square foot of the proposed project. In expensive markets, the price of usable interior space can easily be $1,000 per square foot or more. At this price per interior square foot, a market-housing developer could afford to pay roughly $500 per buildable square foot. In the example given below, I use very round numbers for the sake of simplicity.

In this example, with a market sale price of $1,000 per square foot of usable interior space, the developer would calculate a land-price residual of $500 per buildable square foot because that is what is left after paying for construction (at $250 per square foot) and for fees, consultants, and profits (at a total of $250 per square foot). The developer can afford only up to $500 per buildable square foot, or roughly $4 million for land (i.e., 8,000 interior square feet at $500 per buildable square foot). To pay much more for the land would likely result in bankruptcy. But note the land-price residual has doubled from $2 million to $4 million. And if the developer refuses to pay the $4 million, some other developer certainly will.

However, if the city authorizes only density increases if all of the new units are affordable to those making average incomes, the picture changes considerably. Staying with the Cambridge example, we can work it backwards from the incomes of the people we want to house. To make the math easy, let's say that our target household earns $90,000 per year (or 80 percent of Cambridge household median income as of 2022). Thus it can pay 30 percent of its gross income, or $27,000, to cover the mortgage (at $21,000 per year) and the taxes, utilities, and upkeep (at a total of $6,000 per year). The yearly principle and interest portion of the $27,000 will finance a thirty-year mortgage of $450,000 at an interest rate of 2.7 percent (the rate at time of this writing). Such a household might be able to afford a one-bedroom unit of 600 square feet, meaning that the purchase price will be roughly $750 per square foot.

Working again backwards to the residual value of the land, we have $250 per square foot for construction and $250 per square foot for profit, permitting, and other soft costs. That leaves $250 per buildable square foot to pay for the land. Given that the total allowable built space on this lot measuring 4,000 square feet is 8,000 square feet at the new floor space ration of two (FSR 2), the builder can afford to pay $2 million for the land.

This amount is the residual price for the land, the same as its price under current zoning, which is the only point of this mathematical exercise, the intention being to give the reader a feel for how targeting resident income as a condition for upzoning can drive down or stabilize land price – or land Rent.

In this example, if a nonprofit housing corporation or co-op is assumed, the selling price per square foot drops from $1,000 to $750, with all of this price reduction attributable to lower land cost – that is, lower land Rent. All other costs are the same. This same methodology can be used to find reasonable land Rent extractions for other cities.

With the cost of rent and ownership now unreachable by those with average salaries, the bottom line is that in this new world – where land prices exceed the cost of new construction in virtually all of the major global cities experiencing housing stress – the goal of keeping housing affordable demands that land Rent be controlled. The higher the land Rent, the more crucial it is that control be implemented.

For the sake of accuracy, there are a number of caveats to add here, especially for those familiar with the development industry. Development taxes, such as CAC charges (discussed in Chapter 7), will affect the residual value of each buildable square foot of a subject parcel. When development taxes are added, the land-price residual goes down, and when development costs are removed, the land-price residual goes up. In this way, development taxes do not add to housing prices for new owners but reduce the residual value per buildable square foot of the development site, thus lowering the money that a developer is able to offer the landowner for the land without going broke.

Ultimately, the developer in this example doesn't care whether a dollar goes to the landowner or to the city as long as it's just one dollar. Any dollar claimed by the city is one less dollar that can be offered to the landowner. Therefore, if our goal is to drive down the land Rent residual while streaming land Rent toward a designated social purpose and away from land speculation, it would be a very good thing indeed to adopt a policy device that streams this dollar to affordable housing and away from what would be a deadweight loss[5] to land-price inflation.

A final point to be made is that the calculated land price in the more affordable example is still too high. This example has shown only a way to stabilize land price as a means to ensure more affordable housing. A city that can successfully stabilize land price or, ideally, slowly reverse its rise can become increasingly affordable over time – in the same way that Vienna became increasingly affordable over time, as discussed in Chapter 6 – all through managing land Rents.

Vancouver's CAC tax and Cambridge's Affordable Housing Overlay zone use very different strategies to achieve similar results. It's useful to compare them. Both stream land Rent to social purpose, but Vancouver collects and then distributes the land-lift cash, whereas Cambridge never inflates the land Rent in the first place. Thus there is no cash for Cambridge, and new land Rent value avoids both the pocket of the land speculator and the pocket of the tax collector, literally remaining with the dirt of the development parcel. If sufficient numbers of housing units that are permanently affordable can be produced, it is conceivable that a reasonable mix of housing suitable for a wide range of family incomes may, over time, be achieved in Cambridge – a city that, like many others of its kind, is rapidly becoming a community solely for the rich (or in technical terms, only for the upper quintile of income earners). As long as the city keeps new density approvals contingent on housing supply that is affordable to average wage earners, these Cambridge parcels will become, in effect, a permanent public trust – a fitting public policy in the Commonwealth of Massachusetts.

As you can perhaps understand, this math becomes more and more important as land prices climb. In places like Cambridge, land prices can be higher than the ones in this example, making the need for this approach that much greater.

There are two more important points. First, since the Cambridge ordinance is structured to insist that units be affordable forever, land Rent for subject parcels is forevermore tied to local wage rates. As long as the policy holds, the ultimate cost of land will be 30 percent of prevailing wages. If a substantial percentage of the city is eventually redeveloped in this way, the city's land base will be protected from excessive Rent in perpetuity.

Second, regulating Rent in this way means that the local economy will be more and more tied to the productive value of its local labour pool and active capital (i.e., capital of the entrepreneurial class) without the cash value of those activities being absorbed as Rent. This point makes it clear that pegging land Rents to wages has positive knock-on effects on the local economy as well. In the end, this is the same crucial point that Henry George made so long ago. George was not interested in land per se but in how to direct what was clearly the economic deadweight loss of land Rent to the people who actually created the land's value: the entrepreneurs and wage earners who worked collectively to build up the city.

The Cambridge AHO requirement that 100 percent of new units to be affordable has the net effect of making development land available to nonmarket-housing providers at a price that ensures them a profit. It is not a taxpayer subsidy or an extraction. The AHO model accomplishes this magic by granting new density only if the project produces affordable housing for average wage earners. This restriction prevents the land-price inflation that would otherwise accompany density increases offered without obligation to anyone but the gods of the market.

Finally, this laudatory description of the Cambridge model of land-value capture is not meant to discount using the same AHO process at the district scale or even the block scale. Instead, it is meant to clarify the value of an approach that has the potential to mitigate the land Rent inflation occurring city-wide. Such approaches have an inherently greater chance of influencing city land markets than do policies applied to a smaller planning area.

WHY IS CAMBRIDGE THE EXCEPTION NOT THE RULE?

With its AHO, Cambridge is basically asserting that the unfettered market is no longer capable of supplying affordable housing without being required to do so by rules that insist on this outcome. Many intelligent voices disagree. Proponents of adding density without insisting on affordability claim that land and unit prices will drop as cities add supply, invoking the so-called laws of supply and demand. They insist that this approach is the way to lower prices and that restrictive zoning, which restricts supply, is the problem – an argument made possible by the fact that neoclassical mainstream economists, who dominate academic, public, and corporate circles, do not distinguish between the building and the land that it sits on. Remember that Adam Smith was the first to identify the three factors of production – land, labour, and capital – with land, by its nature, being a necessary but noncontributing factor in the creation of new wealth. In contrast, since the late 1800s, more modern neoclassical mainstream economists have conflated land with capital, narrowing down the factors of production to only two: labour and capital. Although this may not seem important, it is. This difference in their foundational premise leads the neoclassical economists and their real estate experts to exclaim that supply should meet demand and that exorbitant prices can mean only that some exogenous factor is to blame.

Currently, this blame is most often directed at city officials, who presumably legislate under pressure from the NIMBY hordes who are restricting supply – a vastly exaggerated claim in my experience.[6]

To cite the most widely known example, American economists Edward Glaeser and Joseph Gyourko seem to claim that by opening up the zoning floodgates to new supply, the price of urban land could become so cheap that it might not cost anything at all: "Our alternative view is that ... housing is expensive because of artificial limits on construction created by the regulation of new housing. It argues that there is plenty of land in high-cost areas, and in principle new construction might be able to push the cost of houses down to physical construction costs" (Glaeser and Gyourko 2003, 23).

Astonishingly, despite all the real-world evidence to the contrary, Glaeser and Gyourko (2003) offer a theory that urban land price might be zero if controls on land development are removed – and they are considered credible! Why? Because they speak for mainstream economists who accept as valid the assumptions that urban development land is potentially unlimited (if only the NIMBY hordes would finally expire) and that there are really only two factors of production, capital and labour (as if the earth itself did not exist). Moreover, they deny that urban land is a natural monopoly (and as such that it is fundamentally different from moveable or exchangeable capital and labour), and they deny that urban land is capable of absorbing, up to the very last nickel, all of the value created by a city's entrepreneurs and wage earners, making this value a deadweight loss to the local economy. Taking these assumptions and denials as fact results in the belief that open and unrestricted competition between landowners can overcome urban land's natural monopoly and drive down prices. Heterodox economists Cameron Murray and Tim Helm beg to differ: "Granting extra use rights might change land use incentives and the price of housing, but cannot create incentive to compete down land rents. Belief that it can rests on the illusion that dispersion vis-à-vis concentration in ownership of a fixed factor of production affects competitive pressures as it does in product markets with free entry" (Murray and Helm 2022, 12).

Well put.

This author is grateful not to have been trained in neoclassical economics or the various renegade strands of heterodox economic theory. My only claim to methodological facility is as an empiricist; I know it when I see it. And what I observe in the actual world renders absurd Glaeser and Gyourko's (2003) assertion that urban land might settle to zero if restrictions were removed.

I close this chapter with one relevant (and disturbing) empirical example that disproves this theory. Since the 1960s, when Vancouver was already built out, with no undesignated occupied lots, it has more than tripled its number of housing units through infill development. I am not aware of any other centre city in North America that has come close to this benchmark. Housing production in Vancouver has exceeded household formation in every intervening decade. If anywhere was going to show the affordability benefits of adding housing supply, it would have been Vancouver. Yet it has the third highest housing prices in the world, when measured against average incomes (Demographia 2021). That is quite the opposite of what Glaeser and Gyourko (2003) hypothesize. Indeed, the real-world evidence proves that, particularly in the jobs-rich coastal cities where Rent levels are inflating rapidly, increases in allowable density lead to increases in land price – or land Rent – with most of the Rent ending up in the pockets of the land speculators.

Conclusion

It is worth reminding citizens and policy makers of the massive size of the capital flows coursing through the urban lands of the world's major cities. Absent a deep appreciation for the amount of these flows, it is difficult to grasp their relevance.

To take the US example, which is analogous to examples from other corners of the globe, the value of all urban land in every US metropolitan area is in the range of US$30 trillion to US$35 trillion.[1] To give the reader some sense of scale, the annual GDP of the United States is around US$20 trillion (US Bureau of Economic Analysis 2020). Since 2010, the value of America's urban land has roughly doubled (Federal Reserve Economic Data 2022b), increasing in value by US$15 trillion (Manhertz 2020). Yearly increases in American GDP have been in the range of US$1 trillion, meaning that the annual increase in urban land value has substantially exceeded the total annual GDP growth. Of this annual increase of US$1.5 trillion in urban land value, over 80 percent is attributable to the increase in the value of existing housing (ibid.). The annual increases in the value of these homes can be safely ascribed to the increase in urban land value since buildings (according to tax codes) depreciate in value every year, much like cars.

The estimate of US$30 trillion for all metropolitan lands in the United States is likely low given that on Manhattan Island, which has an area of just 23 square miles, the value of only the privately owned land is approximately US$2 trillion (Barr, Smith, and Kulkarni 2018). The value of Manhattan's private lands has increased by 3,000 percent since 1995 (or when adjusted for inflation, by 2,000 percent). The crash that caused the Great Recession of 2008 barely slowed this increase. Although Manhattan is certainly an extreme example, it is not uncharacteristic. Urban and suburban land in the metropolitan areas of America's so-called superstar cities – New York, Los Angeles, San Francisco, Washington, DC, and Chicago – are burdened with land prices per acre that average in the many millions (Florida 2017). This trend is not unique to the United States. All of the English-speaking nations are experiencing similar gains in urban land-asset value, now in the range of 40 to 60 percent of the total national value of nonfinancial assets (Goodhart et al. 2022).

This value increase for urban land does not add one bit to the nation's production of goods and services. In other words, it is not part of the real economy but simply, and frighteningly, a measure of the annual increase in land Rent. It is money that passively fills the pockets of urban landowners and speculators. All of this wealth that is sucked out of the capital-creating collaboration between city wage earners and entrepreneurs is drawn from the real economy.

A scheme to capture only the annual increase in the value of already developed US urban lands would generate over US$900 billion annually, or enough to build between 4 million and 8 million homes each year. This total is actually a large underestimate because the monthly payments supplied by residents of these new units, pegged to 30 percent of average incomes, would amortize the cost of double or triple this number – up to 24 million homes. These massive numbers give us a sense of just how much money is passing through various hands at the municipal level, both in the United States and around the world, and an indication of how much this flow is increasing social and economic inequality. These gains are going largely to real estate investors and to those individuals lucky enough to have bought a home twenty years ago, all of whom are now getting richer through passively acquired gains. If planning and urban development controls were adjusted to capture even a portion of this land value gain, we could strategically address, and substantially alleviate, the racial, economic, intergenerational, epidemiological, and geographic inequities outlined in Chapters 1 and 2 – and the only real losers would be the land speculators.

WIELDING POLICY TOOLS TO INCREASE WELL-BEING AND SOCIAL JUSTICE

Policy solutions already exist that could help to reverse the current harmful trends toward ever-greater geographic inequality that are fuelled by ever-higher land Rent. This is no small thing. Chapters 1 and 2 provided facts that illuminate the connection between geographic inequality and communicable disease, racial injustice, and economic inequality. Accepting this correlation, it is also clear that policies are available to redress these serious dangers. Furthermore, development policies that limit land Rents have passed legal barriers in capitalist liberal democracies worldwide. Policy makers are free to use taxing and planning policies to reverse inequitable and dangerous land-price trends – that is, to reverse the explosion of land Rent. In fact, these policies are already being used in many parts of the world.

However, the crucial issue of the destructive consequence of land Rent is rarely given voice in these policy debates. If it is clear that public bodies must favour the health, safety, and welfare of citizens when in conflict with maximizing land Rents, it follows that actions to reduce or at least to stabilize land Rents should be obligatory. The easiest way to slow or to stop the ever-accelerating rise in urban land Rents is to use zoning and development tools. The strategies outlined in previous chapters *do* slow or reverse the rise in urban land Rents while also increasing the stock of nonmarket housing. It will take time, but with a more aggressive policy, municipal jurisdictions can approach Vienna levels of permanently affordable housing available to nearly every income class at no cost to the taxpayer. The funding would all come from land Rent.

A FINAL NOTE

For four decades, urbanists, including this author, have lobbied hard for walkable, mixed-use, mixed-income, colour-blind, medium-density developments. We have had much success in this combined effort. Although certainly not yet the norm in our urban landscapes, the goals of this movement have been largely incorporated into the planning ambitions of most metropolitan municipalities.

But the hard truth is that our efforts have been ineffective. During these four decades, our communities have become ever more segregated by economic class, and our goal – an affordable home in a suitable neighbourhood where one can raise a family or simply live without stress – has slipped further and further away. Now, up to half of our fellow citizens are experiences housing stress and blocked access to appropriate housing.

Into this uncomfortable reality burst the new threat of a global pandemic. In 2020, the COVID-19 pandemic underlined a problem too long ignored: how we organize our metropolitan landscapes is killing people.

Why is that so? Is there evil intent behind our planning and development decisions? I like to think not. It's not that cities are *trying* to build social and health dysfunctions into their planning decisions. It is rather that they have, for far too long, ignored the real problem: land Rent. All of our cities' best efforts have directed gains only to land speculators and to upper-middle-class families lucky enough to own a plot of land.

Unequal access to land was softened and disguised for three decades after the Second World War. But in recent decades, particularly the past two, the damage inflicted by out of control land price has been unconscionable, most notably in jobs-rich winner cities. As Henry George correctly pointed out 130 years ago, progress, far from being an unreserved good thing, actually *produces* poverty. And the monopoly of land Rent is perhaps *the* main driver. When a city makes progress by adding jobs and skilled labour, nearly all of this creative energy gets inexorably vacuumed into land price – up to and beyond the point where moderate-level wage earners live a precarious existence, such that one life tragedy could put them on the street and leave them in poverty.

This urbanist has reluctantly concluded that there is no way for the free market to overcome this pathology, no matter how much new density is approved. Adding density largely enriches the land speculator and adds fuel to the fires of unbridled land Rent. Landowners gain, but renters do not.

Taming land Rent can be accomplished, as Vienna discovered so long ago, by insisting that land Rent gains be streamed to the commonwealth, not just to the land speculator. Doing so creates security for wage earners (or labour) and opportunity for entrepreneurs (or capital).

What we have forgotten, the thing that George tried valiantly to demonstrate during his short life, is that labour and capital are not opposed. Their common enemy is land Rent.

This closing polemic may seem harsh, but the solutions are surprisingly simple (at least to my mind). Through intelligent use of the no-cost tools of zoning and development controls, both of which are already constitutionally approved, we could stop land Rent inflation and even reverse it.

It's almost too boring a fact to be true, but it is. The rules and regulations of current planning practice at the local level are the Archimedes' lever that we need. One hopes that we can come to understand this reality and then gather the political will to use this lever effectively. Our kids and grandkids are depending on us.

Notes

Preface

1 Although it is true that land-use decisions in the United Kingdom are managed at the national level, and so in this way differ from those in the United States, Canada, New Zealand, and Australia, urban land in the United Kingdom is largely privately owned, with the protection of ownership benefits dating back to the British Enclosure Movement and being long rooted in British common law. In later chapters, these similarities and differences are further explored.

2 If housing precarity had been more substantially mitigated by US pandemic policy, "estimated counterfactuals show that policies that limit evictions could have reduced COVID-19 infections by 14.2% and deaths by 40.7%" (Jowers et al. 2021, 1).

Introduction

1 In 2006, the value of urban land in the United States was estimated at more than US$25 trillion (Albouy, Ehrlich, and Shin 2018, 461; Larson 2015, 4).

2 In this volume, figures are always provided in inflation-adjusted terms.

3 Estimates are based on the increase in average home prices. Home prices are typically based on the value of the structure (or improvements) and on the value of the land. In all the countries mentioned, the land value has increased much faster than building values over this period, with building values often falling or staying the same in many cases. Tax rules acknowledge that buildings depreciate in value yearly. That is not true of land value.

4 The share of the total value attributable to land versus buildings in the United Kingdom has grown from less than 10 percent of the total parcel value before 1930

to over 70 percent now (Christophers 2018). In Vancouver, home of this author, the land-value share approaches an average of 90 percent of the total value (MountainMath Software and Analytics 2021a).

5 For an accessible and riveting look at how housing is now an asset class, see film director Fredrik Gertten's documentary *PUSH* (2019).

6 Much of the content of this volume parallels the emerging work on the issue of general asset-price inflation, a phenomenon now impacting most global economies. A notable new book on this topic is *The Asset Economy: Property Ownership and the New Logic of Inequality* (Adkins, Cooper, and Konings 2020). What distinguishes the present volume from that one and others of its kind is a focus on urban land as the crucial impediment to improved health outcomes and lower levels of economic inequality.

7 The explosive growth of real estate investment trusts (REITs) is evidence of this practice ("REIT Industry Timeline" n.d.).

8 In the United States, thirty-year-old millennial renters are paying, on average, 45 percent of their income on rent at a time when the US Department of Housing and Urban Development (HUD) considers 30 percent to be a maximum sustainable level. This figure compares to the average rent paid by American baby boomers of only 36 percent when they were in their thirties (Sullivan 2018). Statistics are similar or worse in other parts of the English-speaking world.

9 In 2019, the average Vancouver "millennial buyer saving for a 20 [per cent] down payment on an average priced home ($1,050,000) would take 29 years, if saving 15 per cent of their typical pre-tax income each year" (Connolly 2019). At the time of this writing, the number of years required would be substantially more, assuming home prices stop their climb. If prices maintain their climb, the time needed, absent dramatic wage inflation, would be infinity.

10 Whereas white British citizens have accumulated £314,000 of wealth on average, mostly in the value of their homes, Black British citizens hold only £34,000 of wealth on average, indicating a paucity of home equity among this demographic (Kidd 2020).

11 In the United Kingdom, for example, public universities did not charge tuition until 1998. By 2017, tuition was over US$10,000 per year (R. Murphy, Clayton, and Wyness 2017, 7).

12 For more on the urban design consequences of an economy ever more dependent on the service economy, see my previous book *Five Rules for Tomorrow's Cities: Design in an Age of Urban Migration, Demographic Change, and a Disappearing Middle Class* (2020).

13 The net interest rate was near zero till 2022 and 5 percent at the time of this writing. It remains to be seen whether interest rates will trend back near zero again. Economist Paul Krugman (2021) thinks that the greying of the world's people will hold interest rates down for the next thirty years.

14   There is no avoiding the term "neoliberalism," taken from economics. Here, neo-liberalism refers to a philosophy of political economy that favours a reduced role for the state and an increased role for private enterprise as well as a shift from an economy based on wages to one based on assets, or what some call the "democra-tization of finance" (Erturk et al. 2007). It gained political currency in the 1980s when embraced by UK prime minister Margaret Thatcher and by US president Ronald Reagan. It is called neoliberalism because it revives principles of laissez-faire free-market economic thinking from the original liberal period of the eight-eenth century. For the purposes of this volume, neoliberalism and liberalism are largely the same but for a key difference in how they treat the value of land, as discussed in Chapter 2.

15   These trends in inequality are spectacularly similar in the United States, Canada, New Zealand, and Australia, largely spawned by the flow of wealth into the value of urban land. Those owners lucky enough to have held land for a long time (i.e., boomers) and those owners smart enough to have anticipated its climb (i.e., profes-sional investors) have done very well. People without the luck of the boomers or the capital of the smart investors have been left behind. On Australia and New Zealand respectively, see Henwood (2020) and Rashbrooke (2020).

16   The urban land value for all G7 countries is estimated to range from a low of 40 percent to a high of 60 percent (Goodhart et al. 2022). Also, in comparison to previous decades, a larger and larger share of total G7 wages is attributable to the growing share of wage earners who devote their income to managing these assets, with this increase in the wage share that goes to finance being due to the task of managing exploding asset value globally (Christophers 2021).

17   French economist Thomas Piketty (2014) was the first to clearly chart this phenomenon.

18   The "everything bubble" refers to our current global financial circumstances, where national banks intervene to prop up asset values by making money cheaper to borrow if markets start to decline. This intervention, of course, influences the price of land, making it a sounder investment – and thus a more reliable way to attract free capital – than it would be otherwise (Summers 2017).

19   According to a report published by the US Institute for Policy Studies, 43.5 percent of Americans are poor or low-income (Anderson et al. 2018, 9; see also Barber II and Dolan 2018), which means that they are either grindingly poor or just scraping along – unable to buy a home or to acquire other forms of wealth. As a result, 40 percent of Americans cannot come up with US$400 if they need to respond to an emergency (Youn 2019).

20   It is likely that the value of US urban land far exceeds the capital value of American corporations. This is the case because much of the capital value of corporations is tied up in the land that they own – not to mention that many corporations' entire enterprise is the management of urban property.

Chapter 1: Inequality, Disease, and Urban Land

1 In 2019, 43 percent of American millennial homebuyers relied on their parents for the money needed to qualify for mortgages. Previous generations were much more able to finance a home on their own (E. Martin 2019).

2 Parents taking out loans to support their kids' college expenses is laudable, but it begs the question "What about young Americans whose parents don't qualify for these loans?" It suggests yet another roadblock on the path to upward mobility for the financially disadvantaged.

3 "Nearly half of households headed by people ages 18 to 34 are rent-burdened, meaning that more than 30% of their paycheck goes to their landlord" (Nova 2019, citing Freddie Mac 2019).

4 The infection rate for the various COVID-19 variants did increase over time after this study.

5 Blacks were also three times more likely to die of COVID-19 than whites. This is the same discrepancy between the races with respect to the likelihood of Blacks being shot and killed by police (Schwartz and Jahn 2020).

6 This finding suggests the link between COVID-19 outcomes and the urgency of criminal justice reform.

7 The Continental Land Survey, with its impact on the urban and rural landscapes of the United States, is brilliantly described by Andro Linklater in *Measuring America: How an Untamed Wilderness Shaped the United States and Fulfilled the Promise of Democracy* (2002).

8 This land was not entirely free, as there were registration costs and other requirements.

9 *Plessy v. Ferguson*, 163 US 537 (1896).

10 *Jones v. Alfred H. Mayer Co.*, 392 US 409 (1968).

11 For much of this section, I have drawn on the work of historian Richard Rothstein (2017), considered the authoritative contemporary source for this history.

12 *Buchanan v. Warley*, 245 US 60 (1917).

13 The Fair Housing Act was passed with a substantial bipartisan majority, as only sixty-five southern Democrats in the House voted no. It was rushed to the floor of both the House and the Senate two weeks after the assassination of Martin Luther King, with President Lyndon Johnson twisting arms. It gives citizens the power to sue private entities in the case of discrimination. Sadly, the legislation has been ineffective due to a lack of enforcement. Housing advocates estimate that today "there are at least 4 million fair housing violations annually" (National Fair Housing Alliance 2008, 51), most of which remain unresolved. Issued in 2015, Obama's executive order was intended to take enforcement out of the hands of individuals, who are poorly equipped for this role, and to charge municipalities to proactively address the issue instead. If they failed to do so, municipalities would lose the federal funding in various categories that they may have been counting on. The

Obama administration argued that this reliance on municipalities is a simpler and more effective means to ensure compliance with the legislation. Trump disagreed.

14 Although more Black and Brown people were in the ranks of low-wage essential workers and thus more endangered, they were also at least twice as likely to lose their jobs as whites (Luhby 2020).

15 Americans in the top decile of income own 90 percent of all stock. Americans in the top centile captured all of the growth in stock wealth of the previous ten years (Wigglesworth 2020).

16 REITs were granted taxpayer funds to maintain employment. Contention arose around requests to use taxpayer funds, in the words of US politician Alexandria Ocasio-Cortez (2020), "to artificially inflate stock prices, enrich shareholders, or compensate executives with exorbitant pay packages when so many hard-working, ordinary Americans do not know where their next paycheck will come from and in too many cases are ineligible for stimulus checks or unemployment benefits."

17 The Gini coefficient is a measure of inequality that gauges the distribution of income in a culture, where 1 indicates a hypothetical country in which one person owns everything and where 0 indicates a country in which every person owns the same amount. The United States is now the most unequal of the countries in the English-speaking world according to this measure, with the United Kingdom, Australia, and New Zealand being roughly equal. Norway is now the most equal of all developed nations by this measure, with a score of 0.24 (ECD Data. n.d.).

18 This figure is based on an average tax rate of 20 percent and a typical salary of NZ$54,000.

19 On notions of citizenship, including the idea of "old-stock Canadians," see "Stephen Harper Explains" (2015).

Chapter 2: The Economics of Urban Land Value

1 For more on what constitutes a mainstream economist, see heterodox economist Steve Keen's book *The New Economics: A Manifesto* (2022). Keen is often listed among the world's top ten most influential economists, along with Thomas Piketty, Paul Krugman, and Joseph Stiglitz. His core argument is that mainstream economists are stuck adhering to a model of economics that is grounded in a false conception of reality, namely that macroeconomics must be grounded in microeconomics and that microeconomics is fundamentally rational. Adopting this lens, mainstream economists support only the use of linear methodologies to describe how the real-world economy operates. What this approach leads to, in Keen's view, are repeated errors in their conclusions, most notably their failure to anticipate the 2008 global economic collapse. He counters that economics cannot be forced to conform with linear models of description since economics is inherently nonlinear in practice, with attributes more fruitfully examined from the perspective of

complexity or chaos theory. For support, he refers to the revolutionary work of Kyoto Prize winner Edward Lorenz (1972). It was Lorenz who, over fifty years ago, showed how more than two variables may interact in nonlinear ways to produce recurring patterns rather than fixed results. He is best known for the oft-repeated question expressed in the title of his 1972 paper "Predictability: Does the Flap of a Butterfly's Wings in Brazil Set Off a Tornado in Texas?" Keen argues that mainstream economists have ignored the essential complexity of the global economy and that, sadly, all the main bastions in academia are still dominated by mainstream economists.

2 The Reagan-Thatcher revolution is a well-known event in political economy, but for those who want more details, see the article "Revolutionaries" (2013) by American economist Martin Feldstein, who helped to manage it.

3 Real assets are physical assets that have an intrinsic worth due to their substance and properties. Real assets include precious metals, commodities, buildings, land, equipment, and natural resources.

4 Shortly before the time of this writing in 2022, there was an abnormal spike in the costs of building materials caused by pandemic-exacerbated supply chain issues. Lumber prices returned to normal thereafter. For three-year lumber futures, see "Random Length Lumber" (n.d.).

5 The value of land under buildings in Vancouver has increased by 600 percent (MountainMath Software and Analytics 2021a), whereas building values have stayed flat. These unequal value increases are similar in varied places, being as prevalent, for example, in Spokane, Washington, as they are in Los Angeles, California (American Enterprise Institute n.d.).

6 These economists include Nicolaus Tideman, professor of economics, Virginia Polytechnic Institute and State University; William Vickrey, 1992 president, American Economic Association; Mason Gaffney, professor of economics, University of California, Riverside; C. Lowell Harriss, professor emeritus of economics, Columbia University; Jacques Thisse, professor of economics, Center for Operations Research and Econometrics, Université catholique de Louvain, Belgium; Charles Goetz, Joseph M. Hartfield Professor of Law, University of Virginia School of Law; Gene Wunderlich, senior agricultural economist, Economic Research Service, US Department of Agriculture; Daniel R. Fusfeld, professor emeritus of economics, University of Michigan; Carl Kaysen, professor of economics, Massachusetts Institute of Technology; Elizabeth Clayton, professor of economics, University of Missouri at St. Louis; Robert Dorfman, professor emeritus of political economy, Harvard University; Tibor Scitovsky, Emeritus William Eberle Professor of Economics, Stanford University; Richard Goode, Washington, DC; Susan Rose-Ackerman, Eli Professor of Law and Political Economy, Yale Law School; James Tobin, Sterling Professor Emeritus of Economics, Yale University; Richard Musgrave, professor emeritus of political economy, Harvard University;

Franco Modigliani, professor emeritus of economics, Massachusetts Institute of Technology; Warren J. Samuels, professor of economics, Michigan State University; Guy Orcutt, professor emeritus of economics, Yale University; Eugene Smolensky, dean of the School of Public Policy, University of California, Berkeley; Oliver Oldman, Learned Hand Professor of Law, Harvard University; Zvi Griliches, professor of economics, Harvard University; William Baumol, professor of economics, Princeton University; Gustav Ranis, Frank Altschul Professor of International Economics, Yale University; John Helliwell, professor of economics, University of British Columbia; Giulio Pontecorvo, professor of economics and banking, Graduate School of Business, Columbia University; Robert Solow, Institute Professor of Economics, Massachusetts Institute of Technology; and Harvey Levin, Augustus B. Weller Professor of Economics, Hofstra University (Tideman 1990).

7 Perhaps it will be left to Amazon creator Jeff Bezos to finally escape the urban land-value trap by achieving his dream of manufacturing in space (Yilek 2021).

8 Many consider Adam Smith, author of *The Wealth of Nations* (1776), to be the inventor of the economics discipline.

9 That this separation is occurring in both highly regulated and largely unregulated jurisdictions empirically contradicts the widely held position of many housing-policy officials who believe that the housing market would surely provide affordable housing if development restrictions such as zoning were eliminated. Efforts as widely separated as those undertaken by policy leaders in New Zealand ("New Zealand Plans" 2021) and California (Kwok and Lim 2021) attest to the strength of this challengeable commitment.

10 My economist friends will point out that governments and central banks don't actually print $100 bills but instead invent money out of thin air by inserting a line of code somewhere. This line of code puts a very big number on some commercial bank's assets spreadsheet, to be invested as the bank sees fit. Then the central bank puts the same number on its balance sheet, indicating that this amount will be paid back by the bank at some future point. To the lay person, of course, this process appears to differ little from printing money.

11 This analysis depends in part on the *Economist* article "The COVID-19 Pandemic Is Forcing a Rethink in Macroeconomics" (2020), which draws on the paper "Declining Worker Power and American Economic Performance" (2020) by Harvard University scholars Anna Stansbury and Lawrence H. Summers.

12 Krugman (2020) writes, "I hereby propose that the next US president and Congress move to permanently spend an additional 2% of GDP on public investment, broadly defined (infrastructure, for sure, but also things like R&D and child development) – and not pay for it."

13 Transportation, clearly considered by all to be infrastructure, is the other half of a pair with housing. The two are symbiotic. It is odd that they are not yet universally considered to be paired elements of a common infrastructure.

14 There are hundreds of references to the "real estate fundamentals" and hundreds more where the question is raised of why they no longer hold true ("What in the World?" 2019). At the time of writing, there is no consensus among real estate economists as to what is really going on, but most claim that constraints on supply must be the problem. The evidence is to the contrary. This book is one attempt to bring clarity to this problem.

15 If constraints on supply were the cause of high housing prices, Vancouver would have the world's most affordable housing. Since the 1960s, Vancouver, which had been fully built out by then, has nearly tripled the amount of housing units in the city from under 109,000 to over 330,000, all in the form of either "grayfield" or "infill" development. I can find no other North American centre city that has come close to this percentage increase. Yet housing prices in Vancouver are the highest in North America when measured against average wages – which are the lowest of any major Canadian city (Government of Canada 2020).

16 Piketty's book has sold over 10 million copies worldwide. No book on economics has come close since Henry George's *Progress and Poverty*, published in 1879.

17 Although the period from 2008 to 2021 saw interest rates on treasury notes (and other guaranteed-return instruments) below this level, returns on stocks and real estate were higher than 5 percent over the same period.

18 The ten-year averages for GDP growth in the English-speaking world have not been over 5 percent in decades. The post-2009 recovery has been particularly weak, at between 2 and 3 percent per year (Chuck Jones 2020). If Piketty is correct, these figures help to explain why inequality increased after the Great Recession of 2008.

19 This term refers to a three-decade period of economic prosperity in France spanning from 1945 to 1975, following the conclusion of the Second World War. Coined by the French demographer Jean Fourastié in 1979 with the release of his book titled *Les Trente Glorieuses, ou la révolution invisible de 1946 à 1975*, the term draws its inspiration from "Les Trois Glorieuses" ("The Glorious Three"), denoting the three days of revolution that occurred on 27–29 July 1830 in France.

20 Keynesian approaches – named for British economist John Maynard Keynes (1883–1946) – generally signify approaches to managing a nation's economy where the government aggressively intervenes, typically willing to spend itself deep into deficits to keep the economy humming. The 2020 pandemic made even the most ardent neoliberals into instant Keynesians.

21 The "Reagan-Thatcher revolution" is shorthand for the historical moment when both the US and British economies turned away from Keynesian interventionist economic theory and returned to former classical (rebranded as "neoclassical") theories of minimal government intervention in the economy, an approach promoted by Prime Minister Margaret Thatcher's favourite economist, Friedrich Hayek, and by others like him, notably Milton Friedman in the United States. The term "neoclassical economics" is often used interchangeably with "neoliberal economics." Both align in many key respects, particularly on the primacy of the

"free market." Here, the differences are not crucial, except to say that neoclassical economics emerged in the nineteenth century and is grounded in microeconomics, whereas neoliberal economics emerged in the mid-twentieth century and is associated with macroeconomics.

22 The Progressive Era (1896–1917) influenced many aspects of contemporary American political and economic life. Notably, it was during this era that four constitutional amendments were passed: the Sixteenth (on income tax), the Seventeenth (on the direct election of senators), the Eighteenth (on prohibition), and the Nineteenth (on the vote for women). American political economist Henry George, although he passed away earlier, is often given credit for the Sixteenth Amendment, concerning income tax, which was advanced by his son Congressman Henry George Jr. and by his political ally Warren Bailey. Originally, very little of the US income tax applied to ordinary wage earners. It fell almost exclusively on the rich. Not so today.

23 The vast majority of household debt is in the form of real estate mortgages. Homeowners take on this debt, of course, in the hope that their share of urban land will steadily increase in value. The Great Recession of 2008 shook our confidence in this outcome. Household debt varies from country to country, mostly in response to the Great Recession. Households in the United States were most affected by a countrywide housing-value collapse when the bubble burst. Americans had no choice but to deleverage debt as housing values crashed. Debt levels fell from 100 percent of GDP to 75 percent. They are now climbing again. Canada, Australia, and New Zealand, with fewer risky loans, saw a smaller drop or no drop at all in household debt. Consequently, debt levels there continued to track home-price increases until, in the Canadian case, household debt became, as it is now, much larger than national GDP (Richter 2019).

24 Sometimes, the owner and the user are the same person, and GNP calculations include an imputed rent to acknowledge this reality.

25 Economist Friedrich Hayek, in his famous and polemical book *The Road to Serfdom* (1944), came out in opposition to Keynesians prior to the Second World War and picked up adherents among the investor class as advanced economies faltered in the 1970s. He claimed that laissez-faire capitalism was the only guarantee of personal liberty, framing his argument in a way that appealed to political conservatives.

26 Before the Great Depression began in 1929, it was preceded by a real estate correction in 1926 (Nicholas and Scherbina 2013). The Long Depression was triggered in 1873 by the collapse of a speculative market in land around new railways (J. Lee 2008). This bust in land prices stimulated Henry George to understand the damage done to both labour and capital by uncontrolled speculation on urban land. Mason Gaffney (2009), a Henry George scholar, explains how land price drives recurring recessions: "Bank credit swells and shrinks in synch with the land cycle. The two interact in a positive feedback process: swelling bank credit raises land prices;

buyers need more credit to purchase land; the appreciated land than serves as collateral for more bank loans, and so on" Gaffney well explicated his main thesis during his life, that land prices will climb and climb until the paper value of land brings down the real economy. Real estate crashes wipe out the equity that banks and individuals depend on to stay solvent. Because crashes increase foreclosures and damage bank solvency, they freeze up capital markets, leading first to business failures and associated consumer retrenchments and then to recessions like the Great Recession of 2008. That is why many notable contemporary economists blame urban land speculation for business failures and unemployment, a theme that echoes the diagnosis of George.

Chapter 3: Henry George and His Relevance Today

1 Peter Jones (1987, 245) writes, "Henry George, the American social reformer and Single Tax advocate, made six visits to Britain in the last quarter of the 19th century, a period crucial in British labor politics. George became locked in contest for the minds and hearts of British working men and women, as well as all classes, with the advocates of Christian and moderate socialism and with Karl Marx and Frederick Engels, the chief advocates of State socialism [a.k.a. Communism] through political revolution. Though it was Marx's adopted country, George won out for a time, and it was his program for competitive capitalism, with socialization limited to industries unsuited for market discipline, which influenced development of a mixed economy."

2 Not just these two institutions but also individuals of a similar orientation sought to refute George, including Ezra Cornell, the owner of both Western Union and the Associated Press as well as the founder of Cornell University; John D. Rockefeller, who helped to fund the University of Chicago and installed his allies in its economics department, now known as the Chicago School; and J.P. Morgan, an investment banker and early funder of Columbia University. Other railroad magnates who opposed George's ideas invested similarly in economics departments of John Hopkins and Stanford University (Gaffney 1992).

3 Although putting Hayek into such a broad grouping as neoclassical is subject to debate, I think that the debate has been settled.

4 According to legend, at one of her first Cabinet meetings, UK Prime Minister Margaret Thatcher slammed Hayek's *The Road to Serfdom* (1944) down on the table with a thud, telling the startled group, in no uncertain terms, "This is our bible."

5 Pondering this sad history helps us to understand why Henry George, counterintuitively, is revered by many North American YIMBY ("yes in my backyard") advocates for the removal of all government controls on city development. This approach aligns with an ideology that has full faith in capitalism's capacity to solve problems if unfettered. George's critique of capitalism was, as Hudson (2004) points out, much more radical than that.

6 It deserves more attention than can be afforded in this text, but the idea of a

"commonwealth," as a concept integral to the Commonwealth of Massachusetts and the Commonwealth of Australia, is a grounding premise of the rights and responsibilities of representative governments around the English-speaking world, and as such predates any association with the dreaded word "communism."

Chapter 4: Land Rent, Urban Sprawl, and Transport

1   This math also applies to monthly rents, as high ratios of home price to income generally correlate with high area monthly rents as well.

2   The study states, "How have house prices evolved in the long-run? This paper presents annual house price indices for 14 advanced economies since 1870. Based on extensive data collection, we show that real house prices stayed constant from the 19th to the mid-20th century, but rose strongly during the second half of the 20th century. Land prices, not replacement costs, are the key to understanding the trajectory of house prices. Rising land prices explain about 80 percent of the global house price boom that has taken place since World War II. Higher land values have pushed up wealth-to-income ratios in recent decades" (Knoll, Schularick, and Steger 2014, Abstract).

3   This analysis is a distillation of a longer and more mathematical analysis contained in George Miller's *On Fairness and Efficiency: The Privatisation of the Public Income during the Past Millennium* (2000). His main point is that all of our current economy is always verging on recession because land prices are always pushing the economy toward instability, with entrepreneurs barely eking out a profit (after paying the rent) no matter how much they sell.

4   Sadly, the evidence suggests that increasing allowable density, as many public officials propose, in order to increase affordability can have the opposite effect. One study drew much attention for providing strong evidence of this counterintuitive consequence of increasing apparent housing supply in an effort to meet demand and thus lower prices. Instead, doing so raised the price of a house per square foot (Florida 2019).

5   Surviving a nuclear first strike with at least part of the metropolitan area still functioning was a horrifying event to ponder, but it did give impetus for military planners to join with others who favoured a lower-density city that was more spread out.

6   Wilson, who served under President Dwight D. Eisenhower, was a former CEO of General Motors. Stated publicly in confirmation hearings before the Senate Armed Services Committee in response to Senator Robert Hendrickson's question about conflicts of interest, the full quotation is famous: "For years I thought that what was good for our country was good for General Motors, and vice versa. The difference did not exist. Our company is too big. It goes with the welfare of the country. Our contribution to the nation is considerable" (quoted in Safire 2008, 803).

7 The story involves two alternative futures for the main character (played by Jimmy Stewart), one dystopian, where everyone lives in tenements and appears to spend their lives drinking and dancing in jazz clubs, and one utopian, where recent immigrants live in new five-room ranch houses on large lots arranged on cul-de-sacs – with no apparent desire for jazz clubs (Nero 2019).

8 Cars cost slightly more than three times as much now, in inflation-adjusted dollars, as they did in 1953 (Official Data Foundation n.d.).

9 Redlining was the practice of automatically disqualifying any home mortgage within certain parts of the city in favour of newly developing suburban areas. These redlined areas, formerly served by streetcars, were invariably medium-density districts surrounding the centre city. One result of their comparatively lower density was that their housing stock, much of which had been owner-occupied, was bought up at low prices by professional landlords, many of whom let properties decline into slum status – creating prime areas for later slum clearance (Jan 2018).

Chapter 5: Attempts to Provide Affordable Housing

1 The Fifth Amendment reads, "No person shall be held to answer for a capital, or otherwise infamous crime, unless on a presentment or indictment of a Grand Jury, except in cases arising in the land or naval forces, or in the Militia, when in actual service in time of War or public danger; nor shall any person be subject for the same offence to be twice put in jeopardy of life or limb; nor shall be compelled in any criminal case to be a witness against himself, nor be deprived of life, liberty, or property, without due process of law; nor shall private property be taken for public use, without just compensation."

2 The Radburn plan created what is known as the front-door/back-door problem. At Radburn, the architectural language and floor plans of homes placed the formal front side of the home toward the green spaces. This configuration looked fine but meant that visitors, who typically arrived by car at the back of the house, would enter through the mud room and kitchen. Not a satisfactory way to greet your minister.

3 The failure of this project remains controversial. Architects often blame management for its failure, whereas urbanists blame urban design. It is probably fair to blame both, particularly since other city-managed low-income housing projects also had problems, although none failed as spectacularly as Pruitt–Igoe. The more successful projects were those where buildings were more ground-oriented and better integrated into the surrounding streets.

4 It should be noted that in the late 1970s over half of all UK citizens lived in council housing. Margaret Thatcher's government radically increased the Right to Buy program, which allowed residents to buy their flat at below market rate, moving tens of thousands of units out of the public sector. In time, most of these units ended up in the hands of commercial landlords (Beckett 2015).

5 HOPE VI projects were part of a federally funded initiative to turn over public-housing projects to private-sector companies, which would then tear down or alter existing buildings and rebuild the site as a mixed-income privately owned and managed housing complex. Typically, ambitions would include integrating the new project into the fabric of the city in an attempt to blur the previous distinction between the projects and the surrounding city. The longer history of HOPE VI includes seminal work in Boston, where the 1950s-era Columbia Point Housing Project (now named Harbor Point), well located near the water but isolated from the city, was sold in 1984 to the development company Corcoran, Mullins, Jennison via an open competition. In its place, the company built Harbor Point Apartments, a mixed-income community where many, but by no means all, former Columbia Point residents were eventually rehoused. The privatization of Columbia Point became the model for later HOPE VI federal legislation, which passed the US Congress in 1992 ("Boston War Zone" 1991).

6 Section 8 vouchers are intended to allow the poor to rent homes anywhere and thus to escape the pathologies of disadvantaged neighbourhoods (colloquially called ghettos). Critics show that such an escape is rare because rent subsidies enable people to rent only in the same low-income areas that they are supposed to escape (Semuels 2015).

7 Later made into a feature length movie, Michael Lewis's *The Big Short: Inside the Doomsday Machine* (2011) illustrates, among other things, the degree of complicity on the part of ratings agencies such as Moody's. Like other rating agencies, Moody's ignored the risk of mortgage-backed securities, which would fail if the housing market began to slide. And slide it did. Wall Street banks failed, and global finance froze, at a huge eventual cost to taxpayers. Only a few "short sellers" saw the crash coming and bet against these securities by taking out insurance on securities that they didn't even own. When these securities failed, they made billions. More recently, American financier Carl Icahn made a similar killing when he shorted securities backing shopping malls that failed during the COVID-19 pandemic (K. Kelly 2020).

8 This figure is now US$25 billion, down from US$60 billion in 2017, as a result of the Tax Cuts and Jobs Act of 2017. For more information, see "An Economic Analysis of the Mortgage Interest Deduction," Congressional Research Service, June 25, 2020, https://sgp.fas.org/crs/misc/R46429.pdf. In the context of that legislation, it is hard to celebrate this reduction since it merely helped to pay for a small portion of the loss in taxes due to the passage of tax cuts for rich Americans in the same bill. The elimination of the mortgage interest-rate deduction applied only to homes over US$500,000 in value, which hit coastal cities with high housing costs the hardest.

9 Los Angeles is the exception to the rule. Figures for Vancouver are skewed by inclusion of a substantial green zone within the boundaries of an otherwise urbanized area (Demographia 2000).

10 George's ideas had an impact on the thinking of Winston Churchill, who was president of the Board of Trade in the first decade of the twentieth century and a principal author of the People's Budget, a tax proposal tabled by the Liberal government.

11 This Information was gleaned from the publicly accessible real estate website Rightmove at https://www.rightmove.co.uk.

12 Elizabeth Truss, the shortest-serving British prime minister in history, tried to rejuvenate the concept of the property-owning society as part of her 2022 mini-budget, with disastrous results.

13 Nonprofits are private corporations that have an enduring obligation to pour all income into capital, salaries, and maintenance – with anything beyond these expenditures assigned to future requirements. Their mission is typically a charitable one, at least in the housing sphere.

14 Some interesting but also often grim new towns were built, one of which was Milton Keynes, founded in 1967, which had a population of 256,385 in 2021 ("Milton Keynes" n.d.). You can view its grid design and judge for yourself at https://www.google.ca/maps/@52.0395139,-0.762522,3581m/data=!3m1!1e3?hl= en&entry=ttu.

15 As mentioned in other parts of this text, land in high-priced jurisdictions is not sold for its market price per acre but for the market value of each square foot of interior space that the municipality allows through zoning – space that is sold at a price per buildable square foot. Thus, if zoning allows a ten-storey building on a parcel, the price for a square foot of the land might be ten times more than its value would be if zoning allowed only a one-storey building.

16 For example, in nominal terms, Canadian home prices have increased by 500 percent since 1980, whereas New Zealand prices have risen by 2,000 percent ("Global House Prices" 2017).

17 These figures were drawn from *Realestate.com.au* in 2023.

18 Commonwealth Rent Assistance provides approximately AU$5 billion annually to 1.4 million rental households, or roughly 10 percent of the population (National Shelter 2022).

Chapter 6: The Vienna Model and Its Relevance Today

1 Much of this history is distilled from Veronica R. Reiss's (2017) study.

2 The private rental market remains viable, just not usurious. The rate of return is 3 to 4 percent rather than the 10 percent common in other countries. Apartments rent for about 35 percent of the price for similar Paris apartments. New private apartments still get built and are economically viable because rent-control laws keep land prices low (Tirone 2006).

3 Vancouver has tried hard to subsidize new rental-unit construction in the hopes of lowering price by increasing supply. At this time, the opposite seems to be occurring.

4 The correlation between increased construction and the availability of affordable housing is by no means obvious. For example, new migrants to a city can put pressure on housing stock in excess of new construction, but the new construction of high-priced units can also attract immigrants to a city who are capable of paying the price, fostering a "chicken and egg" conundrum. Vancouver is in the latter category to be sure, along with London, New York, Christchurch, and Sydney.

5 Much of this overview of contemporary practices comes from Wolfgang Förster and William Menking's edited volume *The Vienna Model: Housing for the Twenty-First-Century City* (2016).

6 Henry George had more than one connection to Vienna between the wars, most notably through German reformer Silvio Gesell (1862–1930). In Gesell's main work, *The Natural Economic Order through Free-Land and Free-Money* (1916), Gesell opposed the association of blood with land, which of course was the driving ethos of Nazism. Inspired by George and his single tax on land value, Gesell called upon government to buy land for lease to the highest bidder and to forgo taxation since an approach where the purchase price goes to the state achieves the same end as a yearly tax on Rent. A Georgist land tax was attempted in Hungary, and Albert Einstein (1934), living in Switzerland at the time, considered George brilliant: "Men like Henry George are rare, unfortunately. One cannot imagine a more beautiful combination of intellectual keenness, artistic form, and fervent love of justice."

7 Marla Verlič's paper "Emerging Housing Commons? Vienna's Housing Crises Then and Now" (2015) sets out the terms of the ideological debate that is still raging on this topic.

Chapter 7: Policy Solutions and the Quest for Affordable Housing

1 Beginning in the 1970s, some states, including Oregon, Massachusetts, New Jersey, and California, implemented action to reduce or eliminate exclusionary housing practices. For example, in 1973, the New Jersey Supreme Court forced municipalities to accept inclusionary mandates in their housing-development policies. Nevertheless, the evidence of greater and greater metropolitan segregation by income class outlined in Chapter 1 provides ample reason to suspect that these efforts, if laudable and better than nothing, were not in proportion to the problem.

2 Vicki Been (2005) finds that compared to other units for sale in regions that are not required to add affordable units, there is an increase in unit price. But she also observes that over a short time the market adjusts to this demand by means of a reduction in land price – again, in comparison to land sales for similar projects on land not thus encumbered. So the research shows that inclusive-zoning requirements lower land Rent but do not increase the price of market-rate units.

3 High land taxes favour denser development, where land parcels are small and buildings large. This approach favours older, more traditional parts of cities char-

acterized by small lots and tight urban blocks, and it disincentivizes sprawling large-lot subdivisions.

4 Heterodox economist Michael Hudson (2004) is an ardent supporter of land tax but frequently a critic of Henry George and contemporary Georgists, offended by the fact that George spent the last decade of his life fighting the socialists and insisting that his single-tax strategy was sufficient in and of itself to correct all societal wrongs.

5 The Supreme Court chose to return a 2019 case to lower courts without a finding, letting stand an affirmative decision by that court in the case of *Dartmond Cherk v. Marin County California* (Boerne 2020).

6 Options in real estate are agreements between developers and landowners where the landowner offers the developer an option to purchase land at a fixed price at some future date. If developers are successful in getting bank financing and planning approval, they can exercise the option and buy the land at the previously agreed price. If not, the option is not exercised, and the landowner can sell to another person.

7 The question of whether impact fees raise home prices is still contentious. The common sense answer is "Of course they do! Fees add cost!" To make matters worse, studies give different results based on the methodology and duration of each study. The most exhaustive study, a meta-analysis (Been 2005), shows that market prices increased in the short term but equalized in the long term as the land markets and developers adjusted to new costs. This finding conforms to the hypothesis of this text, namely that land taxes, if clearly known in advance by the market, do not increase house prices but lower land costs.

8 *Village of Euclid v. Ambler Realty Co.*, 272 US 365 (1926). In this case before the Supreme Court, Ambler Realty argued that the designation of a client parcel for housing when the parcel was more valuable as industrial land constituted an uncompensated taking. In the end, the court decided against Ambler, arguing that zoning was both a rational extension of "policing" power and a constitutional measure if used in pursuit of health, safety, and welfare (Simpson 1969). Since that time, all US zoning controls have needed to be grounded in justifications based on health, safety, and welfare. Affordable housing has, for over four decades, been accepted as a valid rationale for decisions. Thus landowners must sometimes accept less than the highest and best-use value for their lands, even to the point of paying development taxes for the privilege of developing their land.

9 The Progressive Era debates on inequality and taxes were long and strident. More than a book would be needed to convey the rancour provoked at the time by a tax that we now take for granted. An income tax, or a national land tax for that matter, could not be imposed until the Sixteenth Amendment was passed in 1909. At first, it was a steeply progressive tax, as it was levied almost entirely on the rich. Not so today.

10 Barbara Ehrlich Kautz (2002) provides an excellent and detailed history here. Because the housing crisis hit California first, it has the deepest pool of policy responses and consequent court challenges.

11 This memorandum from a development group in Queenstown gives us insight into the nature of the resistance to inclusive zoning and explains some of the arguments used against it, notably the argument that the city should provide infrastructure and open up more land for development (i.e., sprawl) if city officials want affordability. Queenstown, prized for its rich and protected landscapes, is naturally resistant to this argument (Thorne 2021).

12 Eliminating single-family zoning has a number of sustainability benefits, notably enhanced walkability, transit efficiency, and the adaptation of existing housing stock to different family types. Unfortunately, increased affordability (on the basis of housing costs per square foot) is not usually one of them. The benefits seem to go largely to the landowner in the form of inflated land Rent.

13 For a good (and not too eye-glazing) overview of how Vancouver compares to other major Canadian planning jurisdictions, see the City of Ottawa's *Zoning Best Practices Review* (2022).

14 Larry Beasley was a co-director of Vancouver's urban planning during this period and oversaw redevelopment of the Yaletown neighbourhood. He is often, and in my view correctly, given credit for inventing Vancouverism. In formal terms, Vancouverism is characterized by the use of high-density residential forms called point towers erected atop a mixed-use podium base. The podium was a crucial departure from the previous "tower in the park" forms that had traditionally been used for high-density development. Podiums spatially contained streets, parks, and courtyards, making them positive spaces in ways that late-twentieth-century urbanists strongly favoured. Beasley's lavishly illustrated book *Vancouverism* (2019) has many lessons for similarly motivated urban designers and is highly recommended.

15 Determining the value per buildable square foot is complicated because it is directly influenced by the land-lift tax discussed here. The higher the land-lift tax, the lower the site's value per buildable square foot. Lowering this price is precisely the point of the land-lift tax.

16 The methodology for calculating land lift is clarified in one of many examples from the City of Vancouver Archives (see City of Vancouver 2012).

17 Developable urban land in many places is not sold by the acre of dirt but by how many square feet of interior space the zoning regulations will allow. Thus land is sold at a certain number of dollars per buildable square foot. A site of 10,000 square feet of dirt that allows the construction of four floors out to the lot lines will have 40,000 buildable square feet.

18 "As of right" is a zoning term that connotes what landowners can do with their land without the need to ask for a zoning variance, or zone change, for the subject parcel.

19 Floor surface ratio (FSR) is used as a zoning-density measure to authorize a certain number of built interior square feet in some fixed proportion to site area. Thus a parcel zoned FSR 1 would allow buildings with as many interior square feet as the site area, a parcel zoned FSR 2 would allow double that number, and so forth.

20 Setbacks from the lot lines were required for such a tall building, so the net density of twenty storeys would be less than if the building took up the entire lot area.

21 On the use of CAC funds and some of the controversy that they generated over the decades, see Cheung (2018).

22 The price ranges widely because some projects are aimed only at high-leverage homebuyers, for whom unit purchases are both a luxury item and a sound investment. Most units sell at prices toward the lower end of this spectrum, generating a residual price per buildable square foot (discounting land-lift capture) of approximately Cdn$600.

23 Again, in this volume, land price refers to the price for land whose residual price is not affected by development taxes, which drive down land prices.

24 For example, CACs for new projects along the route of the Cambie Street SkyTrain were under Cdn$125 per square foot, and the land value per buildable square foot was well over Cdn$500, so the city got a land lift here of only 25 percent, nowhere near the 80 percent that it had accrued on earlier projects (Fleguel 2013).

Chapter 8: City-Wide Zoning Approaches and a Modern Tax on Rent

1 Portland's single-family lots are not strictly limited to one building, as Portland already allows a second dwelling (or accessory unit) in areas with single-family zoning.

2 Typically, this control of land Rent inflation is achieved by transferring ownership of strata-titled units to nonprofit housing corporations or by contracting nonprofits to develop and manage these units. Nonprofit housing providers played a significant role in developing the Portland ordinance.

3 Floor surface ratio (FSR) is a near universal measure of housing density. The math is simple. If you have a parcel of 1,000 square feet with a designation of FSR 1, you can construct a building of 1,000 square feet. If the designation is FSR 2, a building of 2,000 square feet is permitted, and so on. The only tricky part is that a typical three-storey building, for example, which you might imagine to be an FSR 3, might be an FSR 1 because the building covers only one-third of the parcel. In this way, suburban communities, which might be full of three-storey homes, could have an average density of FSR of point four (0.4) or less, because most of the lot is devoted to yard space.

4 Whereas the Cambridge ordinance stipulates that units must be built at prices pegged to average incomes forever, most cities' AHO ordinances allow units to become unrestricted with regard to income in thirty years and, in some cases, even less. One assumes that when the constraint period lapses, these units will quickly become unaffordable, as is now apparent with many thousands of the

affordable-housing units built under the tax credits for affordable-housing projects in the 1980s and '90s, as discussed in Chapter 4.

5 As discussed in Chapter 2, a deadweight loss is anything that gets in the way of production. Land Rent is the most severe example of deadweight loss imaginable.

6 In Vancouver, where this author lives, the City Council that sat from 2018 to 2022 reviewed zone-change proposals in well-attended public hearings for 245 sites. In the end, it approved all of them. If the NIMBY hordes existed in the numbers often suggested, they were remarkably ineffective.

Conclusion

1 Estimates of urban land value range broadly due to incompatible and incomplete data. The best estimate includes 324 designated urban metropolitan areas but excludes nonmetropolitan urban areas (Albouy, Ehrlich, and Shin 2018, 459). For a more accessible summary article using the same data, see Florida (2017). These values are from the years 2005 to 2010 and thus include the Great Recession. Urban land prices have generally increased by over 50 percent on average since then.

References

Adkins, Lisa, Melinda Cooper, and Martijn Konings. 2020. *The Asset Economy: Property Ownership and the New Logic of Inequality*. Cambridge, UK: Polity.

–. 2021. "Class in the 21st Century: Asset Inflation and the New Logic of Inequality." *Economy and Space* 53 (3): 548–72. https://journals.sagepub.com/doi/full/10.1177/0308518X19873673.

Ahlfeldt, Gabriel, and Elisabetta Pietrostefani. 2017. *The Economic Effects of Density: A Synthesis*. Munich: Society for the Promotion of Economic Research – CESifo GmbH. https://www.cesifo.org/en/publications/2017/working-paper/economic-effects-density-synthesis.

Albouy, David, Gabriel Ehrlich, and Minchul Shin. 2018. "Metropolitan Land Values." *Review of Economics and Statistics* 100 (3): 454–66. http://www-personal.umich.edu/~gehrlich/landvalue_index.pdf.

Alini, Erica. 2021. "Here's How Home Prices Compare to Incomes across Canada." *Global News*, April 10. https://globalnews.ca/news/7740756/home-prices-compared-to-income-across-canada/.

American Enterprise Institute. n.d. "Land Price and Land Share Indicators." https://www.aei.org/housing/land-price-indicators/.

Anderson, Sarah. 2022. "Vancouver Rent Had Highest Annual Increase Because of Course It Did." *Urbanized*, March 14. https://dailyhive.com/vancouver/vancouver-rent-increase-year-over-year.

Anderson, Sarah, Marc Bayard, Phyllis Bennis, John Cavanagh, Karen Dolan, Lindsay Koshgarian, Aaron Noffke, et al. 2018. *The Souls of Poor Folk: Auditing America 50 Years after the Poor People's Campaign Challenged Racism, Poverty, the War Economy/Militarism and Our National Morality*. Ed. Saurav Sarkar, Shailly

Gupta Barnes, and Aaron Noffke. Washington, DC: Institute for Policy Studies. https://ips-dc.org/wp-content/uploads/2018/04/PPC-Audit-Full-410835a.pdf.

Ang, Carmen. 2022. "Ranked: These Are 10 of the World's Least Affordable Housing Markets." *Visual Capitalist*, June 7. https://www.visualcapitalist.com/10-least-affordable-housing-markets/.

Arrington, Benjamin. 2012. *Free Homes for Free Men: A Political History of the Homestead Act*. Topeka: Digital Commons University of Kansas.

Australian Bureau of Statistics. 2022. "Wage Price Index, Australia." November 2022. https://www.abs.gov.au/statistics/economy/price-indexes-and-inflation/wage-price-index-australia.

Australian Treasury. 2009. "List of Recommendations." In *Australia's Future Tax System: Final Report*, part 1, *Overview*, 79–106. https://treasury.gov.au/sites/default/files/2019-10/afts_final_report_part_1_consolidated.pdf.

Babcock, Richard, and Fred Bosselman. 1973. *Exclusionary Zoning: Land Use Regulation and Housing in the 1970s*. New York: Praeger.

Bacher, John C. 1993. *Keeping to the Marketplace: The Evolution of Canadian Housing Policy*. Montreal and Kingston: McGill-Queen's University Press.

Baker, Linda. 2005. "Spurring Urban Growth in Vancouver, One Family at a Time." *New York Times*, December 25. https://www.nytimes.com/2005/12/25/realestate/spurring-urban-growth-in-vancouver-one-family-at-a-time.html.

Baker, Marissa G. 2020. "Nonrelocatable Occupations at Increased Risk during Pandemics." *American Journal of Public Health*, July 8. https://ajph.aphapublications.org/doi/full/10.2105/AJPH.2020.305738.

Bangham, George, and Jack Leslie. 2019. "Who Owns All the Pie? The Size and Distribution of Britain's £14.6 Trillion of Wealth." Resolution Foundation, December 5. https://www.resolutionfoundation.org/publications/who-owns-all-the-pie/.

Banner, Stuart. 1999. "Two Properties, One Land: Law and Space in Nineteenth-Century New Zealand." *Law and Social Inquiry* 24 (4): 807–52.

Barber, William J., II, and Karen Dolan. 2018. "Trump's War on the Poor Has Just Begun." *Washington Post*, July 18. https://www.washingtonpost.com/opinions/trumps-war-on-the-poor-has-just-begun/2018/07/18/ae0a1b3c-8abc-11e8-85ae-511bc1146b0b_story.html.

Barker, Kate. 2006. *Barker Review of Land Use Planning: Final Report – Recommendations*. Norwich: Controller of Her Majesty's Stationery Office. https://assets.publishing.service.gov.uk/government/uploads/system/uploads/attachment_data/file/228605/0118404857.pdf.

Barker, Nathaniel. 2020. "The Housing Pandemic: Four Graphs Showing the Link between COVID-19 Deaths and the Housing Crisis." *Inside Housing*, May 29. https://www.insidehousing.co.uk/insight/the-housing-pandemic-four-graphs-showing-the-link-between-covid-19-deaths-and-the-housing-crisis-66562.

Barnaby, Catherine, and Nick Pearce. 2017. *Estimation of Land Value Tax Revenues in London*. Bath: Institute for Policy Research, University of Bath. https://www.

bath.ac.uk/publications/estimation-of-land-value-tax-revenues-in-london/ attachments/land-value-tax-report.pdf.

Barr, Jason, Fred H. Smith, and Sayali J. Kulkarni. 2018. "What's Manhattan Worth? A Land Values Index from 1950 to 2014." *Regional Science and Urban Economics* 70: 1–19.

Barrett, Jonathan. 2012. "Land Taxation: A New Zealand Perspective." *eJournal of Tax Research* 10 (3): 573–88. https://papers.ssrn.com/sol3/papers.cfm?abstract_id= 2841132.

Bauman, John F., Roger Biles, and Kristin M. Szylvian, eds. 2000. *From Tenements to the Taylor Homes: In Search of an Urban Housing Policy in Twentieth-Century America*. State College: Pennsylvania State University Press.

Beasley, Larry. 2019. *Vancouverism*. Vancouver: On Point, an imprint of UBC Press.

Beckett, Andy. 2015. "The Right to Buy: The Housing Crisis That Thatcher Built." *Guardian*, August 26. https://www.theguardian.com/society/2015/aug/26/ right-to-buy-margaret-thatcher-david-cameron-housing-crisis.

Been, Vicki. 2005. "Impact Fees and Housing Affordability." *Cityscape: A Journal of Policy Development and Research* 8 (1): 139–85. https://www.huduser.gov/ periodicals/cityscpe/vol8num1/ch4.pdf.

Bell, Michael E., and John H. Bowman. 2006. *Methods of Valuing Land for Real Property Taxation: An Examination of Practices in States That Require Separate Valuation of Land and Improvements*. Cambridge, MA: Lincoln Institute of Land Policy. https://www.lincolninst.edu/sites/default/files/pubfiles/1120_Bowman_ complete_web.pdf.

Bell, Miriam. 2021. "'Dramatic Separation' between House Prices and Wages as Home Affordability Drops Further." *Stuff*, July 1. https://www.stuff.co.nz/life-style/homed/real-estate/125623163/dramatic-separation-between-house-prices-and-wages-as-home-affordability-drops-further.

Bentley, Daniel. 2017. *The Land Question: Fixing the Dysfunction at the Root of the Housing Crisis*. London: Civitas. http://www.civitas.org.uk/content/files/ thelandquestion.pdf.

Berg, Steve. 2014. "Housing Programs Concentrate Poverty in a Few Metro Locations, Report Finds." *MinnPost*, February 7. https://www.minnpost.com/ politics-policy/2014/02/housing-programs-concentrate-poverty-few-metro-locations-report-finds/.

"Berlin Spends Nearly €1 Billion on Apartments." 2019. *Deutsche Welle (DW)*, September 28. https://www.dw.com/en/berlin-spends-nearly-1-billion-buying-back-apartments/a-50617775.

Bertolet, Dan. 2016. "Why Vancouver Trounces the Rest of Cascadia in Allowing ADUs." Sightline Institute, February 17. https://www.sightline.org/2016/02/17/ why-vancouver-trounces-the-rest-of-cascadia-in-building-adus/.

Beyer, Scott. 2016. "What Liberals Don't Get about Affordable Housing: Filtering." *Forbes*, February 19. https://www.forbes.com/sites/scottbeyer/2016/02/19/ what-liberals-dont-get-about-affordable-housing-filtering/?sh=2a1ec04c2879.

Bialik, Kristen, and Richard Fry. 2019. "Millennial Life: How Young Adulthood Today Compares with Prior Generations." Pew Research Center, February 14. https://www.pewsocialtrends.org/essay/millennial-life-how-young-adulthood-today-compares-with-prior-generations/.

Billy-Ochieng, Ranella. 2022. "Unleashing Opportunity: The Economic Gains in Narrowing Canada's Racial Wealth Gap." Royal Bank of Canada, January 13. https://thoughtleadership.rbc.com/unleashing-opportunity-the-economic-gains-in-narrowing-canadas-racial-wealth-gap/.

Bladen, Lucy. 2019. "Why Buying Property in the ACT Is Different from Other States and Territories." Allhomes, August 20. https://www.allhomes.com.au/news/how-buying-property-in-the-act-is-different-to-other-states-and-territories-864975/.

Bloom, Nicholas Dagen. 2016. *Affordable Housing in New York: The People, Places, and Policies That Transformed a City.* Princeton, NJ: Princeton University Press.

Borderless Charity. 2017. "Public Housing in the United States: Where It Is Today." *Medium*, December 15. https://medium.com/@TheCharity/public-housing-in-the-united-states-where-it-is-today-761826f6a43.

Boerne, Dean. 2020. "After Supreme Court Denial, What's Next for NIMBYs and Inclusionary Zoning?" *Bisnow*, January 7. https://www.bisnow.com/national/news/affordable-housing/whats-next-for-inclusionary-zoning-102410.

Borrowell Team. 2021. "Canadian Cities with the Highest & Lowest Millennial Home Ownership Rates." Borrowell, August 5. https://borrowell.com/blog/home-ownership-mortgages-canadian-millennials.

"Boston War Zone Becomes Public Housing Dream." 1991. *New York Times*, November 23. https://www.nytimes.com/1991/11/23/us/boston-war-zone-becomes-public-housing-dream.html.

Bradbury, Bruce. 2023. "The Rent Crisis Is Set to Spread: Here's the Case for Doubling Rent Assistance." *The Conversation*, January 10. https://theconversation.com/the-rent-crisis-is-set-to-spread-heres-the-case-for-doubling-rent-assistance-196810.

Brooks, David. 2020. "How Moderates Failed Black America." *New York Times*, June 18. https://www.nytimes.com/2020/06/18/opinion/black-america-education.html?action=click&block=associated_collection_recirc&impression_id=769041678&index=0&pgtype=Article&region=footer.

Brown, James R. 1967. "A Successful Use of Taxation to Promote Land Reform: The Taiwan Experience." In *Proceedings of the Annual Conference on Taxation under the Auspices of the National Tax Association*, vol. 60, 416–27. Washington, DC: National Tax Association.

Bryan, William Jennings. 1897. "Henry George: One of the World's Foremost Thinkers." *New York Times*, October 30. https://timesmachine.nytimes.com/timesmachine/1897/10/30/105956689.pdf.

Bullard, Robert D. 1991. *The Wrong Complexion for Protection: How the Government*

Response to Disaster Endangers African American Communities. New York: New York University Press.

Burnett, Kimberly, Jill Khadduri, and Justin Lindenmayer. 2008. *Research on State and Local Means of Increasing Affordable Housing*. Washington, DC: National Association of Home Builders. https://www.researchgate.net/publication/266017515_Research_on_State_and_Local_Means_of_Increasing_Affordable_Housing.

Canadian Mortgage and Housing Corporation (CMHC). 1992. *Evaluation of the Federal Co-operative Housing Programs*. Ottawa: Canadian Mortgage and Housing Corporation. https://publications.gc.ca/collections/collection_2017/schl-cmhc/nh15/NH15-566-1992-eng.pdf.

Caro, Robert. 1974. *The Power Broker: Robert Moses and the Fall of New York*. New York: Knopf.

Casselman, Ben. 2015. "The Tax Deductions Economists Hate." *FiveThirtyEight*, April 3. https://fivethirtyeight.com/features/the-tax-deductions-economists-hate/.

Center on Budget and Policy Priorities. 2019. "Federal Rental Assistance Fact Sheets." Accessed December 10. https://www.cbpp.org/research/housing/federal-rental-assistance-fact-sheets#US.

Champlain Heights Archive. 2022. "About." https://champlainheights.info/about/.

Cheung, Christopher. 2018. "Was Vision Vancouver 'Addicted' to Selling Rezoning?" *The Tyee*, October 1. https://thetyee.ca/News/2018/10/01/Vision-Vancouver-Rezoning-Addiction/.

"Chiang Kai-shek." n.d. *Wikipedia*. https://en.wikipedia.org/wiki/Chiang_Kai-shek.

Christiansen, Kat, and Rhys Lewis. 2019. "UK Private Rented Sector: 2018." January 18. https://www.ons.gov.uk/economy/inflationandpriceindices/articles/ukprivaterentedsector/2018.

Christophers, Brett. 2018. *The New Enclosure: The Appropriation of Public Land in Neoliberal Britain*. London: Verso.

–. 2021. "Class, Assets and Work in Rentier Capitalism." *Historical Materialism* 29 (2): 3–28. https://brill.com/view/journals/hima/29/2/article-p3_1.xml?alreadyAuthRedirecting.

City of Cambridge. 2020. "Affordable Housing Overlay." Ordinance of June 10. https://www.cambridgema.gov/-/media/Files/CDD/ZoningDevel/Amendments/2020/affordablehousingoverlay2020refiled/zngamend_aho_petition_20200610.pdf.

City of Ottawa. 2022. *Zoning Best Practices Review*. https://engage.ottawa.ca/28126/widgets/119508/documents/79267.

https://www.portland.gov/sites/default/files/2020-09/accessory-dwelling-units_final_signed_031519.pdf.

–. 2020a. "Introduction and Summary of the Residential Infill Project (RIP)

Amendments." https://www.portland.gov/sites/default/files/2020-08/exhibit_a_ rip_findings_adopted1.pdf.

–. 2020b. "Ordinance No. 190093 as Amended." https://www.portland.gov/sites/ default/files/2020-08/ordinance-190093-as-amended_final.pdf.

City of Vancouver. n.d. "Limiting Land Speculation – Development Contribution Expectations Policy." https://vancouver.ca/home-property-development/limiting-speculation-in-advance-of-planning.aspx.

–. 2009. "Brief Explanation of Zoning and Development Permits in Vancouver." https://development.vancouver.ca/documents/GlossaryofTermsBrief ExplanationofZDPermits.pdf.

–. 2012. "Little Mountain: Intro to the Concept." https://vancouver.ca/docs/ planning/little-mtn-open-house-info-board-intro-to-concept.pdf.

–. 2020. *Vancouver: City Social Indicators Profile 2020.* https://vancouver.ca/files/cov/ social-indicators-profile-city-of-vancouver.pdf.

–. 2017. "Housing Characteristics Fact Sheet." https://vancouver.ca/files/cov/ housing-characteristics-fact-sheet.pdf.

–. 2022a. "Community Amenity Contributions." https://vancouver.ca/home-property-development/community-amenity-contributions.aspx.

–. 2022b. "Creating and Protecting Purpose-Built Rental Housing." https:// vancouver.ca/people-programs/creating-new-market-rental-housing.aspx.

Coates, Brendan, and Carmela Chivers. 2019. "Rising Inequality in Australia Isn't about Incomes: It's Almost All about Housing." *The Conversation*, September 19. https://theconversation.com/rising-inequality-in-australia-isnt-about-incomes-its-almost-all-about-housing-119872.

Coffee, Neil, Emma Baker, and Jarrod Lange. 2016. "Density, Sprawl, Growth: How Australian Cities Have Changed in the Last 30 Years." *The Conversation*, September 28. https://theconversation.com/density-sprawl-growth-how-australian-cities-have-changed-in-the-last-30-years-65870.

Cohen, David. 2022. "Could New Zealand's property bubble bring down Jacinda Ardern?" *The Spectator.* https://www.spectator.co.uk/article/new-zealand-s-soaring-house-prices-spell-big-trouble-for-jacinda-ardern.

Cole, Leslie. 2018. *Under Construction: A History of Co-operative Housing in Canada.* Ottawa: Borealis Press.

Collins, Padraig, and Stephen Johnson. 2022. "Sydney Is the Second Most Unaffordable City in the World and Melbourne Is Barely Any Better – As Alarming Data Shows How Many More Years Australians Must Spend Saving for a Deposit." *Daily Mail*, March 16. https://www.dailymail.co.uk/news/article-10621281/Sydney-second-unaffordable-city-world-Melbourne-barely-better. html.

Condon, Patrick M. 2010. *Seven Rules for Sustainable Communities: Design Strategies for the Post-Carbon World.* Washington, DC: Island.

–. 2018. "How Vienna Cracked the Case of Housing Affordability." *The Tyee*, June

6. https://thetyee.ca/Solutions/2018/06/06/Vienna-Housing-Affordability-Case-Cracked/.

–. 2020a. *Five Rules for Tomorrow's Cities: Design in an Age of Urban Migration, Demographic Change, and a Disappearing Middle Class.* Washington, DC: Island.

–. 2020b. "Portland Just Showed Vancouver How to Fix Its Housing Crisis." *The Tyee*, August 28. https://thetyee.ca/Analysis/2020/08/28/Portland-Showed-Vancouver-Fix-Housing-Crisis/.

–. 2021. *Sick City: Disease, Race, Inequality and Urban Land.* 2nd ed. Vancouver: James Taylor Chair, School of Architecture and Landscape Architecture, University of British Columbia. https://uploads-ssl.webflow.com/5efd1c1c4e2740c1bb1bfb69/60001a4f82797d502d088dcf_Sick%20City%202021.pdf.

–. 2023. "When Will Rents Come Down?" *The Tyee*, February 2. https://thetyee.ca/Analysis/2023/02/02/When-Will-Rents-Come-Down/.

Connolly, Joannah. 2019. "Average Metro Vancouver Home Costs Four Times More Than Millennials Can Afford." *Vancouver Is Awesome*, June 13. https://www.vancouverisawesome.com/real-estate-news/home-prices-four-times-more-millennials-afford-metro-vancouver-bc-1944128.

Convery, Stephanie. 2021. "'I Am Panicking': The Vulnerable Renters at Risk as Housing Subsidy Expires." *Guardian*, November 14. https://www.theguardian.com/australia-news/2021/nov/15/i-am-panicking-the-vulnerable-renters-at-risk-as-housing-subsidy-expires.

Corlett, Eva, and Caitlin Cassidy. 2021. "New Zealand Has Adopted a Radical Rezoning Plan to Cut House Prices – Could It Work in Australia?" *Guardian*, December 15. https://www.theguardian.com/world/2021/dec/15/new-zealand-has-adopted-a-radical-rezoning-plan-to-cut-house-prices-could-it-work-in-australia.

Costello, Greg. 2014. "Land Price Dynamics in a Large Australian Urban Housing Market." *International Journal of Housing Markets and Analysis* 7 (1): 42–60.

"The COVID-19 Pandemic Is Forcing a Rethink in Macroeconomics." 2020. *Economist*, July 25. https://www.economist.com/briefing/2020/07/25/the-covid-19-pandemic-is-forcing-a-rethink-in-macroeconomics.

Cox, LaWanda. 1958. "The Promise of Land for the Freedmen." *Mississippi Valley Historical Review* 45 (3): 413–40.

Crain, Caleb. 2019. "State of the Unions." *New Yorker*, August 19. https://www.newyorker.com/magazine/2019/08/26/state-of-the-unions.

Crook, Tony. 2015. "Capturing Development Value through *De Jure* National Taxation: The English Experience." In *Planning Gain: Providing Infrastructure and Affordable Housing*, ed. Tony Crook, John Henneberry, and Christine Whitehead, 37–62. Hoboken, NJ: John Wiley and Sons.

Dadkhah, Kamran. 2009. "The Reagan-Thatcher Revolution: The Age of Hayek and Schumpeter." In *The Evolution of Macroeconomic Theory and Policy*, 213–30. Berlin: Springer.

Daniel, Pete. 1979. "The Metamorphosis of Slavery, 1865–1900." *Journal of American History* 66 (1): 88–99.

Data USA. 2020. "Fitchburg, MA." https://datausa.io/profile/geo/fitchburg-ma.

Daughherty, Greg. 2022. "History of the Cost of Living." *Investopedia*, October 17. https://www.investopedia.com/ask/answers/101314/what-does-current-cost-living-compare-20-years-ago.asp.

Davey, Melissa, and Josh Nicholas. 2022. "Covid Death Rate Three Times Higher among Migrants Than Those Born in Australia." *Guardian*, February 17. https://www.theguardian.com/australia-news/2022/feb/17/covid-death-rate-three-times-higher-among-migrants-than-those-born-in-australia.

Davidson, Neil. 2011. "The American Civil War Considered as a Bourgeois Revolution." *Historical Materialism* 19 (4): 45–91.

Debusmann, Bernd, Jr. 2022. "Why Is Canada's Covid Death Rate So Much Lower Than US?" *BBC News*, February 15. https://www.bbc.com/news/world-us-canada-60380317.

Demographia. 2000. "International Urbanized Areas Ranked: New Population per New Land Area: 1960–1990." July 29. http://www.demographia.com/db-intlua-popratior.htm.

–. 2021. *Demographia World Urban Areas: 17th Annual Edition*. https://docplayer.net/214326440-Demographia-world-urban-areas-17-th-annual-edition.html.

Dewey, John. 1928. *Significant Paragraphs from Henry George's Progress and Poverty*. New York: Robert Schalkenbach Foundation.

Dickens, Charles. 1842. *American Notes*. London: Chapman and Hall.

Douay, Nicolas. 2015. "Vancouverism: Hybridisation and Spread of an Urban Model." *Metropolitics*, June 12. https://metropolitics.org/IMG/pdf/met-douay2-en.pdf.

Dougherty, Connor. 2020. "12 People in a 3-Bedroom House, Then the Virus Entered the Equation." *New York Times*, August 1. https://www.nytimes.com/2020/08/01/business/economy/housing-overcrowding-coronavirus.html.

Douglas, Erin. 2020. "Wage and Salary Growth in Houston among Slowest Lowest in U.S." *Houston Chronicle*, February 6. https://www.houstonchronicle.com/business/bizfeed/article/Wage-and-salary-growth-in-Houston-among-slowest-15035759.php.

Drum, Kevin. 2019. "Did Workers' Wages Skyrocket during the '70s? Not When You Figure in Inflation." *Mother Jones*, December 10. https://www.motherjones.com/kevin-drum/2019/12/did-workers-wages-skyrocket-during-the-70s-not-when-you-figure-in-inflation/.

Dudley, Michael Quinn. 2001. "Sprawl as Strategy: City Planners Face the Bomb." *Journal of Planning Education and Research* 21 (1): 52–63.

Duffin, Erin. 2020. "U.S. Population Share by Generation 2019." *Statista*, July 20. https://www.statista.com/statistics/296974/us-population-share-by-generation/.

Duncan, Greg J., and Richard J. Murnane, eds. 2011. *Whither Opportunity: Rising*

Inequality, Schools, and Children's Life Chances. New York: Russell Sage Foundation.

Editorial Board. 2019. "America's Millennial Baby Bust." *Wall Street Journal*, May 28. https://www.wsj.com/articles/americas-millennial-baby-bust-11559086198.

Edmunds, Susan. 2021. "$37m a Week in Housing Subsidies: Should Govt Ask for More for Its Money?" *Stuff*, January 31. https://www.stuff.co.nz/business/opinion-analysis/300217564/37m-a-week-in-housing-subsidies-should-govt-ask-for-more-for-its-money.

Einstein, Albert. 1934. "Henry George and His Principles." School of Cooperative Individualism. https://www.cooperative-individualism.org/einstein-albert_henry-george-and-his-principles-1934.htm.

Elflein, John. 2022. "Rate of COVID-19 Cases in the Most Impacted Countries Worldwide as of December 22, 2022." *Statista*, December 22. https://www.statista.com/statistics/1174594/covid19-case-rate-select-countries-worldwide/.

Elsinga, Marja. 2005. "Homeownership and Housing Satisfaction." *Journal of Housing and the Built Environment* 20 (4): 401–24.

Erturk, Ismail, Julie Froud, Sukhdev Johal, Adam Leaver, and Karel Williams. 2007. "The Democratization of Finance? Promises, Outcomes and Conditions." *Review of International Political Economy* 14 (4): 553–75.

"Estate Tax in the United States." n.d. *Wikipedia*. https://en.wikipedia.org/wiki/Estate_tax_in_the_United_States.

Evans, Michele K., Lisa Rosenbaum, Debra Malina, Stephen Morrissey, and Eric J. Rubin. 2020. "Diagnosing and Treating Systemic Racism." *New England Journal of Medicine*, July 16. https://www.nejm.org/doi/full/10.1056/NEJMe2021693.

False Creek South Neighbourhood Association. 2016. *The False Creek South Housing Co-operative's Story.* http://www.falsecreeksouth.org/wp-content/uploads/2016/11/False-Creek-South-Housing-Co-ops-Story-FINAL-October-2016.pdf.

Fearn, Hannah. 2014. "If Housing Were Seen as Infrastructure There Would Be a lot More of It." *Guardian*, January 31. https://www.theguardian.com/housing-network/editors-blog/2014/jan/31/affordable-housing-infrastructure-investment.

Feldstein, Martin. 2013. "Revolutionaries." *Deutsche Welle (DW)*, November 4. https://www.dw.com/en/the-reagan-thatcher-revolution/a-16732731.

Fidler, Derek, and Hicham Sabir. 2019. "The Cost of Housing Is Tearing Our Society Apart." World Economic Forum, January 9. https://www.weforum.org/agenda/2019/01/why-housing-appreciation-is-killing-housing/.

Fink, Camille. 2019. "Opinion: End of Single-Family Zoning Won't Solve Minneapolis' Housing Problems." *Planetizen*, October 8. https://www.planetizen.com/news/2019/10/106557-opinion-end-single-family-zoning-won-t-solve-minneapolis-housing-problems.

Fitzgerald, Karl. 2021. "Runaway Land Prices Undermine Housing Utility." *Fifth Estate*, April 20. https://thefifthestate.com.au/columns/spinifex/runaway-land-prices-undermine-housing-utility/.

Fitzpatrick, Luke. 2021. "The Everything Bubble Sees Investors Flock to Safety." *Yahoo! Finance*, July 12. https://finance.yahoo.com/news/everything-bubble-sees-investors-flock-144838732.html.

Flaherty, Seamus. 2020. *Marx, Engels and Modern British Socialism: The Social and Political Thought of H.M. Hyndman*. London: Springer Nature.

Fleguel, Brady. 2013. "Community Amenity Contributions." *Office Space*, 40–41. https://issuu.com/bivmediagroup/docs/office_space_2013_ebook/40.

Florida, Richard. 2013. "How Walkability Shapes Political Activism." *Bloomberg*, July 5. https://www.bloomberg.com/news/articles/2013-07-05/how-walkability-shapes-political-activism.

–. 2017. "The Staggering Value of Urban Land." *Bloomberg*, November 2. https://www.bloomberg.com/news/articles/2017-11-02/america-s-urban-land-is-worth-a-staggering-amount.

–. 2019. "Does Upzoning Boost the Housing Supply and Lower Prices? Maybe Not." *Bloomberg*, January 31. https://www.bloomberg.com/news/articles/2019-01-31/zoning-reform-isn-t-a-silver-bullet-for-u-s-housing.

Fontinelle, Amy. 2019. "American Debt: Mortgage Debt Reaches $8.94 Trillion in 1Q 2018." *Investopedia*, June 25. https://www.investopedia.com/personal-finance/american-debt-mortgage-debt/.

Förster, Wolfgang, and William Menking, eds. 2016. *The Vienna Model: Housing for the Twenty-First-Century City*. Berlin: Jovis.

Fox, Stephen R. 1981. "The Amateur Tradition: People and Politics." In *The American Conservation Movement: John Muir and His Legacy*, 333–57. Madison: University of Wisconsin Press.

Frank, Thomas. 2020. *The People, No: A Brief History of Anti-populism*. New York: Metropolitan Books/Henry Holt and Company.

Federal Reserve Economic Data. 2022a. "All-Transactions House Price Index for Houston–The Woodlands–Sugar Land, TX (MSA)." February 22. https://fred.stlouisfed.org/series/ATNHPIUS26420Q.

–. 2022b. "All-Transactions House Price Index for the United States." February 22. https://fred.stlouisfed.org/series/USSTHPI.

Freddie Mac. 2019. *Profile of Today's Renter & Homeowner*. http://www.freddiemac.com/fmac-resources/research/pdf/Freddie_Mac_Profile_of_Todays_Renter_and_Homeowner.pdf.

Friedman, Milton. 1962. *Capitalism and Freedom*. Chicago: University of Chicago Press.

Fuchs, Hailey. 2020. "Trump Moves to Roll Back Obama Program Addressing Housing Discrimination." *New York Times*, July 23. https://www.nytimes.com/2020/07/23/us/politics/trump-housing-discrimination-suburbs.html.

Furth, Salim. 2020. "Automobiles Seeded the Massive Coronavirus Epidemic in New York City." *Market Urbanism*, April 19. https://marketurbanism.com/2020/04/19/automobiles-seeded-the-massive-coronavirus-epidemic-in-new-york-city/.

Gaffney, Mason. 1994. "Neo-classical Economics as a Stratagem against Henry George." In Mason Gaffney and Fred Harrison, *The Corruption of Economics*, 29–44. London: Shepheard-Walwyn. https://masongaffney.org/publications/K1Neo-classical_Stratagem.CV.pdf.

–. 2009. "Review: The Secret Life of Real Estate." Earthsharing Australia, May 7. https://www.earthsharing.org.au/2009/05/review-the-secret-life-of-real-estate/.

–. 2013. *The Mason Gaffney Reader: Essays on Solving the "Unsolvable."* New York: Henry George Institute. https://cooperative-individualism.org/gaffney-mason_mason-gaffney-reader-2013.pdf.

Gaffney, Mason, and Fred Harrison. 1994. "The Empire Strikes Back." In Mason Gaffney and Fred Harrison, *The Corruption of Economics*, 45–69. London: Shepheard-Walwyn. https://masongaffney.org/publications/K1Neo-classical_Stratagem.CV.pdf.

Galbraith, John Kenneth. 1958. *The Affluent Society*. Boston: Houghton Mifflin.

Garner, Anne. 2015. "Cholera Comes to New York City." *New York Academy of Medicine Library Blog*, February 3. https://nyamcenterforhistory.org/2015/02/03/cholera-comes-to-new-york-city/.

Gavron, Nicky, Steve O'Connell, Andrew Boff, Tom Copley, and Navin Shah. 2016. *Tax Trial: A Land Value Tax for London?* London: London Assembly Planning Committee/Greater London Authority. https://www.london.gov.uk/sites/default/files/final-draft-lvt-report_2.pdf.

George, Henry. 1879. *Progress and Poverty*. Reprint, New York: D. Appleton and Company, 1881. https://archive.org/details/progresspovertyi00georiala/mode/2up.

George, Henry, Jr. 1900. *The Life of Henry George*. New York: Doubleday/McClure Company. https://archive.org/details/lifehenrygeorge01georgoog.

George de Mille, Agnes. n.d. "Who Was Henry George?" Henry George Foundation of America. https://web.archive.org/web/20060212232234/http://www.henrygeorgefoundation.us/who.

George de Mille, Anna. 1948. "Henry George: The Australian Tour." *American Journal of Economics and Sociology* 7 (3): 369–77.

Gertten, Fredrik, dir. 2019. *Push*. WG Film. https://www.wgfilm.com/push.

Gesell, Silvio. 1916. *Die natürliche Wirtschaftsordnung durch Freiland und Freigeld* [The natural economic order through free-land and free-money]. Bern: n.p.

Glaeser, Edward, and Joseph Gyourko. 2003. "The Impact of Building Restrictions on Housing Affordability." *Economic Policy Review* 9 (2): 21–39. https://www.newyorkfed.org/medialibrary/media/research/epr/03v09n2/0306glae.pdf.

"Global House Prices." 2017. *Economist*, March 9. https://www.economist.com/graphic-detail/2017/03/09/global-house-prices.

Goodhart, Charles, Michael Hudson, Michael Kumhof, and Nicolaus Tideman. 2022. "Post-Corona Balanced Budget Fiscal Stimulus: The Case for Shifting Taxes onto Land." *VoxEU*, January 14. https://cepr.org/voxeu/columns/post-corona-balanced-budget-fiscal-stimulus-case-shifting-taxes-land.

Gotham, Kevin Fox. 2000. "Separate and Unequal: The Housing Act of 1968 and the Section 235 Program." *Sociological Forum* 15 (1): 13–37.

Gougeon, Annik, and Oualid Moussouni. 2021. "Residential Real Estate Sales in 2018: The Relationship between House Prices and Incomes." Statistics Canada, October 27. https://www150.statcan.gc.ca/n1/pub/46-28-0001/2021002/article/00003-eng.htm.

Gov.UK. 2020. "Renting Social Housing." February 4. https://www.ethnicity-facts-figures.service.gov.uk/housing/social-housing/renting-from-a-local-authority-or-housing-association-social-housing/latest.

Government of British Columbia. 2014. *Community Amenity Contributions: Balancing Community Planning, Public Benefits and Housing Affordability.* Victoria, BC: Ministry of Community, Sport and Cultural Development. https://www2.gov.bc.ca/assets/gov/british-columbians-our-governments/local-governments/planning-land-use/community_amenity_contributions_guide.pdf.

Government of California. 2021. "The California HOME Act." https://focus.senate.ca.gov/sb9.

Government of South Australia. 2017. *The 30-Year Plan for Greater Adelaide.* Adelaide: Department of Planning, Transport and Infrastructure. https://livingadelaide.sa.gov.au/__data/assets/pdf_file/0003/319809/The_30-Year_Plan_for_Greater_Adelaide.pdf.

"Govt Formally Putting Brakes on State House Sales." 2017. *Radio New Zealand (RNZ),* December 20. https://www.rnz.co.nz/news/political/346609/govt-formally-putting-brakes-on-state-house-sales.

Graeber, David. 2012. "Occupy's Liberation from Liberalism: The Real Meaning of May Day." *Gardian,* May 7. https://www.theguardian.com/commentisfree/cifamerica/2012/may/07/occupy-liberation-from-liberalism.

Granwal, Lynda. 2022. "Average Residential House Price in New Zealand in January 2022, by Region." *Statista,* April 2. https://www.statista.com/statistics/1028580/new-zealand-median-house-prices-by-region/.

Greenaway-McGrevy, Ryan. 2022. "New Zealand's Bipartisan Housing Reforms Offer a Model to Other Countries." Brookings Institution, January 24. https://www.brookings.edu/blog/the-avenue/2022/01/24/new-zealands-bipartisan-housing-reforms-offer-a-model-to-other-countries/.

Gutheil-Knopp-Kirchwald, Gerlinde, and Justin Kadi. 2017. "Housing Policy and Spatial Inequality: Recent Insights from Vienna and Amsterdam." In *Public or Private Goods? Redefining Res Publica,* ed. Bridgette Unger, Daan van der Linde, and Michael Getzner, 175–96. Cheltenham, UK: Edward Elgar.

Gutman, David. 2020. "After Months of Pleading for Social Distancing, Health Officials Support Protests. Seattle Black Lives Matter Warns of Dangers." *Seattle Times,* June 4. https://www.seattletimes.com/seattle-news/health/after-months-of-pleading-for-coronavirus-social-distancing-health-officials-supportive-of-protests-black-lives-matter-calls-them-too-dangerous/.

"Henry Tax Review." n.d. *Wikipedia*. https://en.wikipedia.org/wiki/Henry_Tax_Review#cite_note-4.

Habberman, Maggie. 2017. "Mnuchin's Wife Mocks Oregon Woman over Lifestyle and Wealth." *New York Times*, August 22. https://www.nytimes.com/2017/08/22/us/politics/mnuchin-louise-linton-treasury-instagram.html.

Hardwick, Walter. 1994. "Responding to the 1960s: Designing Adaptable Communities in Vancouver." *Environment and Behavior* 26 (3): 338–62.

Harris, Catherine. 2018. "Housing Analyst Says Soaring Land Prices Auckland's Key Housing Obstacle." *Stuff*, November 17. https://www.stuff.co.nz/business/property/108676571/housing-analyst-says-soaring-land-prices-aucklands-key-housing-obstacle.

Harris, Greg. 2014. "Land Tax Myths." *Tax Alert*, October, 1–2. https://www2.deloitte.com/content/dam/Deloitte/nz/Documents/tax/Tax-alert/2014/nz-en-tax-alert-october-2014.pdf.

Harris, Jeffrey E. 2020a. "The Subways Seeded the Massive Coronavirus Epidemic in New York City." National Bureau of Economics Research, Working Paper No. 27021. http://web.mit.edu/jeffrey/harris/HarrisJE_WP2_COVID19_NYC_24-Apr-2020.pdf.

–. 2020b. "Why the Subways Are a Prime Suspect: Scientific Evidence That NYC Public Transit Spread the Coronavirus." *New York Daily News*, April 19. https://www.nydailynews.com/opinion/ny-oped-why-the-subways-are-a-prime-culprit-20200419-kkqwbd5yx5gk7awngy4d7j4zfa-story.html.

Harris, John. 2016. "The End of Council Housing." *Guardian*, January 4. https://www.theguardian.com/society/2016/jan/04/end-of-council-housing-bill-secure-tenancies-pay-to-stay.

Harvard T.H. Chan School of Public Health. n.d. "Coronavirus and Air Pollution." https://www.hsph.harvard.edu/c-change/subtopics/coronavirus-and-pollution/.

Hawes, Michael. 2010. "The Law of Rent – The Concept." *Ethical Economics*, August 25. https://www.ethicaleconomics.org.uk/2010/08/the-law-of-rent-the-concept/.

Hayek, Friedrich. 1944. *The Road to Serfdom*. Chicago: University of Chicago Press.

Hays, R. Allen. 1995. *The Federal Government and Urban Housing: Ideology and Change in Public Policy*. Albany: State University of New York Press.

Hein, Scot. 2022. *Zoning Must Evolve: You Forgot about Me*. Morrisville, NC: Lulu.

Heisz, Andrew, and Elizabeth Richards. 2019. "Economic Well-Being across Generations of Young Canadians: Are Millennials Better or Worse Off?" Statistics Canada, April 18. https://www150.statcan.gc.ca/n1/pub/11-626-x/11-626-x2019006-eng.htm.

Helm, Tim. 2019. *Stamp Duty to Land Tax: Designing the Transition*. Melbourne: Prosper Australia. https://www.prosper.org.au/wp-content/uploads/2019/07/Designing-the-Transition_Final_Helm.pdf.

Helman, Christopher. 2022. "Housing Market Crash 2022: What to Expect as Interest Rates Rise." *Forbes*, October 16. https://www.forbes.com/sites/

qai/2022/10/16/housing-market-crash-2022-what-to-expect-as-interest-rates-rise/?sh=2a0aab6f120d.

Henry George Foundation of America. 2010. "Winston Churchill & Henry George." *Ethical Economics*, October 25. https://www.ethicaleconomics.org.uk/2010/10/winston-churchill-henry-george/.

"Henry George Theorem." n.d. *Wikipedia*. https://en.wikipedia.org/wiki/Henry_George_theorem.

Henwood, Belinda. 2020. "Income and Wealth Inequality in Australia Was Rising before COVID-19." *Newsroom*, September 2. https://newsroom.unsw.edu.au/news/social-affairs/income-and-wealth-inequality-australia-was-rising-covid-19.

Hepburn, Cameron, Brian O'Callaghan, Nicholas Stern, Joseph Stiglitz, and Dimitri Zenghelis. 2020. "Will COVID-19 Fiscal Recovery Packages Accelerate or Retard Progress on Climate Change?" *Oxford Review of Economic Policy* 36 (suppl. 1): S359–81. https://academic.oup.com/oxrep/article/36/Supplement_1/S359/5832003.

Hobbs, Dylan. 2019. "The Use of Land Value Tax in New Zealand (1891–1991)." PhD diss., Victoria University of Wellington. https://researcharchive.vuw.ac.nz/xmlui/bitstream/handle/10063/9006/thesis_access.pdf?sequence=1.

Holmes, Kristen, and Kevin Bohn. 2020. "Azar Lays Part of Blame for COVID-19 Death Toll on State of Americans' Health." *CNN*, May 17. https://www.cnn.com/2020/05/17/politics/us-health-conditions-coronavirus-alex-azar-cnntv/index.html.

Home for All. n.d. "Housing Overlay Zones (HOZs)." https://homeforallsmc.org/toolkits/housing-overlay-zones/.

"Home Ownership Rate." 2022. *Trading Economics*. https://tradingeconomics.com/country-list/home-ownership-rate.

Horowitz, Evan. 2018. "Go a Few More Miles in Your Career." *Boston Globe*, February 16. https://www.bostonglobe.com/business/2018/02/16/few-more-miles-your-career/kjz1TuspX1i02dLYS1NHjL/story.html.

"House Prices Continue to Go through the Roof." 2021. *Economist*, August 12. https://www.economist.com/graphic-detail/2021/08/12/house-prices-continue-to-go-through-the-roof.

Howard, Ebenezer. 1898. *To-morrow: A Peaceful Path to Real Reform*. Reprint, Cambridge, UK: Cambridge University Press, 2010.

Hudson, Michael. 2004. "Has Georgism Been Hijacked by Special Interests?" *Ground Swell* 17 (1): 1–2, 4–12. https://commonground-usa.net/hudson-michael_has-georgism-been-hijacked-by-special-interests-2004-jan-feb.pdf.

Huebl, Steve. 2019. "Homeownership Rates in Canada Still among Highest Globally." *Canadian Mortgage Trends*, March 4. https://www.canadianmortgage-trends.com/2019/03/homeownership-rates-in-canada-still-among-highest-globally/.

Inclusionary Housing. 2019a. "Commercial Linkage Fees." https://inclusionary-housing.org/designing-a-policy/program-structure/linkage-fee-programs/commercial-linkage-fees/.

–. 2019b. "Linkage Fee Programs." https://inclusionaryhousing.org/designing-a-policy/program-structure/linkage-fee-programs/.

Jackson, Kenneth T. 1985. *Crabgrass Frontier: The Suburbanization of the United States*. New York: Oxford University Press.

Jacobs, Jane. 1961. *The Death and Life of Great American Cities*. New York: Random House.

Jan, Tracy. 2018. "Redlining Was Banned 50 Years Ago. It's Still Hurting Minorities Today." *Washington Post*, March 28. https://www.washingtonpost.com/news/wonk/wp/2018/03/28/redlining-was-banned-50-years-ago-its-still-hurting-minorities-today/.

Jenkins, Simon. 2021. "Covid Has Made Inequality Even Worse. The Only Answer: Squeeze the Super-Rich." *Guardian*, January 26. https://www.theguardian.com/news/commentisfree/2021/jan/26/covid-inequality-worse-squeeze-super-rich.

Johns Hopkins University. 2023. "COVID-19 Dashboard." https://coronavirus.jhu.edu/map.html.

Jones, Chuck. 2020. "Ignore GDP Plunging 33%. Pay Attention to the 9.5% Decline." *Forbes*, July 31. https://www.forbes.com/sites/chuckjones/2020/07/31/ignore-gdp-plunging-33-pay-attention-to-the-95-decline/.

Jones, Colin, and Alan Murie. 2006. *The Right to Buy: Analysis and Evaluation of a Housing Policy*. London: Blackwell.

Jones, Jonathan. 2022. "U.S. Cities with the Highest Home Price-to-Income Ratios in 2021." *Construction Coverage*, April 26. https://constructioncoverage.com/research/cities-with-highest-home-price-to-income-ratios-2021.

Jones, Peter. 1987. "Henry George and British Labor Politics." *American Journal of Economics and Sociology* 46 (2): 245–56.

Jowers, Kay, Christopher Timmins, Nrupen Bhavsar, Qihui Hu, and Julia Marshall. 2021. "Housing Precarity & the COVID-19 Pandemic: Impacts of Utility Disconnection and Eviction Moratoria on Infections and Deaths across US Counties." National Bureau of Economic Research, January. https://www.nber.org/papers/w28394.

Kadi, Justin. 2015. "Recommodifying Housing in Formerly 'Red' Vienna?" *Housing, Theory and Society* 32 (3): 247–65.

Karácsonyi, Dávid, Sigurd Dyrting, and Andrew Taylor. 2021. "A Spatial Interpretation of Australia's COVID-Vulnerability." *International Journal of Disaster Risk Reduction* 61: 102299. https://www.sciencedirect.com/science/article/pii/S221242092100265X.

KATU Staff. 2020. "Portland City Council Passes Residential Infill Project." *KATU2*, August 12. https://katu.com/news/local/portland-city-council-passes-residential-infill-project.

Kautz, Barbara Ehrlich. 2002. "In Defense of Inclusionary Zoning: Successfully Creating Affordable Housing." *University of San Francisco Law Review* 36 (4): 971–1032. https://repository.usfca.edu/cgi/viewcontent.cgi?article=1060&context=usflawreview.

Keen, Steve. 2022. *The New Economics: A Manifesto*. Medford, MA: Polity.

Kelly, Jane-Frances. 2013. *Renovating Housing Policy*. Melbourne: Grattan Institute. https://grattan.edu.au/wp-content/uploads/2014/03/800_Renovating_Housing.pdf.

Kelly, Kate. 2020. "'The Big Short 2.0': How Hedge Funds Profited off the Pain of Malls." *New York Times*, August 24. https://www.nytimes.com/2020/08/24/business/mall-short-hedge-funds.html.

Keyser Marston Associates. 2016. *Summary, Context Materials and Recommendations: Affordable Housing Nexus Studies*. Prepared for the City of Albany, California. https://alamedamgr.files.wordpress.com/2018/07/albany-affordable-housing-nexus-study-december-2016.pdf.

Khadduri, Jill, Carissa Climaco, Kimberly Burnett, Laurie Gould, and Louise Elving. 2012. *What Happens to Low-Income Housing Properties at Year 15 and Beyond?* Washington, DC: Office of Policy Development and Research, US Department of Housing and Urban Development. https://permanent.fdlp.gov/gpo52524/what_happens_lihtc.pdf.

Kidd, Carla. 2019. "Total Wealth in Great Britain: April 2016 to March 2018." Office for National Statistics, December 5. https://www.ons.gov.uk/peoplepopulationandcommunity/personalandhouseholdfinances/incomeandwealth/bulletins/totalwealthingreatbritain/april2016tomarch2018.

–. 2020. "Household Wealth by Ethnicity, Great Britain: April 2016 to March 2018." Office for National Statistics, November 2020. https://www.ons.gov.uk/peoplepopulationandcommunity/personalandhouseholdfinances/incomeandwealth/articles/householdwealthbyethnicitygreatbritain/april2016tomarch2018.

King, Martin Luther. 2003. *A Testament of Hope: The Essential Writings and Speeches*. New York: Harper Collins.

Knoll, Katharina, Moritz Schularick, and Thomas Michael Steger. 2014. *No Price Like Home: Global House Prices, 1870–2012*. Center for Economic Studies and Ifo Institute, Working Paper Series No. 5006. https://papers.ssrn.com/sol3/papers.cfm?abstract_id=2512724.

Kohler, Marion, and Michelle van der Merwe. 2015. "Long-Run Trends in Housing Price Growth." Reserve Bank of Australia, September 17. https://www.rba.gov.au/publications/bulletin/2015/sep/3.html.

Krugman, Paul. 2010. "The New Economic Geography, Now Middle Aged." Paper presented to the Association of American Geographers, April 16. http://www.princeton.edu/~pkrugman/aag.pdf.

–. 2020. "The Case for Permanent Stimulus." *VoxEU*, May 10. https://voxeu.org/article/case-permanent-stimulus.

–. 2021. "Learning to Live with Low Fertility." *New York Times*, May 17. https://www.nytimes.com/2021/05/17/opinion/low-population-growth-economy-inflation.html.

Kumhoff, Michael, Nicolaus Tideman, Michael Hudson, and Charles Goodhart. 2021. *Post-Corona Balanced-Budget Super-Stimulus: The Case for Shifting Taxes onto Land*. Centre for Economic Policy Research, Discussion Paper No. 16652. https://papers.ssrn.com/sol3/papers.cfm?abstract_id=3954888.

Kwok, Iris, and Samantha Lim. 2021. "Gov. Gavin Newsom Signs SB 9, Ending Single-Family Zoning in CA." *Daily Californian*, September 23. https://www.dailycal.org/2021/09/23/gov-gavin-newsom-passes-sb-9-ending-single-family-zoning-in-ca/.

La Grange, Adrienne, Chin-Oh Chang, and Nm Yip. 2005. "Commodification and Urban Development: A Case Study of Taiwan." *Housing Studies* 21 (1): 53–76. https://www.researchgate.net/publication/241196412_Commodification_and_Urban_Development_A_Case_Study_of_Taiwan/figures?lo=1.

Landis, John, Michael Larice, Deva Dawson, and Lan Deng. 2001. *Pay to Play: Residential Development Fees in California Cities and Counties, 1999*. Sacramento: California Department of Housing and Community Development. https://www.novoco.com/sites/default/files/atoms/files/pay2play.pdf.

Larsen, Karin. 2018. "Vancouver's New Duplex Rules Explained." *CBC News*, September 20. https://www.cbc.ca/news/canada/british-columbia/vancouver-s-new-duplex-rules-explained-1.4831741.

Larson, William. 2015. "New Estimates of Value of Land of the United States." US Bureau of Economic Analysis, April 3. https://www.bea.gov/system/files/papers/WP2015-3.pdf.

Le Corbusier. 1967. *The Radiant City: Elements of a Doctrine of Urbanism to Be Used as the Basis of Our Machine-Age Civilization*. Trans. Pamela Knight, Eleanor Levieux, and Derek Coltman. London: Faber.

Lee, Geoffrey. 2008. *The People's Budget: An Edwardian Tragedy*. London: Shepheard-Walwyn.

Lee, Jennifer. 2008. "New York and the Panic of 1873." *New York Times*, October 14. https://cityroom.blogs.nytimes.com/2008/10/14/learning-lessons-from-the-panic-of-1873/.

Lee, Mark. 2021. "How to Build Affordable Rental Housing in Vancouver." Canadian Centre for Policy Alternatives, March 16. https://policyalternatives.ca/publications/reports/how-build-affordable-rental-housing-vancouver.

Leonhardt, David. 2020. "The Black-White Wage Gap Is as Big as It Was in 1950." *New York Times*, June 25. https://www.nytimes.com/2020/06/25/opinion/sunday/race-wage-gap.html.

Lewis, Michael. 2011. *The Big Short: Inside the Doomsday Machine*. New York: Norton.

Linklater, Andro. 2002. *Measuring America: How an Untamed Wilderness Shaped the United States and Fulfilled the Promise of Democracy*. New York: Walker & Company.

Livabl. n.d. "Oakridge x Clémande." https://www.livabl.com/vancouver-bc/oakridge-x-clemande.

Locke, John. 1689. *Two Treatises of Government*. London: Awnsham Churchill. https://archive.org/details/twotreatisesofgo00lock_1/mode/2up.

Longtermtrends. n.d. "Home Price to Income Ratio (US & UK)." https://www.longtermtrends.net/home-price-median-annual-income-ratio/.

Lorenz, Edward. 1972. "Predictability: Does the Flap of a Butterfly's Wings in Brazil Set Off a Tornado in Texas?" Paper presented to the American Association for the Advancement of Science, December 29. https://static.gymportalen.dk/sites/lru.dk/files/lru/132_kap6_lorenz_artikel_the_butterfly_effect.pdf.

Lloyd, Alcynna. 2019. "U.S. Housing Market Value Climbs to $33.3 Trillion in 2018." *HousingWire*, January 4. https://www.housingwire.com/articles/47847-us-housing-market-value-climbs-to-333-trillion-in-2018/.

Luhby, Tami. 2020. "Nearly 40% of Low-Income Workers Lost Their Jobs in March." *CNN*, May 15. https://www.cnn.com/2020/05/14/economy/low-income-layoffs-coronavirus/index.html.

Lupton, Ruth, Rebecca Tunstall, Wendy Sigle-Rushton, Polina Obolenskaya, Ricardo Sabates, Elena Meschi, Dylan Kneale, and Emma Salter. 2009. *Growing Up in Social Housing in Britain: A Profile of Four Generations, 1946 to the Present Day*. London: Tenant Services Authority and Joseph Roundtree Foundation. https://www.jrf.org.uk/report/growing-social-housing-britain-profile-four-generations-1946-present-day.

Maclaren, Andrew. 2019. "Henry George and Churchill's 'The People's Rights': Part 1." Churchill Project, Hillsdale College, March 20. https://winstonchurchill.hillsdale.edu/henry-george-land-taxation/.

Mallach, Alan. 2010. "The Global Reach of Inclusionary Housing." In *Inclusionary Housing in International Perspective: Affordable Housing, Social Inclusion, and Land Value Recapture*, ed. Nico Calavita and Alan Mallach, 323–58. Cambridge, MA: Lincoln Institute of Land Policy.

Manhertz, Treh. 2020. "Recovery Riches: The U.S. Housing Market Gained $11 Trillion in Value in the 2010s." *Zillow*, January 16. https://www.zillow.com/research/us-total-housing-value-2019-26369/.

Marom, Nathan. 2015. "Housing Studies: Affordable Housing Plans in London and New York: Between Marketplace and Social Mix." *Housing Studies* 30 (7): 993–1015.

Marquardt, Susanne, and Daniel Glaser. 2023. "How Much State and How Much Market? Comparing Social Housing in Berlin and Vienna." *German Politics* 32 (2): 361–80. https://doi.org/10.1080/09644008.2020.1771696.

Martin, Chris, Hal Pawson, and Ryan van den Nouwelant. 2016. *Housing Policy and the Housing System in Australia: An Overview*. Sydney: City Futures Research Centre, University of South Wales. https://www.researchgate.net/publication/331771856_Shaping_Futures_Changing_the_Housing_Story_Final_report

Martin, Emmie. 2017a. "Here's How Much Housing Prices Have Skyrocketed over the Last 50 Years." *CNBC*, June 23. https://www.cnbc.com/2017/06/23/how-much-housing-prices-have-risen-since-1940.html.

–. 2017b. "Here's How Much More Expensive It Is for You to Go to College Than It Was for Your Parents." *CNBC*, November 29. https://www.cnbc.com/2017/11/29/how-much-college-tuition-has-increased-from-1988-to-2018.html.

–. 2019. "Here's How Many Millennials Got Money from Their Parents to Buy Their Homes." *CNBC*, March 12. https://www.cnbc.com/2019/03/11/how-many-millennials-got-money-to-buy-homes-from-their-parents.html.

Massachusetts Department of Public Health. 2020. *Weekly COVID-19 Public Health Report*. July 8. https://www.mass.gov/doc/weekly-covid-19-public-health-report-july-8-2020/download.

Mathiesen, Karl. 2015. "How and Where Did UK Lose City-Sized Area of Green Space in Just Six Years?" *Guardian*, July 2. https://www.theguardian.com/environment/2015/jul/02/how-where-did-uk-lose-green-space-bigger-than-a-city-six-years.

Mawby, Nathan. 2021. "Australia's Building Boom Will Be 13,000 Homes Bigger Than First Forecast: HIA." *Realestate.com.au*, May 20. https://www.realestate.com.au/news/australias-building-boom-will-be-13000-homes-bigger-than-first-forecast-hia/.

Mayor of London. 2017. *Homes for Londoners: Affordable Housing and Viability Supplementary Planning Guidance 2017*. London: Greater London Authority. https://www.housinglin.org.uk/Topics/type/Homes-for-Londoners-Affordable-Housing-and-Viability-Supplementary-Planning-Guidance-2017/.

McDonald, Patrick Range. 2021. "Trickle-Down Housing Is a Failure. Here's What You Need to Know." Housing Is a Human Right, May 25. https://www.housingisahumanright.org/trickle-down-housing-is-a-failure-heres-what-you-need-to-know/.

McDonnell, Tim. 2017. "Slum Dwellers in Africa's Biggest Megacity Are Now Living in Canoes." *NPR*, May 15. https://www.npr.org/sections/goatsandsoda/2017/05/15/528461093/slum-dwellers-in-africas-biggest-megacity-are-now-living-in-canoes.

McDowell, Heather. 2022. "Understanding Housing Price to Income Ratio Like a Pro." *Canadian Real Estate Wealth*, October 18. https://www.canadianrealestate-magazine.ca/expert-advice/understanding-housing-price-to-income-ratio-like-a-pro-335224.aspx.

McGerr, Michael. 2003. *A Fierce Discontent: The Rise and Fall of the Progressive Era*. New York: Free Press.

McGowan, Michael. 2022. "More Than $3bn of Social Housing Sold by NSW Government since Coalition Took Power." *Guardian*, April 15. https://www.theguardian.com/australia-news/2022/apr/16/more-than-3bn-of-social-housing-sold-by-nsw-government-since-coalition-took-power.

McIntosh, Kriston, Emily Moss, Ryan Nunn, and Jay Shambaugh. 2020. "Examining the Black-White Wealth Gap." Brookings Institution, February 27. https://www.brookings.edu/blog/up-front/2020/02/27/examining-the-black-white-wealth-gap/.

Meen, Geoffrey. 2018. *Policy Approaches for Improving Affordability*. London: UK Collaborative Centre for Housing Evidence. https://housingevidence.ac.uk/wp-content/uploads/2018/09/R2018_02_02_policy-approaches-for-improving-affordability.pdf.

Meja, Merisol, and Paulette Cha. 2020. "Overcrowded Housing and COVID-19 Risk among Essential Workers." Public Policy Institute of California, May 12. https://www.ppic.org/blog/overcrowded-housing-and-covid-19-risk-among-essential-workers/.

Merritt, Keri Leigh. 2016. "Land and the Roots of African-American Poverty." *Aeon*, March 11. https://aeon.co/ideas/land-and-the-roots-of-african-american-poverty.

–. 2017. *Masterless Men: Poor Whites and Slavery in the Antebellum South*. Cambridge, UK: Cambridge University Press.

Miller, George. 2000. *On Fairness and Efficiency: The Privatisation of the Public Income during the Past Millennium*. Bristol, UK: Policy.

Miller, Jonathan. 2011. "Change Is the Constant in a Century of New York City Real Estate." *Elliman Magazine*, October 13. https://millersamuel.com/papers/change-is-the-constant-in-a-century-of-new-york-city-real-estate/.

"Milton Friedman Talks about Property Taxes." 2014. *YouTube*, January 26. https://www.youtube.com/watch?v=yS7Jb58hcsc.

"Milton Keynes." n.d. *Wikipedia*. https://en.wikipedia.org/wiki/Milton_Keynes.

Molnar, Coleman. 2021. "Vancouver Is Officially the Most Expensive City in North America." *Complex*, October 27. https://www.complex.com/life/vancouver-officially-most-expensive-city-in-north-america.

"Modal Share." n.d. *Wikipedia*. https://en.wikipedia.org/wiki/Modal_share.

Monk, Sarah. 2010. "England: Affordable Housing through the Planning System: The Role of Section 106." In *Inclusionary Housing in International Perspective: Affordable Housing, Social Inclusion, and Land Value Recapture*, ed. Nico Calavita and Alan Mallach, 123–68. Cambridge, MA: Lincoln Institute of Land Policy.

Monro, Dugald. 1997. *Public Rental Housing Policy: Learning the Lessons from Overseas*. Parliament of Australia, November 10. https://parlinfo.aph.gov.au/parlInfo/download/library/prspub/G5N30/upload_binary/G5N30.pdf;fileType=application%2Fpdf.

Montgomery, Roger. 1987. *Pruitt-Igoe: An Annotated Bibliography*. Chicago: Council of Planning Librarians.

Moore, Antonio. 2016. "Black Wealth in America Hardly Exists." *Inequality*, October 18. https://inequality.org/research/black-wealth-exists/.

Moore, Rowan. 2014. "Margaret Thatcher Began Britain's Obsession with Property. It's Time to End It." *Guardian*, April 6. https://www.theguardian.com/society/2014/apr/06/margaret-thatcher-britains-obsession-property-right-to-buy.

MountainMath Software and Analytics. 2021a. "1755 West Broadway, Vancouver." https://mountainmath.ca/map/assessment?zoom=16&lat=49.2622&lng=-123.1536&layer=5&mapBase=2.

–. 2021b. "Vancouver Assessment Map." https://mountainmath.ca/map/assessment.

Mundt, Alexis, and Wolfgang Amann. 2010. "Indicators of an Integrated Rental Market in Austria." *Housing Finance International* 25 (2): 35–45. http://iibw.at/documents/2010%20(Art.)%20Amann_Mundt.%20Integrated%20Rental%20Market%20Austria%20(HFI).pdf.

Murphy, Luke. 2018. *The Invisible Land: The Hidden Force Driving the UK's Unequal Economy*. London: Commission on Economic Justice, Institute for Public Policy Research. https://www.ippr.org/files/2018-08/cej-land-tax-august18.pdf.

Murphy, Richard, Judith Scott Clayton, and Gill Wyness. 2017. "The End of Free Tuition in England." *Centrepiece*, Summer, 7–9. https://cep.lse.ac.uk/pubs/download/cp503.pdf.

Murray, Bruce K. 1973. "The Politics of the 'People's Budget.'" *Historical Journal* 16 (3): 555–70.

Murray, Cameron. 2022. "A Social Housing Fund Is Bad Policy." *Fresh Economic Thinking*, April 24. https://fresheconomicthinking.substack.com/p/a-social-housing-fund-is-bad-policy?s=r.

Murray, Cameron, and Tim Helm. 2022. "Ownership Illusions: When Ownership Really Matters for Economic Analysis." https://osf.io/cw8ze/.

Nareit. n.d. "History of REITs & Real Estate Investing." https://www.reit.com/what-reit/history-reits.

National Fair Housing Alliance. 2008. *Dr. King's Dream Denied: Forty Years of Failed Federal Enforcement*. New York: National Fair Housing Alliance. https://nationalfairhousing.org/wp-content/uploads/2017/04/2008_fair_housing_trends_report.pdf.

National Housing Law Project, Poverty and Race Research Action Council, Sherwood Research Associates, and Everywhere and Now Public Housing Residents Organizing Nationally Together (ENPHRONT). 2002. *False HOPE: A Critical Assessment of the HOPE VI Public Housing Redevelopment Program*. https://www.nhlp.org/files/FalseHOPE.pdf.

National Museum of Australia. n.d. "Daceyvile." https://www.nma.gov.au/exhibitions/glorious-days/social-laboratory/daceyville.

National Shelter. 2019. *Inclusionary Zoning*. http://shelter.org.au/site/wp-content/uploads/190325-Inclusionary-Zoning-Report-V6-Final.pdf.

–. 2022. "National Shelter 2022–23 Federal Budget Analysis." https://shelter.org.au/site/wp-content/uploads/20220411-Federal-Budget-Analysis-1.0.pdf.

Nero, Dom. 2019. "In *It's a Wonderful Life*, Pottersville Actually Looks Way More Fun Than Bedford Falls." *Esquire*, December 24. https://www.esquire.com/entertainment/movies/a30315437/its-a-wonderful-life-pottersville-better-than-bedford-falls/.

New Zealand Legislation. 2021. *Resource Management (Enabling Housing Supply and Other Matters) Amendment Bill*. December 8. https://www.legislation.govt.nz/bill/government/2021/0083/latest/LMS566049.html.

"New Zealand Plans New Housing Density Laws to Tame Red-Hot Property Market." 2021. *Reuters*, October 18. https://www.reuters.com/article/newzealand-housing-idUSL4N2RF01C.

Newman, Oscar. 1972. *Defensible Space: Crime Prevention through Urban Design*. New York: Macmillan.

Nicholas, Tim, and Anna Scherbina. 2013. "Real Estate Prices during the Roaring Twenties and the Great Depression." *Real Estate Economics* 41 (2): 278–309. https://www.hbs.edu/faculty/Pages/item.aspx?num=41283.

"1978 California Proposition 13." n.d. *Wikipedia*. https://en.wikipedia.org/wiki/1978_California_Proposition_13.

Nova, Annie. 2019. "Here's Why Millions of Millennials Are Not Homeowners." *CNBC*, August 30. https://www.cnbc.com/2019/08/30/homeownership-eludes-millions-of-millennials-heres-why.html.

Numbeo. n.d. "Cost of Living Comparison between Paris and Vienna." https://www.numbeo.com/cost-of-living/compare_cities.jsp?country1=France&city1=Paris&country2=Austria&city2=Vienna.

–. 2022. "Property Price to Income Ratio by Country 2022." https://www.numbeo.com/quality-of-life/rankings_by_country.jsp?title=2022&displayColumn=5.

Nygaard, Christian A., George Galster, and Stephen Glackin. 2022. "The Size and Spatial Extent of Neighborhood Price Impacts of Infill Development: Scale Matters?" *Journal of Real Estate Finance and Economics*, August 8. https://doi.org/10.1007/s11146-022-09916-x.

Nzau, Bernard, and Claudia Trillo. 2020. "Harnessing the Real Estate Market for Equitable Affordable Housing Provision: Insights from the City of Santa Monica, California." *Housing Studies* 36 (7): 1086–121. https://www.tandfonline.com/doi/ref/10.1080/02673037.2020.1746244?scroll=top.

Ocasio-Cortez, Alexandria. 2020. "Ahead of Hearing, Ocasio-Cortez Condemns the Real Estate Industry's Request to Use Federal Bailout Funds to Enrich Shareholders." *Progressive Newswire*, July 14. https://www.commondreams.org/newswire/2020/07/14/ahead-hearing-ocasio-cortez-condemns-real-estate-industrys-request-use-federal.

OECD Data. n.d. "Income Inequality." https://data.oecd.org/inequality/income-inequality.htm.

Official Data Foundation. n.d. "Prices for Cars, 1935–2023 ($15,000)." https://www.in2013dollars.com/New-cars/price-inflation.

O'Keefe, Dereck. 2018. "Landlord B.C. Is Wrong – Vancouver Tenants Can't Afford These Rent Hikes." *Georgia Straight*, September 19. https://www.straight.com/news/1139081/derrick-okeefe-landlord-bc-wrong-vancouver-tenants-cant-afford-these-rent-hikes.

Olick, Diana. 2018. "Want to Buy a House? How Long You'll Have to Save Depends on Where You Live." *CNBC*, July 13. https://www.cnbc.com/2018/07/13/want-to-buy-a-house-this-is-how-long-youll-have-to-save.html.

–. 2022. "Housing Wealth Is Setting New Records for Both Owners and Sellers." *CNBC*, February 3. https://www.cnbc.com/2022/02/03/housing-wealth-is-setting-new-records-for-both-owners-and-sellers.html.

Olorunnipa, Toluse, and Colby Itkowitz. 2020. "Trump Tries to Win Over 'Suburban Housewives' with Repeal of Anti-segregation Housing Rule." *Washington Post*, July 23. https://www.washingtonpost.com/politics/trump-suburbs-biden-housing-suburban-housewives/2020/07/23/2f269980-ccf5-11ea-bc6a-6841b28d9093_story.html.

Oppel, Richard A., Jr., Robert Gebeloff, K.K. Rebecca Lai, Will Wright, and Mitch Smith. 2020. "The Fullest Look Yet at the Racial Inequity of Coronavirus." *New York Times*, July 5. https://www.nytimes.com/interactive/2020/07/05/us/coronavirus-latinos-african-americans-cdc-data.html.

Parker, Kim, Juliana Menasce Horowitz, Anna Brown, Richard Fry, D'Vera Cohn, and Ruth Igielnik. 2018. "Demographic and Economic Trends in Urban, Suburban and Rural Communities." Pew Research Center, May 22. https://www.pewsocialtrends.org/2018/05/22/demographic-and-economic-trends-in-urban-suburban-and-rural-communities/.

Parker-Pope, Tara. 2020. "Can I Get Coronavirus from Riding an Elevator?" *New York Times*, May 13. https://www.nytimes.com/2020/05/13/well/live/can-i-get-coronavirus-from-riding-an-elevator.html.

Perry, Bryan. 2016. *Household Incomes in New Zealand: Trends in Indicators of Inequality and Hardship 1982 to 2015*. Wellington: Ministry of Social Development. https://www.msd.govt.nz/about-msd-and-our-work/publications-resources/monitoring/household-incomes/household-incomes-1982-2015.html.

–. 2021. *Housing Affordability for Renters and Owners: International Comparisons*. Wellington: New Zealand Ministry of Social Development. https://www.msd.govt.nz/documents/about-msd-and-our-work/publications-resources/monitoring/household-income-report/2021/international-comparisons-of-housing-affordability.docx.

Perry, Nick. 2018. "New Zealand Bans Foreigners from Buying Homes." *Global News*, August 15. https://globalnews.ca/news/4388427/new-zealand-bans-foreign-home-buyers/.

Pettinger, Tejvan. 2022. "UK House Price to Income Ratio and Affordability." *Economics Help*, September 21. https://www.economicshelp.org/blog/5568/housing/uk-house-price-affordability/.

Piketty, Thomas. 2014. *Capital in the Twenty-First Century*. Cambridge, MA: Harvard University Press.

–. 2020. *Capital and Ideology*. Cambridge, MA: Harvard University Press.

Piketty, Thomas, and Joseph Stiglitz. 2015. "Thomas Piketty and Joseph Stiglitz on Inequality." *YouTube*, April 8. https://www.youtube.com/watch?time_continue=7500&v=Fg6UwAQJUVo&feature=emb_logo.

Pinsker, Joe. 2020. "The New Boomerang Kids Could Change American Views of Living at Home." *Atlantic*, July 3. https://www.theatlantic.com/family/archive/2020/07/pandemic-young-adults-living-with-parents/613723/.

Planning Tank. 2018. "What Is New Urbanism? | Definition, Concept & Benefits." September 9. https://planningtank.com/urbanisation/new-urbanism-definition-concept-benefits.

"Political Bubbles and Hidden Diversity: Highlights from a Very Detailed Map of the 2016 Election." 2018. *New York Times*, July 25. https://www.nytimes.com/interactive/2018/07/25/upshot/precinct-map-highlights.html.

Pope, Alexandra. 2016. "Mapping 40 Years of Canadian Urban Expansion." *Canadian Geographic*, March 23. https://canadiangeographic.ca/articles/mapping-40-years-of-canadian-urban-expansion/.

Porter, Douglas R., and Elizabeth B. Davison. 2009. "Evaluation of In-Lieu Fees and Offsite Construction as Incentives for Affordable Housing Production." *Cityscape* 11 (2): 27–59.

Power, John. 2021. "No Way Home: Overseas New Zealanders Despair at Tightened Borders." *Aljazeera*, December 22. https://www.aljazeera.com/economy/2021/12/22/no-way-home-overseas-new-zealanders-despair-at-border-rules.

Prager, Alicia. 2018. "Vienna Battles Rising Housing Costs – Can a New Policy Fix It?" *Euronews*, October 30. https://www.euronews.com/2018/10/30/vienna-battles-rising-housing-costs-can-a-new-policy-fix-it.

Preiss, David L. 2017. "California 'In Lieu' Affordable Housing Fees withstand Constitutional Challenge." *Holland & Knight Alert*, October 31. https://www.hklaw.com/en/insights/publications/2017/10/california-in-lieu-affordable-housing-fees-withsta.

Prudential. 2019. *Gig Economy Impact by Generation*. Newark, NJ: Prudential Insurance Company of America. https://www.prudential.com/wps/wcm/connect/1b4fcef8-afc0-4c87-bc12-2ace844aecb3/Gig_Economy_Impact_by_Generation.pdf?MOD=AJPERES&CVID=mMoGiuO.

Pullen, John. 2005. "Henry George in Australia: Where the Landowners Are 'More Destructive Than the Rabbit or the Kangaroo.'" *American Journal of Economics and Sociology* 64 (2): 683–713.

Punwasi, Stephen. 2021. "Canadian Residential Real Estate Now Worth over $6.1 Trillion, More Than 3x GDP." *Better Dwelling*, November 25. https://betterdwelling.com/canadian-residential-real-estate-now-worth-over-6-1-trillion-more-than-3x-gdp/.

Quealy, Kevin. 2020. "The Richest Neighborhoods Emptied Out Most as Coronavirus Hit New York City." *New York Times*, May 15. https://www.nytimes.com/interactive/2020/05/15/upshot/who-left-new-york-coronavirus.html.

Radford, Gail. 1996. *Modern Housing for America: Policy Struggles in the New Deal Era*. Chicago: University of Chicago Press.

"Random Length Lumber Continuous Contract." n.d. *Wall Street Journal*. https://www.wsj.com/market-data/quotes/futures/LUMBER.

Rashbrooke, Max. 2014. "How New Zealand's Rich-Poor Divide Killed Its Egalitarian Paradise." *Guardian*, December 12. https://www.theguardian.com/commentisfree/2014/dec/12/how-new-zealands-rich-poor-divide-killed-its-egalitarian-paradise.

–. 2020. "New Zealand's Astounding Wealth Gap Challenges Our 'Fair Go' Identity." *Guardian*, August 31. https://www.theguardian.com/world/2020/aug/31/new-zealands-astounding-wealth-gap-challenges-our-fair-go-identity.

Reiss, Veronica R. 2017. "Viennese Planning Culture: Understanding Change and Continuity through the Hauptbahnhof." MA thesis, University of British Columbia.

"REIT Industry Timeline: Celebrating 50 Years of REITs and Nareit." n.d. *REIT.com*. https://web.archive.org/web/20121113221303/http://www.reit.com/timeline/timeline.php.

"Residual Techniques in Real Estate Valuation." 2019. *PropertyMetrics*, July 23. https://propertymetrics.com/blog/residual-techniques-in-real-estate-valuation/.

Ricardo, David. 1817. *On the Principles of Political Economy and Taxation*. London: John Murray.

Rice, Douglas. 2016. "Chart Book: Cuts in Federal Assistance Have Exacerbated Families' Struggles to Afford Housing." Center on Budget and Policy Priorities, April 12. https://www.cbpp.org/research/housing/chart-book-cuts-in-federal-assistance-have-exacerbated-families-struggles-to-afford.

Richter, Wolf. 2019. "The State of the Canadian Debt Slaves, How They Compare to American Debt Slaves, and the Bank of Canada's Response." *Wolf Street*, December 13. https://wolfstreet.com/2019/12/13/the-dreadful-state-of-the-canadian-debt-slaves-how-they-compare-to-american-debt-slaves-and-the-bank-of-canadas-response/.

Riley, Frederick J. 2020. "Amid Racial Injustice and COVID-19, There's Still Hope America Will Become a Better Place." *USA Today*, July 8. https://www.usatoday.com/story/opinion/2020/07/08/why-even-amid-racial-injustice-and-covid-19-theres-hope-america-column/5389201002/.

Rognlie, Matthew. 2015. "Deciphering the Fall and Rise in the Net Capital Share: Accumulation or Scarcity?" *Brookings Papers on Economic Activity*, 1–69. https://www.brookings.edu/wp-content/uploads/2016/07/2015a_rognlie.pdf.

Rohde, Jeff. 2022. "The Houston Real Estate Market: Stats & Trends for 2022." *Roofstock*, July 7. https://learn.roofstock.com/blog/houston-real-estate-market.

Rosenthal, Stuart S. 2014. "Are Private Markets and Filtering a Viable Source of Low-Income Housing? Estimates from a 'Repeat Income' Model." *American Economic Review* 104 (2): 687–706.

Rothstein, Richard. 2017. *The Color of Law: A Forgotten History of How Our Government Segregated America.* New York: Liveright.

Russell, Tonya. 2020. "Racism in Care Leads to Health Disparities, Doctors and Other Experts Say as They Push for Change." *Washington Post,* July 11. https://www.washingtonpost.com/health/racism-in-care-leads-to-health-disparities-doctors-and-other-experts-say-as-they-push-for-change/2020/07/10/a1a1e40a-bb9e-11ea-80b9-40ece9a701dc_story.html.

Ryan, Paul. 2021. "If Housing Price Growth Seems Unusually High, That's Because It Is." *Realestate.com.au,* November 24. https://www.realestate.com.au/insights/if-housing-price-growth-seems-unusually-high-thats-because-it-is/.

Ryan-Collins, Josh, and Cameron Murray. 2021. "When Homes Earn More than Jobs: The Rentierization of the Australian Housing Market." In *Housing Studies* 38 (10): 1888–917, https://doi.org/10.1080/02673037.2021.2004091.

Saad, Lydia. 2020. "Americans Rapidly Answering the Call to Isolate, Prepare." Gallup, March 20. https://news.gallup.com/poll/297035/americans-rapidly-answering-call-isolate-prepare.aspx.

Safire, William. 2008. *Safire's Political Dictionary.* Oxford: Oxford University Press.

Salsberg, Bob, and Angeliki Kastanis. 2018. "Analysis: Blacks Largely Left Out of High-Paying Jobs, Government Data Shows." *USA Today,* April 2. https://www.usatoday.com/story/money/2018/04/02/analysis-blacks-largely-left-out-high-paying-jobs-government-data-shows/477845002/.

Samarasinghe, Don Amila Sajeevan. 2020. "The Housing Crisis in Australia and New Zealand: A Comparative Analysis through Policy Lenses." *International Journal of Construction Supply Chain Management* 10 (2): 212–23.

Scanlon, Kath. 2017. "Social Housing in England: Affordable vs 'Affordable.'" *Critical Housing Analysis* 4 (1): 21–30. https://doi.org/10.13060/23362839.2017.4.1.321.

Schrader, Ben. 2014. "The Origins of Urban Sprawl in New Zealand." In *UHPH_14: Landscapes and Ecologies of Urban and Planning History,* ed. Morten Gjerde and Emina Petrović, 749–58. Wellington: Victoria University Press. https://apo.org.au/sites/default/files/resource-files/2014-04/apo-nid213746.pdf.

Schwartz, Gabriel L., and Jaquelyn L. Jahn. 2020. "Mapping Fatal Police Violence across U.S. Metropolitan Areas: Overall Rates and Racial/Ethnic Inequities, 2013–2017." *PLoS One* 15 (6): 1–16. https://journals.plos.org/plosone/article?id=10.1371/journal.pone.0229686.

Scruggs, Gregory. 2018. "'Everything We've Heard about Global Urbanization Turns Out to Be Wrong' – Researchers." *Thompson Reuters Foundation News,* July 12. http://news.trust.org/item/20180712130016-lwnc2/.

"Segregation in America." 2018. *Economist*, April 4. https://www.economist.com/graphic-detail/2018/04/04/segregation-in-america.

Semuels, Alana. 2015. "How Housing Policy Is Failing America's Poor." *Atlantic*, June 24. https://www.theatlantic.com/business/archive/2015/06/section-8-is-failing/396650/.

Shaw, Kate. 2022. "Why We Need to Fight for Inclusionary Zoning in Victoria." *Overland*, May 9. https://overland.org.au/2022/05/why-we-need-to-fight-for-inclusionary-zoning-in-victoria/comment-page-1/.

Sheil, Christopher, and Frank Stilwell. 2019. "What the Bureau of Statistics Didn't Highlight: Our Continuing Upward Redistribution of Wealth." *The Conversation*, August 20. https://theconversation.com/what-the-bureau-of-statistics-didnt-highlight-our-continuing-upward-redistribution-of-wealth-121731.

Shrubsole, Guy. 2019. *Who Owns England? How We Lost Our Green and Pleasant Land, and How to Take It Back*. London: William Collins.

Silver, Johnathan. 2019. "Here's How Much Houston Home Prices Have Jumped in Just 5 Years." *Culture Map*, March 26. https://houston.culturemap.com/news/real-estate/03-20-19-point2-houston-home-price-increase-north-america-report/.

Simpson, Michael. 1969. "Village of Euclid v. Ambler Reality Co." *Encyclopedia of Cleveland History*. https://case.edu/ech/articles/v/village-euclid-v-ambler-realty-co.

Small, Zane. 2019. "PM Jacinda Ardern Refuses to Stand by Major KiwiBuild Goal." *Newshub*, August 5. https://www.newshub.co.nz/home/politics/2019/05/pm-jacinda-ardern-refuses-to-stand-by-major-kiwibuild-goal.html.

Smith, Adam. 1776. *The Wealth of Nations*. London: W. Strahan and T. Cadell. https://archive.org/details/TheWealthNations/mode/2up.

Smith, Nicole. n.d. "Neoliberalism." *Britannica*. https://www.britannica.com/topic/neoliberalism.

Smyth, Jaime. 2021. "New Zealand's Housing Crisis Poses Big Test for Jacinda Ardern." *Financial Times*, January 4. https://www.ft.com/content/2ec734f0-23b4-4aef-9675-f89d357ce0e1.

Sparkes, Sam. 2019. "Poorest Cities in Massachusetts for 2020." *RoadSnacks*, December 24. Accessed April 12, 2020. https://www.roadsnacks.net/poorest-places-in-massachusetts/.

Sprigings, Nigel, and Duncan H. Smith. 2012. "Unintended Consequences: Local Housing Allowance Meets the Right to Buy." *People, Place and Policy* 6 (2): 58–75. https://doi.org/10.3351/PPP.0006.0002.0001.

Stahl, Ashley. 2020. "New Study: Millennial Women Are Delaying Having Children Due to Their Careers." *Forbes*, May 1. https://www.forbes.com/sites/ashley-stahl/2020/05/01/new-study-millennial-women-are-delaying-having-children-due-to-their-careers/.

Stamm, Everett, and Taylor LaJoie. 2020. *An Overview of the Low-Income Housing*

Tax Credit. Washington DC: Tax Foundation. https://files.taxfoundation. org/20200810100355/An-Overview-of-the-Low-Income-Housing-Tax-Credit.pdf.

Stansbury, Anna, and Lawrence H. Summers. 2020. "Declining Worker Power and American Economic Performance." *Brookings Papers on Economic Activity*, March 19. https://www.brookings.edu/wp-content/uploads/2020/03/Stansbury-Summers-Conference-Draft.pdf.

State of Black America. 2020. *Unmasked: Executive Summary*. New York: National Urban League. http://sobadev.iamempowered.com/sites/soba.iamempowered. com/files/NUL-SOBA-2020-ES-web.pdf.

Statistics Canada. 2022. "Building Construction Price Indexes, Percentage Change, Quarterly, Inactive." November 1. https://www150.statcan.gc.ca/t1/tbl1/en/tv. action?pid=1810013502.

Stats NZ. 2016. "Wealth Patterns across Ethnic Groups in New Zealand." November 3. https://www.stats.govt.nz/reports/wealth-patterns-across-ethnic-groups-in-new-zealand.

–. 2018. *Living in a Crowded House: Exploring the Ethnicity and Well-Being of People in Crowded Households*. https://www.stats.govt.nz/assets/Uploads/Reports/Living-in-a-crowded-house-exploring-the-ethnicity-and-well-being-of-people-in-crowded-households/living-in-a-crowded-house-exploring-the-ethnicity-and-well-being-of-people-in-crowded-households.pdf.

Steele, Marion. 1998. "Canadian Housing Allowances Inside and Outside the Welfare System." *Canadian Public Policy* 24 (2): 209–32.

Stein, Clarence S. 1957. *Toward New Towns for America*. Rev. ed. Cambridge, MA: MIT Press.

"Stephen Harper Explains 'Old-Stock Canadians' Comment." 2015. *CBC News*, September 18. https://www.cbc.ca/news/politics/canada-election-2015-harper-debate-1.3233785.

Stiglitz, Joseph E. 2015. "The Origins of Inequality, and Policies to Contain It." *National Tax Journal* 68 (2): 425–48.

–. 2020. "Priorities for the COVID-19 Economy." *Project Syndicate*, July 1. https:// www.project-syndicate.org/commentary/covid-2020-recession-how-to-respond-by-joseph-e-stiglitz-2020-06?barrier=accesspaylog.

Stolba, Stefan Lembo. 2019. "Baby Boomers' Student Loan Debt Continues to Grow." *Experian*, July 18. https://www.experian.com/blogs/ask-experian/research/baby-boomers-and-student-loan-debt/.

Sullivan, Bob. 2018. "Millennials Spend a Large Percent of Income on Rent." *Credit. com*, May 9. https://www.credit.com/blog/millennials-spend-a-large-percent-of-income-on-rent-183309/.

Summers, Graham. 2017. *The Everything Bubble: The Endgame for Central Bank Policy*. Scotts Valley, CA: CreateSpace.

Sun, Yat-sen. 1918. *Memoirs of a Chinese Revolutionary: A Programme of National Reconstruction for China*. London: Hutchinson & Co. https://babel.hathitrust.org/cgi/pt?id=hvd.32044044473106&seq=1.

Talora, Joe. 2021. "London Is 'Epicentre' of Housing Crisis as 250,000 Londoners Await Council Homes." *Evening Standard*, October 13. https://www.standard.co.uk/news/london/london-housing-crisis-sadiq-khan-council-homes-b960327.html.

Tartar, Brent. n.d. *Encyclopedia Virginia*. https://www.encyclopediavirginia.org/Vagrancy_Act_of_1866.

Tate, Luke. 2007. "Fighting Poverty and Creating Opportunity: The Choice Neighborhoods Initiative." *Edge*. https://www.huduser.gov/portal/pdredge/pdr_edge_frm_asst_sec_101911.html.

Taylor, Alan. 2011. "Occupy Wall Street Spreads Worldwide." *Atlantic*, October 17. https://www.theatlantic.com/photo/2011/10/occupy-wall-street-spreads-worldwide/100171/.

Taylor, W.A. 1975. *Crown Lands: A History of Survey Systems*. Victoria, BC: Registries and Titles Department, Ministry of Sustainable Resource Management. https://web.archive.org/web/20110706184529/http://www.ltsa.ca/data/img/publication/Crown-Lands-A-History-of-Survey-Systems.pdf.

Tencer, Daniel. 2019. "Overcrowding in Housing Is Worst in Toronto, Western Canada: StatCan." *Huffington Post*, December 2. https://www.huffpost.com/archive/ca/entry/overcrowded-housing-canada_ca_5de555fde4b00149f733d6af.

Thaden, Emily, and Ruoniu Wang. 2017. *Inclusionary Housing in the United States: Prevalence, Impact, and Practices*. Cambridge, MA: Lincoln Institute of Land Policy. https://www.lincolninst.edu/sites/default/files/pubfiles/thaden_wp17et1_0.pdf.

Thompson, Derick. 2014. "Homeownership in America Has Collapsed – Don't Blame Millennials." *Atlantic*, October 28. https://www.theatlantic.com/business/archive/2014/10/homeownership-is-historically-weakdont-blame-millennials/382010/.

Thompson, Megan, and Melanie Saltzman. 2019. "How Minneapolis Became the First to End Single-Family Zoning." *PBS News Weekend*, November 23. https://www.pbs.org/newshour/show/how-minneapolis-became-the-first-to-end-single-family-zoning.

Thorne, Daniel. 2021. "Planning for Affordable Housing / Homes Strategy Fulton Hogan Land Development Limited." Town Planning Group, Queenstown, New Zealand, September 24. https://letstalk.qldc.govt.nz/70800/widgets/347921/documents/221311.

Thrush, Glenn. 2020. "Trump Attacks a Suburban Housing Program. Critics See a Play for White Votes." *New York Times*, July 1. https://www.nytimes.com/2020/07/01/us/politics/trump-obama-housing-discrimination.html.

Tideman, Nicolaus. 1990. "Open Letter to Mikhail Gorbachev." *Wikisource*, November 7. https://en.wikisource.org/wiki/Open_letter_to_Mikhail_Gorbachev_(1990).

"The Time May Be Right for Land-Value Taxes." 2018. *Economist*, August 9. https://www.economist.com/briefing/2018/08/09/the-time-may-be-right-for-land-value-taxes.

Turbov, Mindy, and Valerie Piper. 2005. *HOPE VI and Mixed-Finance Redevelopments: A Catalyst for Neighborhood Renewal: Atlanta Case Study*. Washington, DC: Brookings Institution Metropolitan Policy Program. https://web.archive.org/web/20160304060849/http://www.brookings.edu/metro/pubs/AtlantaCaseStudy.pdf.

UK Land Registry. 2023. "UK House Price Index." https://landregistry.data.gov.uk/app/ukhpi.

Urback, Robyn. 2022. "Pierre Poilievre Is onto Something When He Rants about Canada's Housing Nightmare." *Globe and Mail*, April 13. https://www.theglobeandmail.com/opinion/article-pierre-poilievre-is-onto-something-when-he-rants-about-canadas-housing/.

Urban Institute. n.d. "Property Taxes." https://www.urban.org/policy-centers/cross-center-initiatives/state-and-local-finance-initiative/projects/state-and-local-backgrounders/property-taxes.

US Bureau of Economic Analysis. 2020. "Gross Domestic Product, Fourth Quarter and Year 2019 (Advance Estimate)." January 30. https://www.bea.gov/news/2020/gross-domestic-product-fourth-quarter-and-year-2019-advance-estimate.

US Bureau of Labor Statistics. 2012. "Occupational Employment by Race and Ethnicity, 2011." *TED: The Economics Daily*, October 26. https://www.bls.gov/opub/ted/2012/ted_20121026.htm.

US Department of Defense. n.d. "Charles E. Wilson." https://history.defense.gov/Multimedia/Biographies/Article-View/Article/571268/charles-e-wilson/.

US Department of Housing and Urban Development (HUD). n.d. "About Hope VI." https://www.hud.gov/program_offices/public_indian_housing/programs/ph/hope6/about.

–. n.d. "Choice Neighborhoods." https://www.hud.gov/program_offices/public_indian_housing/programs/ph/cn.

–. n.d. "Low-Income Housing Tax Credit (LIHTC)." https://www.huduser.gov/portal/datasets/lihtc.html.

US General Accounting Office. 2000. *Local Growth Issues – Federal Opportunities and Challenges*. Washington DC: US General Accounting Office. https://www.gao.gov/assets/240/230572.pdf.

US Government. 1865. *An Act to Establish a Bureau for the Relief of Freedmen and Refugees*. http://www.freedmen.umd.edu/fbact.htm.

US President's Economic Recovery Advisory Board. 2010. *The Report on Tax Reform Options: Simplification, Compliance, and Corporate Taxation*. https://web.archive.org/web/20101105201333/http://www.whitehouse.gov/sites/default/files/microsites/PERAB_Tax_Reform_Report.pdf.

Valentine, Ashish. 2020. "'The Wrong Complexion for Protection.' How Race Shaped America's Roadways and Cities." *NPR*, July 5. https://www.npr.org/2020/07/05/887386869/how-transportation-racism-shaped-america?utm_campaign=storyshare&utm_source=twitter.com&utm_medium=social.

Verlič, Mara. 2015. "Emerging Housing Commons? Vienna's Housing Crises Then and Now." Paper presented at the RC21 International Conference on "The Ideal City: Between Myth and Reality: Representations, Policies, Contradictions and Challenges for Tomorrow's Urban Life," Urbino, Italy, August 27–29. https://www.rc21.org/en/wp-content/uploads/2014/12/E8_Verlic.pdf.

Vincent, Joshua. 2019. "Non-glamorous Gains: The Pennsylvania Land Tax Experiment." Strong Towns, March 6. https://www.strongtowns.org/journal/2019/3/6/non-glamorous-gains-the-pennsylvania-land-tax-experiment.

Wade, Jill. 1986. "Wartime Housing Limited, 1941–1947: Canadian Housing Policy." *Urban History Review* 15 (1): 40–59. https://www.erudit.org/fr/revues/uhr/1986-v15-n1-uhr0856/1018892ar.pdf.

Washington, Jesse. 2020. "Why Did Black Lives Matter Protests Attract Unprecedented White Support?" *Andscape*, June 18. https://andscape.com/features/why-did-black-lives-matter-protests-attract-unprecedented-white-support/.

Wasmer, Etienne, Guillaume Chapelle, Alain Trannoy, and Odran Bonnet. 2021. "Land Is Back – It Should Be Taxed, It Can Be Taxed." *VoxEU*, March 16. https://voxeu.org/article/land-back-it-should-be-taxed-it-can-be-taxed.

"What in the World Are 'Real Estate Fundamentals'?" 2019. *Toronto Realty Blog*, October 21. https://torontorealtyblog.com/blog/what-in-the-world-are-real-estate-fundamentals/.

Whitehead, Christine. 2007. "Housing Studies Planning Policies and Affordable Housing: England as a Successful Case Study?" *Housing Studies* 22 (1): 25–44.

Wigglesworth, Robin. 2020. "How America's 1% Came to Dominate Stock Ownership." *Financial Post*, February 11. https://financialpost.com/investing/how-americas-1-came-to-dominate-stock-ownership.

Williams, Linda Faye. 2010. *Constraint of Race: Legacies of White Skin Privilege in America*. State College: Pennsylvania State University Press.

Williamson, Elizabeth J., Alex J. Walker, Krishnan Bhaskaran, Seb Bacon, Chris Bates, Caroline E. Morton, Helen J. Curtis, et al. 2020. "Factors Associated with COVID-19-Related Death Using OpenSAFELY." *Nature*, July 8. https://www.nature.com/articles/s41586-020-2521-4.

Williamson, Mary Lou. 1987. *Greenbelt: History of a New Town, 1937–1987*. Norfolk, VA: Donning.

Wiltshire, Trent, and Danielle Wood. 2017. "Three Charts On: The Great Australian Wealth Gap." *The Conversation*, October 1. https://theconversation.com/three-charts-on-the-great-australian-wealth-gap-84515.

Wisconsin Historical Society. n.d. "Garden Homes Historic District." https://www.wisconsinhistory.org/Records/NationalRegister/NR1906.

Wolfe, Jonathan. 2022. "From 'Zero' to Surge." *New York Times*, March 3. https://www.nytimes.com/2022/03/03/briefing/hong-kong-new-zealand-covid-surge.html.

Wong, Daniel. 2018. "Canadian Real Estate Prices See Biggest Drop Worldwide." *Maclean's*, January 29. https://www.macleans.ca/economy/economicanalysis/canadian-real-estate-prices-see-biggest-drop-worldwide/.

Wong, Martin. 2017. "Revisiting the Wealth Effect on Consumption in New Zealand." Reserve Bank of New Zealand, March 30. https://www.rbnz.govt.nz/research-and-publications/analytical-notes/2017/an2017-03.

Wood, Gordon S. 2002. *The American Revolution: A History.* New York: Modern Library.

Wu, Katherine. 2020. "Study of 17 Million Identifies Crucial Risk Factors for Coronavirus Deaths." *New York Times*, July 8. https://www.nytimes.com/2020/07/08/health/coronavirus-risk-factors.html?searchResultPosition=1.

Yates, Judith. 2016. "Why Does Australia Have an Affordable Housing Problem and What Can Be Done about It?" *Australian Economic Review* 49 (3): 328–39.

Yilek, Caitlin. 2021. "Jeff Bezos on Future of Spaceflight: 'We can move all heavy industry and all polluting industry off of Earth.'" *CBS News*, July 21. https://www.cbsnews.com/news/jeff-bezos-space-heavy-industry-polluting-industry/.

Yiqing, Xia, Huiting Ma, Gary Moloney, Héctor A. Velásquez García, Monica Sirski, Naveed Z. Janjua, David Vickers, et al. 2022. "Geographic Concentration of SARS-CoV-2 Cases by Social Determinants of Health in Metropolitan Areas in Canada: A Cross-sectional Study." *Canadian Medical Association Journal* 194 (6): E195–204. https://www.cmaj.ca/content/194/6/E195.

Youn, Soo. 2019. "40% of Americans Don't Have $400 in the Bank for Emergency Expenses: Federal Reserve." *ABC News*, May 24. https://abcnews.go.com/US/10-americans-struggle-cover-400-emergency-expense-federal/story?id=63253846.

Zarenski, Ed. 2016a. "Construction Inflation." *Construction Analytics*, October 24. https://edzarenski.com/2016/10/24/construction-inflation-index-tables-e08-19/.

–. 2016b. "Construction Inflation Cost Index." *Construction Analytics*, January 31. https://edzarenski.com/2016/01/31/construction-inflation-cost-index/.

Zaveri, Mihir. 2020. "'I Need People to Hear My Voice': Teens Protest Racism." *New York Times*, June 23. https://www.nytimes.com/2020/06/23/us/teens-protest-black-lives-matter.html.

Index

Printed and bound in Canada by Friesens

Set in Sabon and Myriad by Julie Cochrane

Copy editor: Robert Lewis

Indexer: Emily LeGrand

Cover designer: John van der Woude